COMPUTERS IN THE CURRICULUM SERIES
Howard Budin and Diane S. Kendall, Editors

Using Computers in the Social Studies
Howard Budin, Diane S. Kendall, and James Lengel

Using Computers in the Teaching of Reading
Dorothy S. Strickland, Joan T. Feeley, and Shelley B. Wepner

Using Computers—in the Teaching of Reading

Dorothy S. Strickland
Joan T. Feeley
Shelley B. Wepner

With a Foreword by George E. Mason

Teachers College, Columbia University
New York and London

Published by Teachers College Press, 1234 Amsterdam Avenue,
New York, N.Y. 10027

Library of Congress Cataloging-in-Publication Data

Strickland, Dorothy S.
  Using computers in the teaching of reading.

  (Computers in the curriculum series)
  Bibliography: p.
  Includes index.
  1. Reading—United States—Computer-assisted
instruction. I. Feeley, Joan T., 1932–   .
II. Wepner, Shelley B., 1951–   . III. Title.
IV. Series.
LB1050.37.S77 1987   371.3'9445   86-14567
ISBN 0-8077-2823-3

Manufactured in the United States of America

92 91 90 89 88   2 3 4 5 6

To our families —
Maurice, Mark, Randy, and Michael
Bob, John, and Maura
Roy, Leslie, and Meredith
                    With love

Contents

Foreword

To the best of my knowledge, this new book, *Using Computers in the Teaching of Reading*, is the first attempt to incorporate Taylor's concepts of the three major functions of the computer into a set of strategies for the teaching of reading. But it is wrong to classify this book as an attempt; it is a success! Writing for teachers, the authors call upon that which teachers know best as the major way of making their thinking explicit. From beginning to end, they provide vignettes, personal experiences, and descriptions of real classroom practices to bring home their message to their readers.

Needless to say, I like this book. I'm especially impressed with the guidelines for using computers in the reading program that appear at the end of the first chapter. Another fine characteristic of this work is its accurate descriptions of recommended programs, categorized not only by use but also by level. I also must give credit for the excellent section on accessing data bases in Chapter 3. And finally, I applaud the authors' stand on piracy and their clear discussion of the keyboarding and equity issues in Chapter 8.

I believe this to be a noteworthy addition to our rapidly accumulating body of literature. It reads well; it's highly informative; it's current and complete. I'm grateful to the authors for letting me read it in draft so that I could write this foreword.

University of Georgia   GEORGE E. MASON

Acknowledgments

Like a good play, it's the people behind the scenes who deserve to be acknowledged for their invaluable assistance and support. This book is based on the contributions of many:

Teachers who shared—Maureen Armour, Gaye Carabillo, Chris Chakmakian, Janet Forer, Joyce and Larry Giblin, Roberta Hart, Frieda Helmstetter, Spence Hook, Sharyn Kost, Joe Lanni, Gail Okun, Rosalie Pagano, Virginia Radonich, Phil Restaino, Mary Savino, Jeffrey Seise, Lucille Van Eck, Judi Vihonski;

Administrators who assisted—John Cowen, Susan Ginsberg, Av Green, Steven Kramer, Maxine Pearce;

Colleagues who helped—Ernest Balajthy, Jane Bambrick, Beva Eastman, Myrna Erhlich, Ken Komoski, Michael Labuda, George Mason, Dorothy Minkoff, Dorothy Mulligan, Marie Murphy, David Reinking;

Typists who worked quickly—Robert (Rocky) Schwartz; Jean Montanari;

Our talented artist—Nancy Deneka;

Our honest reader—Vida Welsh;

Our patient editor—Sonia DiVittorio;

And all the children who shared their reactions and insights about learning with computers.

We recognize that without their help our production would not measure up to the expectations of our targeted audience.

Introduction

Computers, often referred to as protean machines, are being used in a multiplicity of ways by forward-looking educators. Once regarded merely as "teaching machines," these electronic devices are beginning to be utilized more creatively by even the most cautious educators. Reasons for these pioneering efforts in classrooms across the country stem from the prophetic sentiments of computer advocates such as Robert Taylor. In his book *The Computer in the School: Tutor, Tool, Tutee* (1980), Dr. Taylor has provided educators with a cogent framework for thinking about computers. He views computers as vehicles for instruction (tutor), assistance (tool), and creative problem solving (tutee).

In the tutor mode, the computer is used to teach new material or reinforce previously acquired information. Programmed to present specific material and respond accordingly, the computer can be used to accommodate individual differences in learning. In the tool mode, the computer assists in typically laborious tasks such as calculation, statistical analysis, information retrieval, and word processing. As in the tutor mode, the user does not need involved computer experience to use the computer as a tool. In the tutee mode, though, the computer user teaches the computer via a compatible programming language. The computer user must be able to communicate intelligibly with the computer in order to elicit sensible responses. All three modes can serve important functions in today's schools.

Since computers are appearing in schools in ever-increasing numbers, teachers want to know how to use them easily, effectively, and efficiently. As reading teachers, we researched useful, realistic ways in which computers could be used immediately with minimal knowledge of programming languages. This book is the result of these efforts. Adapting Taylor's framework, we attempt to show how the computer can be used as tool, tutor, and tutee with currently available software in the reading/language arts curriculum for the teacher of reading, whether functioning in a classroom or in a reading resource center. While software development is occurring at an incredibly rapid rate, existing software has tremendous potential, if used creatively within each of these modes.

To set the stage for how computers can be used in reading, Chapter 1 defines the reading process in terms of its relationship to background experiences and language cue systems. Based on this philosophy, we describe how the computer can be used productively.

Chapters 2 and 3 describe how the computer can be used as a tool in the reading/language arts curriculum. Chapter 2 provides suggestions for using word processing as a writing tool at all levels, including its applicability to the Language Experience Approach. Chapter 3 discusses the nature and use of teacher utilities, readability and reading assessments, and computerized filing systems.

Chapters 4 and 5 delineate how the computer can be used as a tutor. Chapter 4 deals with drill-and-practice packages; Chapter 5 describes interactive reading/writing software packages, including simulations. Selected programs for different developmental levels are included.

How the computer as tutee might fit into the reading/language arts curriculum is discussed in Chapter 6. Along with software programs that students can manipulate, two programming languages, Logo and BASIC, are described in terms of reading/thinking skill development.

Chapter 7 introduces practical considerations for organizing the computer program, including evaluation of computer software. Chapter 8 closes the text with a look at critical issues and trends related to the computer and the teaching of reading/language arts. The appendix contains a guide to resources that can be used as a convenient reference for teachers to use in developing a computer-literate environment in their schools.

A wide variety of programs are described throughout this book. These are meant to serve as good examples of topics under discussion and not as an exhaustive guide to computer software. These examples help fulfill the goal of providing a readable and practical guide to those interested in using computers in reading instruction.

Using Computers
in the Teaching of Reading

□ 1 □

The Reading Process
and the Role of the Computer

First and foremost, this book is concerned with improving the teaching of reading. It is about helping young children at the early stages of reading development and helping older students as they extend and refine their reading abilities throughout the grades. As teachers of reading, we realize the importance of a school's literacy program to all areas of the school curriculum. The child who is unsuccessful in learning to read is likely to be unsuccessful in social studies, science, and math. Moreover, the child will probably have problems coping with ordinary daily activities outside of school as well. It is not surprising that educators are constantly seeking new and better ways to make reading instruction more effective. Certainly, it came as no surprise to find educators turning to the new computer technologies as a possible "new and better way." Computers, we are told, can help individualize instruction, maximize children's attention, present material in new ways, provide immediate feedback, be infinitely patient, keep records of progress, and help free the teacher for other instructional duties. In schools everywhere, teachers are learning that using computers in the teaching of reading can offer many instructional advantages. They are also learning about the limitations of the new technology and about the need to consider its use carefully along with their beliefs about the reading process and the goals of the reading curriculum they are attempting to put in place.

In many ways, the most effective reading instruction is that which provides students with an optimal set of conditions in which to learn. That set of conditions results from an orchestration of methods, materials, and classroom context. We call it the curriculum. Administrators and teachers are constantly at work juggling the various components of the

1

curriculum to obtain just the right mix for the students in their charge. When new materials are considered, it does not matter whether they are microscopes, textbooks, or the most advanced computer technologies; educators must consider their purchase in terms of the students to be served, the existing materials and methods in use, and the potential effect on classroom organization and management.

Reading, perhaps more than any other area of the curriculum, offers teachers a wide variety of methods and materials from which to choose. In addition to textbooks, trade books (library books), and periodicals for children, there is a wide range of instructional kits and audiovisual materials available for classroom use. Historically, reading instruction has been the focus of virtually every new technology available in education. The use of computer technology is no exception. C. B. Smith reports, "Reading holds the number-two position below math, for the heaviest use of microcomputers in the elementary grades in U.S. schools. Usage patterns are limited at present but a wide array of thinking and comprehension activities are beginning to appear" (1985, p. 11). Our work in schools not only confirms Smith's observations but suggests that the use of computers in reading instruction is becoming less and less limited.

As the number of schools with computers increases, more and more teachers of reading are attempting to make use of computer technology in their programs. Often these teachers have had little experience with or interest in computers. The purchase of computers is often initiated by a school administration eager to introduce programs that reflect a more up-to-date, effective image. Ironically, whenever new technologies are added to the curriculum, they not only bring the potential for making the teaching task more exciting and more effective, they also bring the challenge of requiring a new and more complicated set of teaching skills and tasks. Very often, it is not until after the computer arrives that teachers and administrators begin to ask a host of familiar questions regarding the availability and quality of software for reading and how best to organize and manage time and space so that the computer is used most effectively.

All this makes curricular decision making extremely complex. Making the right decisions requires the ability to combine knowledge of the new technologies with a clear understanding of how students learn to read. Making computers work for us in the reading classroom means selecting and using them and their related materials within a framework of how reading is learned and taught. The following is an overview of the current research and methodology upon which this book is based. It provides the framework for *Using Computers in the Teaching of Reading.*

☐ ## OVERVIEW OF THE READING PROCESS ☐

Learning to Read Is a Process of Constructing Meaning. Through the medium of print, the reader must focus on the task of constructing meaning from the author's message. The meanings that are constructed do not reside in the text; they are the product of the interaction between the reader and the text. For example, psycholinguists F. Smith (1983) and Goodman (1984) tell us that as readers we are constantly making predictions as we read. The predictions are based on our prior knowledge of the world and of the language being read. As we move through the text, we continually confirm the predictions we have made. We do this by applying a variety of strategies. Decoding clues (phonics), semantic clues (word meanings), and syntactic clues (sentence structure) are used in conjunction with one another as readers press on in the search for meaning. The degree to which these strategies are used is largely determined by the degree to which the text matches the reader's predictions. It is only when comprehension appears to break down that readers need to attend closely to all of the available clues. As long as understanding is taking place, we readers continue to move through the text with relative ease, confirming and disconfirming predictions based on our prior knowledge and experiences with printed language and with the topic at hand.

It follows that the more readers know about a topic, the better their predictions will be and, thus, the better their comprehension. The importance of prior knowledge has been explained by researchers through schema theory. Durkin (1981) describes schema theory as an attempt to explain how new information acquired while reading is meshed with old information already in our heads. Pearson and Spiro (1982) describe a schema as "the little pictures of associations you conjure up in your head when you hear a word or a sentence" (p. 46). For example, when we see the word *automobile* in a text, we may conjure up images of auto bodies, wheels, traffic, or anything else that might be associated with cars. Our prior knowledge of things associated with automobiles largely determines the meanings that will be constructed.

A reader's schemata (plural) are never complete. All of us are constantly in the process of adding new information to the schemata already in our heads, and empty slots always remain waiting to be filled. Reading comprehension involves filling those empty slots. Reading, then, is a process that both develops a reader's schemata and depends on them. Not only does our prior knowledge of the world affect our understanding of old information, it helps us make connections to information that is new. Thus, existing schemata are expanded and modified.

When we view reading as a process of constructing meaning, some implications for computer-based instruction clearly emerge. Certainly, computer-based instruction that fosters comprehension is the most valuable type. Since reading comprehension involves making predictions, teachers need to look for activities that offer learners opportunities to test and confirm their predictions. These might involve predictions about what might happen next in a particular story or about what questions might be answered in an informational passage.

Readers construct meaning best when they have whole, meaningful texts with which to interact rather than fragments. Programs that focus on word recognition and word meanings are apt to be most effective when they offer these skills in context and in conjunction with one another. Programs that isolate skills and fail to provide for their application in context are least helpful, because they often foster habits that are ineffective in authentic reading situations, where understanding the message is essential. Whether the reader is using the computer to gain information entered by others or to enter information for others to read, background knowledge is involved. Teachers should be aware of the need to build students' background knowledge and to help them use the knowledge they already possess as they attempt to comprehend and compose with computer-based materials. Most important, the search for meaning requires materials and situations that are meaningful to the learner. It is unlikely that students will learn very much about reading from programs that defy all efforts to make sense of them. Constructing meaning can be accomplished only when the reading task itself is meaningful.

Learning to Read Requires the Learner's Active Involvement and Control of the Process. Whether we are functioning as speakers, writers, listeners, or readers, we are actively involved. The very nature of the word *learning* implies active participation rather than the passive absorption of skills and knowledge. Unfortunately, however, the receptive nature of reading and listening has frequently caused them to be treated as passive modes of language. For example, in the teaching of reading, there has traditionally been far less concern for the reader's purpose than for the author's. Too often teachers fail to capitalize on the rich variety of interpretations and perceptions that readers with different backgrounds may construct with the same text.

In addition to being active participants in the process, good readers are clearly in control of what they are about. They are aware of what the reading situation requires, whether it be a picture storybook or a word problem in a mathematics text, and they monitor their own comprehension as they read. Research done under the rubric of metacognition suggests that the knowledge and control of one's own thinking and learning is an important aspect of reading comprehension. Brown (1982) suggests two categories of metacognition. The first category involves the reader's understanding of the purpose of the reading task. This requires the ability to separate the relevant from the trivial. The second category relates to the reader's knowledge of when he or she understands the text and the recognition of when comprehension has broken down. This involves the ability to self-question and self-correct when needed. Researchers in the area of metacognition tell us that poorer readers are often unaware that they are supposed to make sense of the text. They approach reading as a decoding process rather than as a search for meaning. They are less likely to reflect upon what they read or ask questions of themselves or others about the meaning of a passage even when they don't understand it. They are less likely to take remedial action or use alternative strategies when their attempts at remediation fail. To learn to read, individuals must view themselves as actively involved in the process. Such readers are most likely to see themselves as competent learners, possessing the power and responsibility to effect their own learning.

When the learner's active involvement and control in the process of learning to read are considered, several implications for computer-based instruction come to mind. Computer materials are most effective when they allow the learner some degree of decision making and control over the task. Interactive materials, which encourage students not only to respond to stimuli but to influence or control outcomes, are imperative. Whenever possible, students should be able to self-check by looking back at previous work or calling up other help features. Preference should be given to programs that require the reader to make decisions about the progression or direction of the content, because these decisions promote active involvement. In all cases, students should be fully informed about the purpose of the computer task and what it requires of them. They should be encouraged to ask questions about the purpose and requirements and to assess their own capability to successfully complete the task: What is this supposed to teach or help me to do? What do I need to know in order to do it? How will I know whether or not I am succeeding? These are good questions for *students* to ask themselves as they spend their valuable time using the computer to help them learn to read. Questions of this type are also appropriate for the *teacher* who is considering the use of a particular computer program.

Learning to Read Involves a Knowledge of Text Structures.   Research indicates that readers use their knowledge of the nature and internal structure of a text to help them organize, interpret, and recall information. The work of

Mandler and Johnson (1977), Rumelhart (1977), and Whaley (1981) suggests that stories have an underlying structure that can be described in terms of their narrative parts and relationships. Although the various components may be labeled differently by different researchers, the following elements are generally agreed upon:

> *Setting*—introduces the main characters, time, and place.
> *Initiating Events*—lead the characters to formulate goals.
> *Internal Response "Goals"*—include reactions to initiating events and formation of goals.
> *Major Actions*—include attempts of the characters to achieve goals.
> *Conclusions*—include consequences of actions, final responses of story characters.

Knowledge of the structure of stories might aid comprehension by helping the reader decide whether a portion of a story is complete or incomplete or predict what types of information might be forthcoming. It seems likely that readers who pay attention to the overall structure of informational texts may also be better able to access and interpret the information in them. Whether students are reading or writing and whether the text is narrative or expository, their knowledge of text structures can assist them in the process of constructing meaning.

Activities that help readers develop a knowledge of text structures are desirable. Students may be required to analyze, complete, or make predictions about texts written by others or to create their own texts using the computer. The almost limitless possibilities for restructuring and reformatting text on the computer provide excellent opportunities for students to experiment with various ways to organize texts. This kind of experimentation can help them gain insight into the relationships between the organization of a passage and how easy or difficult it is to understand it.

Learning to Read Requires Content That Is Appropriate in Difficulty and Interest.   One of the major goals of teachers of reading is to find materials that their students can comprehend and enjoy. They seek to match reader with text. Computers can assist teachers in this effort by saving valuable time when readability formulas are to be employed; however, the use of readability formulas should always be in conjunction with the consideration of other factors. Some of the factors that influence whether or not a text is readable have already been discussed, and they apply whether the text is offered via a computer monitor or presented in some traditional print medium. Whether we are referring to "user-friendly" software or "considerate" textbooks, we are speaking of the factors that affect their comprehensibility to the learner. For example, the use of information section headings, spacing between sections, and illustrations with captions that enhance the text are all techniques that authors and publishers of textbooks and computer software use to aid the reader. A student's background knowledge or prior experience with a topic also plays a major role in determining how well he or she comprehends. Students who are highly motivated because of their interest in a topic will frequently expend an enormous amount of effort to comprehend a text that they might otherwise have abandoned. The use of the computer in reading instruction is often a powerful motivating force in itself. The format or graphic design of a text can assist or impede the reader's comprehension. The very context in which the reading is assigned or selected by the student and completed can also influence the reader's ability to comprehend. Classrooms where care is given to provide successful reading assignments, where personal involvement in the reading is encouraged, and where sharing, discussion, and other activities related to reading are frequent are more apt to promote reading comprehension.

Obviously, what makes a text readable goes far beyond the use of a formula to determine readability. While readability formulas may be useful as general estimates of difficulty, they fall far short of being precise. This is true because these formulas are usually based on word or sentence length. They do not take into account such factors as sentence complexity, word frequency, concept density, or level of abstraction, which also influence a reader's comprehension.

Readability formulas may be useful to teachers as one guide to text difficulty. Computer programs designed to estimate readability can be helpful to that end. But, as Dreyer states, "A book is readable only if it is readable for the intended reader regardless of its formula score" (1984, p. 335). This might very well be applied to computer-based materials as well.

Learning to Read Shares Many Similarities with Learning to Write. No discussion of reading and computers would be complete without a strong emphasis on the relationship between reading and writing. This is especially so since many teachers are finding the use of word processing to be one of the most important means of extending literacy via the computer in the classroom. In recent years, a number of researchers (Rosenblatt, 1978; Squire, 1983; Stotsky, 1982) have turned their attention to the investigation of the relationships between reading development and writing development. Traditionally, these two language processes have been treated as mirror images or opposites of each other. Current emphasis has been placed on the ways in which the development of reading and that of writing are similar and how each may enhance the other. In her review of the research on the relationship of reading and writing, Stotsky (1982) reports that correlational studies almost consistently show that better writers tend to be better readers (of their own writing as well as the writing of others) and that better readers tend to produce more syntactically mature writing than poorer readers do. Although the research offers no evidence to suggest that reading and writing instruction be undertaken for purposes other than those with which they have been traditionally associated, there is consistent evidence of a strong natural influence affecting the outcome of instruction. Reading experiences may be as critical a factor in developing writing ability as writing instruction itself (pp. 636–637). Writing is a complementary aspect of the reading program, particularly where meaning is being emphasized.

There are many ways in which reading and writing are similar. They are both fostered by the learner's natural desire to communicate, and they both involve the construction of meaning in order to communicate. Whether students are writing their own stories or reading stories written by others, they are actively engaged in a search for meaning using written language.

Miscues or mistakes are a natural part of both reading development and writing development. A certain degree of risk taking is involved as learners attempt to make sense of their world through print. The mistakes they make are a necessary and natural outcome of that risk taking. The nature and quality of the errors can reveal a great deal about how students are developing and how they can best be assisted in that development.

Whole language (not fragments) is necessary for constructing meaning through both reading and writing. Whether students are comprehending text or composing it, they must have the ability to see the interrelationships among words in sentences, sentences within paragraphs, and paragraphs within longer passages. The word *mean*, for example, takes on meaning only when it appears in a context. "The mean temperature for September was seventy-five degrees." "Mr. Glover proved how mean he could be." "I didn't mean to hit you." "What does that sentence really mean?" These examples help to illustrate the importance of making associations among chunks of language.

Reading and writing are both dependent on the learner's prior experience and general facility with language. An individual's overall language development is a good indicator of achievement in both reading and writing. Students who have rich vocabularies are more apt to express themselves well orally, bring a greater set of understandings to a task, and achieve more with it.

Both readers and writers tend to be pragmatic. They are guided by their own purpose and that of others. When readers comprehend, they are concerned with the author's intent as well as their own. Writers compose with a sense of audience as well as their own goals in mind. In both, the need to maintain direction in thinking about the intended meaning is critical.

Finally, reading and writing involve both the cognitive and the affective aspects of learning. Readers and writers do what they do for intellectual as well as personal fulfillment.

It becomes obvious that word processing with computers is highly linked to reading development. Composing one's own text structures is an important way to demonstrate how such structures are understood. While it may be possible to perform many computer activities without thinking about writing, it is virtually impossible to engage in word processing without reading. A great deal of reading occurs during writing, particularly at the revision and proofreading stages, which word processing helps us do more efficiently.

The following guidelines serve to summarize the information offered in this chapter. They may also be used as a checklist to help teachers of reading match their use of computers with what is known about the reading process. It is our hope that the checklist will be used in a context where students are given opportunities to work in all the various computer modes: tool, tutor, and tutee.

☐   GUIDELINES FOR COMPUTERS AND READING   ☐

1. Computer instruction in reading should focus on meaning and stress reading comprehension.
   a. Learners should have opportunities to work with whole, meaningful texts. Programs that offer learners a chance to process large chunks of related text, rather than bits and pieces of unrelated language fragments, allow students to use and extend what they know about reading comprehension.
   b. Learners should have opportunities to work with word-recognition programs that stress the use of word meanings in conjunction with phonics and structural analysis. Care must be taken to make sure that, when programs feature the study of individual words and phrases, they are offered within a contextual framework that helps them make sense to the learner. Assessment programs for teachers should also be provided in meaningful context.
   c. Learners should have opportunities to apply the skills being taught in some meaningful way. Programs that deny the learner an oppor-

tunity to make use of what is being "taught" are merely assessment tools and do little to further the learner's growth.

    d. Learners should have opportunities to work with computer materials that use content and language that are within the range of their conceptual development. Tasks should be challenging but not frustrating. Student interests, previous experiences, and purpose play a role in determining whether or not a computer task is comprehensible and worthwhile.

2. Computer instruction in reading should foster active involvement and stimulate thinking.

    a. Learners should have opportunities to discuss the purpose of the computer task or program as well as its nature. They should be aware not only of what they are supposed to do but also of why doing it is important.

    b. Learners should have opportunities to make decisions that control or influence the computer task. Programs that build in opportunities for students to make choices and test predictions help them learn to think and act on their own rather than merely react to someone else's thinking.

    c. Learners should have opportunities to monitor their own learning. Tasks that offer students opportunities to self-check and correct their own errors support the development of independent learners.

3. Computer instruction in reading should support and extend students' knowledge of text structures.

    a. Learners should have opportunities to encounter a wide variety of text structures upon which to apply and refine their comprehension skill. A variety of narrative and expository structures should be provided. Commercially prepared teacher-authored and student-authored materials also should be included. Reading instruction can take place through all kinds of computer-based materials, not merely those designated specifically for that purpose.

    b. Learners should have opportunities to experiment with text in creative ways to suit their purposes. When students reorganize a story or an informational piece on the computer, they are employing and strengthening what they know about the structure of texts.

4. Computer instruction in reading should make use of content from a wide range of subject areas.

    a. Learners should have opportunities to use the computer as a means of applying reading strategies to all areas of the curriculum. Programs related to science, social studies, and math require the use of strategies for reading comprehension. Unless students are being helped to use what they know about reading comprehension under these circumstances, they are not progressing as competent readers.

b. Learners should have opportunities to use the computer in conjunction with other modes of instruction. The computer should not operate as a separate and isolated means of learning. Its use should be integrated with that of books and other learning materials. Students need to think of the computer as one additional means of sharing and retrieving information and practicing skills in interesting and meaningful ways.

5. Computer instruction in reading should link reading to writing.

a. Learners should have opportunities to create text with the computer for sharing and use by others. When students enter information into the computer for someone else to retrieve and use, they must compose with the reader in mind. This frequently involves making explicit use of what they know about what makes a text comprehensible. For example, decisions might be made about how much information to give, what to stress, whether or not to use topic headings, whether or not the ideas are clearly stated, whether or not spelling, punctuation, and other writing conventions are accurately applied, and so on. Revision and proofreading strategies such as these clearly involve the combined application of reading and writing skills.

b. Learners should have opportunities to use the computer as an information-retrieval system. Classroom data bases, where several students input information on a particular topic, are excellent opportunities for students to collect, organize, and store information for others to retrieve, reorganize, and use. The information collected may be lists of items or short passages on various topics. In either case students are acting as readers and writers as they peruse information to make decisions about what to collect and store. Later, they search and sample the stored information to make decisions about what to retrieve and how to use or report it in some written fashion.

☐   SUMMARY   ☐

The foregoing discussion of the reading process has been presented in an effort to provide a framework for you, our readers, as you construct your own personal meanings with this text. It is our hope that you will allow this information to enter your existing schema of reading and computers and that it will help guide you in the many important decisions to be made regarding the use of this new technology in the teaching of reading.

□ 2 □

The Computer as Tool
Word Processing

Lynn Rice, a fifth-grade teacher, was not convinced that writing with pencil and paper could be replaced by the "revolutionary" ways of word processing. During one of her sessions in a reading-and-computers course, she was introduced to a simple word processing program for children. Although still reluctant, she decided to introduce her students to the simple tutorial provided with the program. To her amazement, the students not only responded positively to the opportunity to process their ideas but also seemed to want to experiment more with their writing. They were thrilled with the idea of being able to erase whatever they wrote and seemed to be writing more freely, without fear of making mistakes. After several weeks of experimenting, Mrs. Rice incorporated word processing into her letter-writing unit by having her students write formal and informal letters to the staff and students in the school.

Hal Brier, an eighth-grade language arts teacher, was often frustrated by the record keeping involved with his 125-plus students. Whenever parent conferences were on the horizon, he would berate himself for his disorganized handling of students' files. At an in-service session on a simple data-base-management system, he thought about putting his students' records on file. If he took time initially to file the necessary information, he could easily update the files throughout the year. He also knew that his overwhelming pile of papers could be reduced to a few disks of organized data that could be saved for future reference. Being able to retrieve information instantly without constantly having to shuffle through a stack of papers would help to alleviate a great deal of his filing frustration.

•   •   •

These examples describe two teachers who discovered that the computer can serve them as a tool for teaching and organizing in the classroom. Similarly, our experiences with computers have helped us to appreciate the myriad ways in which computers can be used by teachers and students to perform usually time-consuming tasks at an incredibly rapid rate.

In the next two chapters, specific examples are offered for using the computer as a tool to assist you and your students in a variety of classroom situations. In the present chapter, word processing will be discussed in terms of its applicability to the Language Experience Approach for teaching reading and its use as a writing tool at all levels. In Chapter 3, teacher utility and readability software packages will be described to show the efficiency with which a variety of everyday teacher tasks can be performed. Examples of computerized filing systems will be explained to demonstrate how files can be created and used for classroom teaching and management. Also discussed will be software packages for assisting in the assessment of students' reading skills. Chapter 3 will conclude with examples of computer data bases that teachers and students can access to retrieve many different kinds of information.

Although the following may merely scratch the surface of how the computer can be used to lighten the load of burdensome tasks, we feel that the examples cited can serve as stepping stones for your adaptation of the computer as a tool in your particular teaching situation.

☐   WORD PROCESSING: A TOOL FOR TEACHERS   ☐

Word processing is the general term for software programs that permit you to write, edit, store, and print text. There are programs with varying levels of sophistication available for just about every computer on the market (McWilliams, 1983). A powerful tool for both teachers and students engaged in creating text, word processing is a computer application whose potential is just beginning to be tapped.

Word Processing and the Language Experience Approach

Word processing is made to order for reading teachers who use the Language Experience Approach with beginning readers at any level. In the Language Experience Approach (LEA), as described by M. Hall (1981), Nessel and Jones (1981), and Stauffer (1980), the teacher draws on a student's experiences to elicit language, which is then written down to be read back by the student. This approach assures a match between the reader and the text. The content is well within the reader's schemata, since it is based on real experiences (either supplied directly by the teacher or shared by the student, who relates something that has happened outside of school). Because the student's own natural language patterns are used, the text is usually highly predictable (Bridge, Winograd, & Haley, 1983).

The teacher writes the text (usually in manuscript) on charts, on the chalkboard, or on paper and uses it to introduce concepts about print (for example, a word, a sentence, capital and lowercase letters) and how reading works (directionality, voice-print match, search for meaning). Students usually read the stories with the teacher and take home copies to practice reading by themselves. Through their LEA stories, students build a basic sight vocabulary, gain insights into the phoneme-grapheme system, and learn firsthand how reading and writing are interrelated. This approach is highly recommended for beginners, remedial readers, the linguistically different, and adult illiterates (M. Hall, 1981).

Word processing is a perfect vehicle for LEA. As students generate language about real experiences, the teacher can type it right into the computer through the word processing program. The text can be read back immediately from the screen, stored on disk, and printed out for the student to take away. The teacher can call up the story to work on during subsequent sessions.

Classroom Applications with LEA

In the primary grades, teachers often use a form of LEA when they have children talk about their drawings and then print the words on the picture for the child to read back. Warasch (1984) described a "Computer Language Experience Approach" developed at the West Virginia University Nursery School. Children drew pictures on the screen of an Apple computer using a special program developed in MIT Logo by West Virginia professor Roy Moxley (1984). A press of a key produced an object such as a boy, a girl, a house, or a tree; four other keys allowed the children to move these objects around on the monitor. When their pictures were complete, they composed stories about them, which the teacher typed beneath. Since this nursery school teacher added the computer activity to a traditional LEA program, she was able to compare stories generated with and without word processing. Warasch reported that the children verbalized significantly more and produced longer stories with the computer than they did when they worked in the traditional way.

Although we prefer that children draw their own perceptions of the world on paper or on a screen, we report this application because it is an example of educators' recognizing how the computer can be used to teach reading. Whether the West Virginia people got their positive outcomes because of the "Computer Language Experience Approach" itself or because of the children's excitement about using computers, the results do indicate that combining LEA and word processing can have beneficial effects. Today's children need to learn to deal with text through a variety of media.

Scholastic's *Story Maker: A Fact and Fiction Tool Kit* and *Bank Street Storybook* are two commercial programs now available that combine predrawn graphics with word processing. Both allow users to select pictures from their files, place them anywhere on the screen, and add text to go along with the picture array. These can work much like any pictorial story starters for children who have trouble generating text in an LEA situation. We have dubbed these programs "electronic picture files," suggesting they be used in the same way that teachers use their own picture files. Children can go from generating captions and sentences for pictures to captioning picture storybooks as teachers type in their oral compositions. When these texts are printed out with the child as author, they become very personalized and professional-looking beginning reading materials.

Bradley (1982) described a word processing LEA project carried out with three groups of average or above-average first-graders who had been composing language experience stories in the traditional manner with the teacher writing their dictations on a chart. In the experiment, the teacher recorded the stories on an Apple computer, using a different word processing program with each group. Each group wrote collective stories about a large stuffed rabbit that was used as a stimulus.

Several advantages were reported. When the teacher wrote the stories on charts, the text seemed to become immediately permanent, whereas when she wrote on the computer, the children made spontaneous revisions both during and after the composing. While the average lined chart held about forty words and appeared to determine the length of the line (teachers and children seemed relieved to write "The End" on the bottom line), the computer-written stories averaged about one hundred words. Children were eager to contribute ideas and read back the display, enjoying the speed at which their dictated words could be transcribed. Getting printed copies immediately after the composing session stimulated rereadings as children shared the text with others.

A Reading Center Application

We tried word processing and LEA with a remedial student attending the college reading center. Using *Bank Street Writer* with an Apple II computer we typed his stories as he dictated them. *Bank Street Writer*, probably one of the easiest word processing programs to learn, was developed for children and can be learned by most in a short period of time.

The following story dictated by Bill, a second-grader, shows how we used the dynamic capabilities of the software to teach reading.

> After school yesterday I went into *Mr. Kleinberg's* backyard with my friend Jack. We had matches and there were a lot of leaves.
>
> Just for fun we started a small fire. It smelled so good and crackled and popped. But it started to spread. *Mr. Kleinberg* came home just in time. He pulled out the hose and put it out.
>
> *Mr. Kleinberg* made *us* sign a paper saying that we *were* sorry and that we would never do it again. We *were* glad to sign it and get home that night.

After we read it together, Bill took a printed copy home to read to his family and his now famous neighbor. When he returned the next week, it was easy to call up his story, which had been stored on the disk. (And a good thing, too, since he had forgotten to bring his copy.) He did bring a piece of paper on which he had penciled *Klernberg*, saying that his mom and the neighbor had pointed out that we had misspelled the name. Well, that was easy to correct; we immediately changed all the *Kleinberg*s to *Klernberg*s.

Then we worked on sight words with which Bill had been having trouble (*were/where*). We searched the text to see if either word appeared in the story. No *where* was found, but *were* appeared highlighted in the text in two places. Bill practiced reading the word in and out of context.

At this time Bill also confessed that, although when he first dictated the story he had used *we*, indicating that both he and his friend Jack shared the blame, in truth Jack was just an innocent bystander. This gave us an opportunity to work with syntax. First we replaced *we* with *I* throughout the text and began to reread it. The first sentence of the last paragraph now jarred us. It read, "Mr. Klernberg made *us* sign a paper saying that I *were* sorry and that I would never do it again." We found that we had to change *us* and *were* to have the text make sense and sound right. Again, this was easy to do with word processing.

Next, we looked at the text as a whole to see if any parts could be moved without changing the sense of the story. Could we start the story in any other way? Now we were authors looking for a new "lead." Bill suggested moving the last paragraph up to the beginning. The new draft read as follows:

> Mr. Klernberg made me sign a paper saying that I was sorry and that I would never do it again. I was glad to sign it and get home that night.

> After school yesterday I went into Mr. Klernberg's backyard with my friend Jack. I had matches and there were a lot of leaves.
>
> Just for fun I started a small fire. It smelled so good and crackled and popped. But it started to spread. Mr. Klernberg came home just in time. He pulled out a hose and put it out.

We cannot report that Bill learned to read better because we used a computer, but we can say that combining LEA with word processing allowed us to do a great deal of on-the-spot teaching, quickly and easily, as we manipulated text with this young reader.

Software Made Specifically for LEA

George Mason of the University of Georgia has developed a software package just for LEA. Called *Language Experience Recorder,* it allows the teacher to type in and revise children's stories, just as all word processing packages do, but it also will produce word counts and lists of sight words that can be used by the teacher for testing, teaching, and research purposes. (See Chapter 5 for a more comprehensive description.)

The *Talking Screen Textwriting Program,* created by Terri Rosegrant of State University of New York at Buffalo and Laura Meyers of the University of Southern California, augments typical word processing capabilities with speech. The addition of a voice synthesizer to this specialized word processing program permits students to hear their stories read back to them. Although the first edition was flawed by the robotlike voice used with all early voice synthesizers, subsequent versions promise to have the realistic, easy-to-understand voices that characterize the newer voice synthesizer programs. Reviewer Jean Casey calls this "an outstanding tool for all educators, K through adult education, as well as special education, and bilingual. . . . it is appropriate for any age group that is developmentally functioning at beginning literacy levels" (1983, p. 53).

Software such as these programs, which link a whole-language learning activity like LEA with the powerful tool of word processing, has tremendous implications for teaching and research.

☐   WORD PROCESSING: A TOOL FOR STUDENTS   ☐

As children gain more control over written language and the keyboard (software packages that teach keyboarding will be discussed in a later chapter), they can begin to use this powerful tool directly. From primary grades through postsecondary school, students are being introduced to word processing as the newest instrument for communicating through print.

Primary

Phenix and Hannan (1984) report that word processing helped their grade 1 children come to a better understanding of the writing process. Although many were using only consonants and invented spellings, these children were accustomed to daily writing, conferencing, and revising of stories, following the approach suggested by Don Graves (1983) and Lucy Calkins (1983). After three months of writing and publishing their own books for their class library, they had an opportunity to add word processing to their repertoire of writing instruments. The experience proved very worthwhile.

A perfectionist who wanted every word spelled correctly and who consequently wrote very short pieces, Althea at first carried this behavior over to the computer. Because her teacher agreed to correct the spelling in the first drafts before they were printed out, Althea gained confidence and produced a five-page piece on whales, the longest she had ever written. Josie, a good reader and mathematician, found composing difficult; her "blank sheet" was at first replaced by a "blank screen." After realizing she could easily change anything she wrote, Josie began to experiment with free writing, gradually finding it easier to get a first draft going. Word processing helped these two girls overcome problems faced by beginning writers at any level.

Good writers became better as they worked with the new tool. Shibu, the best speller in the class, found printing laborious. His lengthy stories were hard to read because of his tightly packed lettering. He was thrilled with word processing, which took over the most difficult part of the composing act for him. Jay, an enthusiastic writer, loved experimenting with the word processing program. Instead of just adding to his piece about a family picnic, he inserted details and described events more fully at each revision. But finally he ran out of real happenings and began adding irrelevant material just to stay at the machine. During a conference with his teacher, he admitted that many of the add-ons were unnecessary and readily deleted them. He carried over the inserting and deleting when writing with pencil, crossing out here and cutting/pasting there; he seemed to have internalized the revising process by using word processing.

Several effects of this writing with word processing were noted. Instead of starting new pieces each day, the children generally chose to continue works in progress, revising and adding to them; the pieces became longer and more detailed. They read over their pieces critically, increasing the effectiveness of their peer and teacher conferences. Because they could look at successive drafts (printouts were saved in folders, just as were written drafts), they became aware that writing could be manipulated, that it evolved over time. Those who had trouble with the physical act of writing and subsequent transcribing were thrilled with the ease of the mechanical part and with the appearance of their finished products. This new tool proved to be an extremely positive addition to this primary writing program.

Elementary

Most schools reporting the use of word processing as a tool appear to introduce it in grade 4. One teacher in Ridgewood, New Jersey, combines teaching about computers with word processing. She has her fourth-graders compose letters to people connected with computers (for example, Messrs. Jobs and Wozniak, founders of Apple Computer) asking about what they do and how they became interested in the field. Then they use the computer to write the final drafts. The recipients are so impressed that the children's letters are written with a word processing tool that they invariably reply.

Maureen Armour, a fourth-grade teacher in Demarest, New Jersey, has added word processing to the many writing tools (assorted pens, pencils, and magic markers) already in use in her writing-as-process classroom. Class members wheel two or three computers into her room and boot up a simple word processing program (*Bank Street Writer*). Children who want to use word processing sign up for a specific day and period. While most avail themselves of the opportunity to use word processing to write a final draft of a piece that has been revised after peer and teacher conferences, a few choose to ignore the new tool and stay with the more conventional instruments. During one writing period we observed children writing final drafts of poems they had composed over the last week. Word processing allowed them to move words around and realign their poems with ease. (Figure 2.1 shows some samples of their poems.) They were planning a Poet's Day to which parents and school staff would be invited to hear the children read their poems, which would be bound in a collection with everyone receiving a copy.

Bruce, Michaels, and Watson-Gegeo (1985) report how the social interaction that takes place around the computer can affect children's writing. One sixth-grade class was engaged in writing critical reviews of a school assembly production. They had written first drafts at their desks

Figure 2.1. *Poems written by fourth graders in Maureen Amour's class.*

The Sparkling Fields
The sun shines upon the fields of white,
Making them sparkle
As if they were sprayed with stars.
Laura Woodson●

Data Disk
Data disk with his square head,
And sometimes two eyes.
The eyes, of course,
Are the stickers.
The data disk also has a nose
And a freckle next to it.
The best thing he does
Is save things in his memory
For people.

● Alex Hayden

poets
who
know
it!

Medicine
Medicine in your mouth
Medicine in your tummy
Pink medicine for cherry-itis
Green for greenpox
Red for strep strawberry
And Blue for blue flu.
●Alyssa Winkler

and, after an editing conference with their teacher, were assigned numbers to enter their reviews into the computer. As they were awaiting their turns, they had the opportunity to read each other's drafts. When she used the word processing tool, Margaret, who had written a straightforward critique at first, added to her piece a narrative discrediting Marine, a fellow reviewer whose work she had just read. Marine's review was highly critical of the glee club, but Margaret knew Marine wrote this because she had been turned down by the glee club. Margaret, acting as critic and as exposer of another critic with ulterior motives, moved toward composing at the keyboard. The computer as tool, because of the change it made in the overall writing system in that classroom, affected both the content and the form of student writing. Daiute (1985a) points out that writing is a social process, especially when students write at computer stations, since they tend to read and comment on each other's writing and get immediate reader-writer interaction.

Much social interaction and peer critiquing takes place in Roberta Hart's fifth-grade writing-as-process program at Montclair-Kimberley Academy in Montclair, New Jersey. In the computer lab, students can be seen engaged in peer conferencing and shared composing both at computers and in small groups around the room. During one visit we noticed the following interactions.

As Saurabh read aloud his story "The Case of the Diamond and Ruby Clock," Yung typed the text into the Apple computer. Since Yung, who had already finished his piece, was a fast typist, he had volunteered to help Saurabh get his contribution to the class literary collection into print. Some on-the-spot revising and editing were taking place. They discussed cohesion, pronoun antecedents ("But you didn't say who *they* are in this part"), the spelling of specific words, and the organization of the text into paragraphs.

Next to them, Marnie and Amy, who had been collaborating on a piece that had gone through several revisions, were taking turns typing in their story about surprise happenings at a carnival. They didn't have their drafts with them, but they knew the story so well that they were able to write this final draft directly on the computer. They could easily erase, insert, or move blocks of text as they wrote and read aloud the unfolding story.

At the next station, Diane, who had also picked up the carnival setting, was typing her finished piece "Kidnapped at the Carnival" from voluminous drafts in her writing folder. Also working alone, Rachel was scrolling through her piece about a boy who had died and gone to heaven but still had to earn his wings. She stopped to change words, correct typos and misspellings (checking with Kelli at her right), and add punctuation marks.

Three boys who were working on illustrations for the booklet sat at a table in the middle of the lab while three other students, who were quietly discussing their group story before beginning to type it into a computer, sat on the floor in a corner. Others were at various stages of composing, revising, and editing, using either conventional writing tools or the word processor. One girl, who had completely finished her piece and printed it out, was using words from the book the class had just read (William Pène Du Bois's *Twenty-one Balloons*) to make a crossword puzzle with a piece of software called *Crossword Magic* (this will be described in the next chapter).

Although this was a writing class, there was plenty of reading going on as the children read each other's pieces on the screens or in their writing folders. As noted by Daiute (1985a), writing and reading were going on in a social context to which the computer had added a new dimension.

Students at Valley Middle School in Oakland, New Jersey, use word processing to produce a school newspaper. As an after-school activity, ten or more students (a different group each marking period) meet with teacher Chris Chakmakian to write feature stories and news stories for their paper, *The Valley Voice.* After assignments are given and deadlines set, students gather their information, write their articles, and revise/edit after receiving feedback from peers and their teacher. Then they type the finished pieces onto a disk using *Bank Street Writer*, print them out, and cut and paste them into a newspaper format, which is duplicated for the whole school.

Chris Chakmakian is planning to introduce her students to a specialized word processing program called *Newsroom.* This piece of software allows the user to set up banners and columns and supplies a file of special graphics that can be used to produce a newspaper. Once they become familiar with it, these young journalists will be able to get out a professional-looking paper more easily and more quickly than is possible with the general word processing program they are presently using.

Secondary and Postsecondary

Phil Restaino, an English teacher at Mamaroneck High School, Mamaroneck, New York, has set up a computer lab just for writing. All ninth- and tenth-graders are introduced to word processing as an integral part of a one-semester English course. We observed a tenth-grade class on their first day in the lab. They had written several drafts of an autobiography, interspersed with peer and teacher conferences, and were ready to write the next draft on the computer. After a brief introduction to the *PFS: Write* program, they were all off and writing within twenty minutes.

The next day they finished entering their pieces and, after running them through a spelling checker (*Sensible Speller*), had them printed out. Phil reads these first drafts and confers with each student in class. They have one or two more sessions in the lab before submitting their papers for a final grade. Phil has the students bring their journals to the lab so that they can free-write from journal entries should they finish the target piece ahead of others. Thus they move easily and naturally into composing directly with their new writing tool.

The supervised writing lab is open before and after classes and during the lunch hour so students can work independently on writing projects. Since they have had the introduction to word processing in the context of a course, juniors and seniors come during open times and free periods to write papers for all their courses. Word processing is regarded as a valuable tool to use in completing assignments across the curriculum.

Okun (1984) wanted to see whether word processing would affect the quality of writing generated by students in a postsecondary secretarial school. She taught developmental reading/writing to one group that also learned word processing from her. In writing class, she had them choose their own topics for descriptive paragraphs, write first drafts, revise after conferences, edit, and write final drafts. Then they learned to use a dedicated word processing system similar to those found in many offices. The next descriptive piece, following the same process approach, was done entirely on the computer. Pre- and post-word-processing final copies were compared for overall content and delivery (holistic scores) and syntactic maturity (mean length of *t*-unit; Hunt, 1970). The pieces composed on the word processor had longer *t*-units and significantly higher holistic scores. Okun concluded that her students produced more mature, higher-quality compositions when they wrote with a word processing system.

Jersey City State College introduced word processing to their ESL students who were trying to learn to produce coherent papers with identifiable thesis statements. English instructors were able to work with syntax and semantics while the text was still in the formative stages. Students were delighted with their printed versions, which soon appeared relatively error-free and read like standard American English. Because of the successful use of this tool with this specialized population, Jersey City State is introducing word processing into its freshman writing program.

Daiute (1985a) reports that word processing is becoming increasingly popular in college composition classes. Spelling checkers and text-analysis programs like *Writer's Workbench* can help students produce papers that don't have to be read for mechanics, allowing instructors to spend conference time on more important issues like logical development and the actual content of the papers.

Bortnick (1986) has just developed an easy-to-use program that helps writers take an objective look at their pieces. Called *Ghost Writer*, it will give you a readability level based on the Fry formula (see Chapter 3 for more on readability) and a picture of your text's organization — the text, with only conjunctions printed, is shown by lines with indentations indicating new paragraphs. Writers who string together sentences with numerous *and*'s come face to face with their problems when they see their text devoid of content but packed with the often overused coordinating conjunction.

The program also contains a homonym checker that works like most spelling checkers. For example, for every *there,* the writers will see the other possible spellings (*their, they're*) and can check their texts to determine which one they intended. Of course, not all writers need this kind of check, but for those who do confuse common homonyms, working with them in the context of their own pieces is a much more valuable way of learning than by doing drill-and-practice exercises.

Two other features of this new tool are a clarity checker, which will do such things as identify prepositions and *to be* verbs, and a vocabulary analyzer, which will count the number of different words in a piece and the number of times words are used.

While Bortnick has used parts of *Ghost Writer* with middle-school students, starting with the text organization option in grade 6 and working up to the other options by grade 8, we have recommended it to instructors who teach basic skills writing at William Paterson College. Some classes are using *Apple Writer* and can therefore subject their disks to any or all of the options. Run-on sentences and misspelled homonyms are problems for some writers even at the college level.

While some colleges and universities (Stevens Institute of Technology, Drexel Institute, and Dartmouth) are requiring students to purchase their own micros, others are providing labs dedicated to writing. Bucknell is a case in point. They have set up a lab of Apple Macintosh micros for composition courses only. Text-analysis programs are fast becoming available for most commonly used word processing packages.

Daiute also describes an interesting software program being developed by the Harvard University composition program. Called *Notewriter*, it permits the instructor to insert symbols in students' files that tell them to see the instructor's discussion of that section. They press an appropriate key to read the comments and can return to their text to make changes if they wish. She notes, "Such a commenting procedure offers the student feedback in the context of the text, which remains clear of handwritten remarks that could distract the student from reading the text" (1985, p. 220).

Since there are over three hundred word processing programs now available, no attempt has been made here to recommend specific software packages. We have named those we have seen in use, but the choice of what to buy must remain with you, the users, who are constrained by the type of hardware you own, the level of students you teach, and, of course, budget considerations.

We would like to share with you the titles of a few programs that have special features useful for some populations. For instance, *Magic Slate* is one piece of word processing software that "grows" with children. You can adjust the size of type (20, 40, 80 columns) to fit the reading needs of your students. The Macintosh *MacWrite* program, which permits nine font styles in five print sizes, is also an excellent choice for teachers who deal with readers and writers of varying age levels.

Most elementary school teachers find that children in grades 4 and up can easily handle the menu-driven *Bank Street Writer*. The new augmented version for the Apple IIe and IIc has cleared up some of the problems encountered with the earlier edition. For older students, who generally need more powerful programs with more formatting and editing options, teachers can investigate a wide variety of word processing packages, from the very sophisticated but easy-to-learn *Word Perfect* with its indexing, table of contents, and footnoting features to *AppleWorks*, which is an integrated package including word processing, data base, and spreadsheet programs. An excellent resource for helping you to select word processing programs is Colette Daiute's *Writing and Computers* (1985a). In Part III, she discusses the needs of writers of various ages and stages, and in her resources section she lists the most widely used programs with brief descriptions. Teachers need to select carefully, trying out different programs with their students. Leslie Eiser, who teaches in the Computers in Education program at McGill University in Montreal, says, "Choose with care; more powerful word processing may be a better investment in the long run if you will be able to take advantage of the extra power. You do not have to teach your kids all the possibilities right now—they can grow into their word processing program slowly" (1985, p. 55).

Another integrated program developed by Andee Rubin and Bertram Bruce at Bolt, Beranek, and Newman and now being distributed by D. C. Heath is *Quill*. This complex of programs was designed to help teach writing by means of the classic process approach: prewriting, composing, revising/editing, and sharing. "Planner" is the prewriting program, which helps students generate and organize ideas before writing. They can brainstorm alone or in groups, then select points to develop further, grouping them into frameworks for written pieces. Teachers also can use "Planner" as a simple authoring system, setting up questions to guide students in the prewriting period.

"Library" is an information-storage system that allows students to type in pieces, index them according to keywords, and retrieve them much as you do any data base information. "Writer's Assistant" is a text editor that enables students to revise and edit pieces they have written and stored in "Library." "Mailbag" is an electronic communications system that permits teachers and students to send messages within the classroom, school, district, or network of users.

In reviewing *Quill*, Judith Newman (1985) noted that it is based on a linear view of writing, with the manual suggesting that "Planner" be used before "Library" or "Mailbag." She points out that this isn't always the way writing happens. Sometimes it is best to begin to free-write, so that your first efforts can act as a powerful prewriting experience. She also noted that, when entering text into "Library," you can't edit. All revising/editing must be done when using the text editor. This can be very annoying if you like to make changes as you write.

All fourth- and fifth-graders in the Bridgewater-Raritan school district in New Jersey are introduced to *Quill*. Contrary to the manual's suggestions, this district appears to be using *Quill* mainly for word processing. We observed children typing pieces from their writing folders into "Library," first entering their names, titles, and keywords and finally calling for a printed copy to give to the teacher. (Prewriting, composing, and some revising had already taken place with conventional tools in their writing workshops.) Their teachers, Frieda Helmstetter and Virginia Radonich, read the printed versions, offering suggestions and editing points; then the students returned to the Apple, using the text editor to produce the final, edited copy. These printed pieces were placed in their writing folders along with their handwritten compositions for the term.

Frieda, the fourth-grade teacher, told us that, although her class didn't regularly use "Planner," they had found it helpful for one class writing project, a booklet on Christmas customs around the world. Once the class developed questions to be answered on "Planner," they arranged themselves into groups to do the research, and finally entered their finished reports into "Library," creating their own data base.

These middle-grade children were not using "Mailbag" much when we observed them in the latter half of the school year. Frieda explained that she had introduced them to writing on the computer through "Mailbag" at the beginning of the year so that they could get used to the keyboard by typing in short messages. They started out by typing in "problems" that required responses. For example, "Going Crazy" asked the

"Quick Quaint Quill Editorial Group" (QQQEG) how to solve a local noise problem (Figure 2.2). However, on the whole, the potential for this program as an inter- or intraclass communications network appeared not to be realized as yet. These teachers are still experimenting with ways to integrate all the components of this package into their program.

Quill was also being used, but differently, in the Bridgewater-Raritan high school English workshops. These were small classes of students from all high school levels who needed remedial work in reading and writing. For the most part, they were reading paperbacks and high-interest/low-readability materials from an extensive collection. Their teachers were using "Planner" as an authoring system, putting in questions to help the students respond to what they had just read. For instance, one student had just finished a novel with strongly drawn characters. Her teacher, Sharyn Kost, suggested she call for "Fiction: Characterization" (Figure 2.3) from "Planner" and work through the questions. The student was able to type in her responses, often referring to the book to support her answers. When she finished, she printed out a copy and placed it in the teacher's "in" basket. Sharyn Kost says that she can readily assess her students' level of understanding from their answers; she also points out that her students prefer to use the "Planner" response mode rather than to write the usually assigned book reports. She feels they are internalizing book review and other writing conventions through working with this program. She and her fellow teacher George Connors have developed "Planners" for types of fiction and nonfiction reading/writing activities. Figure 2.4 shows one for reading letters to the editor in newspapers.

Quill is valuable because it encourages students to share their writing, makes them think about keywords for storing and accessing information, and permits the linking of reading and writing in innovative contexts with products appearing both on the screen and in printout form. However, most of the activities could be done with many word processing packages now available; we tend to agree with Newman, who wrote, "While an

---

Figure 2.2. *A "Mailbag" message (*Quill*) in a fourth-grade classroom.*

To: QQQEG
From: Going Crazy
Subject: Problem to Solve

    I don't know what to do with these children on our block. They are outside playing before we are ready to wake up in the morning. It wouldn't be so bad, except they are extremely noisy. They are constantly yelling and screaming. What do you suggest we do?

Figure 2.3. *An application of the "Planner" (Quill) with fiction in a high school resource room (Bridgewater-Raritan).*

Planner: Fiction
Fiction: Characterization

Sharyn Kost

Having to write a book report forces you to read your book carefully. Then you must analyze and comment on certain aspects of the work.

A novel contains certain elements: characters, setting, conflict, and plot structure. This planner deals with characterization.

This characterization planner contains 15 questions.

Answer each of the following questions in as much detail as possible. When you have finished answering all of the questions, press N (none of the above) and print 1 copy.

* What is your name? Class period? Today's date?
* What is the exact title of your book?
* Who is the author?
* Who is the audience that the author is addressing?
* Who is the most important character? Explain.
* What other characters have important roles? Name them and tell their importance.
* Minor characters enrich a story by providing further complications for the major characters. Describe a minor character and explain why this character is special.
* Physically describe each major character. Consider such things as sex, age, height, weight, coloring, appearance, facial expressions, clothing, habits, etc.
* Do you think the major character is capable of a deep, strong love? Tell why or why not.
* Is the major character capable of fierce hate? Explain.
* Is the character motivated by emotion (fear, pain, love, guilt, or hate)? Explain.
* Has anyone in the book been victimized or treated unfairly? Explain.
* If you had to make a dangerous journey with a character from the book, whom would you choose? Explain why you would choose this particular person.
* Does the character suffer alienation from society? Friends? Family? Self? Explain.
* Some people may be described as "selfish takers" and others as "unselfish givers." Whom would you describe as a "taker"? A "giver"? Explain your reasons by giving specific examples from the book.

Keywords: /Novel/Characters/

Figure 2.4. *An application of the "Planner" (Quill) with nonfiction in a high school resource room (Bridgewater-Raritan).*

Planner: Nonfiction
Letter to the Editor

George G. Connors   Sharyn H. Kost

Editorials tell you what the paper thinks. Columnists tell you what the experts think. But to find out just what average people like ourselves think, read letters to the editor.

Sometimes people have strong feelings about what is going on around them and want to let others know how they feel. Letters may be about . . . news events, taxes, nuclear weapons, low student test scores, and other issues.

Readers are encouraged to send in their views on virtually any topic. Some stipulations (rules/requirements) are that the letters be signed (although the signature does not have to appear in the paper), kept within a maximum word limit, and show good taste.

1. Turn to the page on which the letters to the editor are located.
2. List the name of the newspaper and the date.
3. How many letters to the editor appear on the page?
4. Clip *one* of the letters from the paper. Attach it to this printout when you are finished with the assignment.
5. What does the letter concern, that is, what is the topic of the letter?
6. Is the writer in favor of or against the topic?
7. What main points does the writer make?
8. How is the letter signed?
9. Do you agree or disagree with the letter? Why?
10. Type in your name, period, and date.
11. Type in number twelve (12) and press return.

Keywords: /Editorial/Letter - Read/Opinions - Read/

imaginative teacher having experience with word processing and file systems could improvise these activities without much difficulty using any standard word processor, *Quill* is a useful tool for teachers who are themselves still novice computer users" (1985, p. 300).

☐   SUMMARY   ☐

This chapter has shown how word processing can be a valuable tool for both teachers and students at all levels as they draft, compose, revise, edit, and read dynamic text that can be easily manipulated on a computer screen, stored for later use, and printed out as hard copy. Teachers already are using this tool in exciting ways in classroom and lab settings; the potential seems almost limitless as more and more teachers gain access to the new technology and work it into their reading-writing programs. The next chapter will deal with other ways in which teachers of reading can use the computer as a tool.

□ 3 □

The Computer as Tool
Utilities, Assessments, and Data Bases

As was shown in Chapter 2, the beneficial effects of word processing are beginning to be felt in many classroom situations. In a similar vein, other "tool" uses of the computer can enhance the learning environment. This chapter describes how five other computer applications can be used to help teachers implement their reading programs. Three of the applications — teacher utility, readability assessment, and informal reading assessment packages — are described in terms of their ability to tailor the learning environment to students' needs. The other two, personalized filing and information-retrieval systems, are discussed in terms of their ability to organize and retrieve data for a variety of purposes. Although presented separately here for purposes of clarity, these tools become even more effective when they are integrated into the total curriculum.

□   TEACHER UTILITY PROGRAMS   □

Teacher utility packages enable computer novices to tailor software to students' academic needs. They provide frameworks consisting of an activity format (replete with graphics and reinforcement) and directions for supplying the content to be produced on or off the computer. A particularly appealing aspect of these packages is how expeditiously activities that normally take much of a teacher's time to create can be prepared.

Creating Skill Exercises and Tests

Some software packages, such as *Word Wise, Create — Vocabulary, Words for the Wise,* and the Arcademic Drill builders (*Wiz Works, Idea Invasion,* and *Master Match*), contain utility options for inserting your own entries in lieu of the original predetermined skill exercises. *Word Wise*, for example, enables the teacher to create sight vocabulary exercises for primary-level students. Students have the option of filling in a sentence blank with a word or phrase or matching a word or phrase with a preprogrammed picture. *Wiz Works* provides a beat-the-clock format for spelling practice. Students need to select quickly from four options the letter that completes the correct spelling of a word. Although *Wiz Works* is presented as a game of isolated drill, the ability to supply choice words enhances its appeal.

Other teacher utility packages are more open-ended in that the teacher creates rather than alters the content used within the program. Often referred to as "authoring systems" or "mini-authoring systems," these software packages provide a structured framework for typing questions, answers, clues, and feedback so that tests, drill-and-practice exercises, tutorial lessons, or puzzles can be created.

Test packages such as *Quizley Test Worm* and *Exam Builder* enable the teacher to create extensive files of content-area questions in objective formats such as multiple-choice, matching, true-false, or fill-in-the-blank. Options for adding, deleting, or editing questions are usually available, along with some type of feedback and student management system. Variations in cost, space availability, physical appeal, graphics capabilities, and record-keeping devices are the critical considerations for purchase.

Drill-and-practice exercises and tutorials can be created with such packages as *Kid Bits Words Fair, Create—Lessons*, and *ZES Authoring System. Kid Bits Words Fair* is a nicely designed program for primary children. The disk starts out with ten drill-and-practice lessons. Each time students get the correct answer, they get to add another feature to a colorful clown face. At the end of the lessons, the students can enjoy a slide show of the clown faces created. Up to twenty drill-and-practice lessons on any topic can be added, edited, and printed easily with an option to monitor the progress of up to eighty students in four classes.

With programs like *Create—Lessons*, the teacher can provide hints for answering questions missed on the first round and explanations for any series of questions answered incorrectly. Because editing features are available, the teacher can alter the hints and explanations periodically to help students close any conceptual gaps. With more sophisticated programs like *ZES Authoring System*, teachers can include branching so that students are presented continually with the appropriate level of information or skill exercises. However, the excitement of tailoring instruction on a disk must be tempered with consideration for the way in which it is used. While they are an invaluable aid for organizing content material or differentiating instructional presentations, isolated skill-development exercises often become a substitute for holistic learning. Emphasis should be given to the contextual application of skill development. For instance, if at the elementary level homonym exercises are entered in a multiple-choice format, they then should be included in whole-text exercises. Similarly, if at the secondary level literary terms such as *simile* and *metaphor* are included in a true-false exercise, their figurative effects on language can be best appreciated in cloze-type exercises.

Creating Word Games and Puzzles

Increasingly popular are the utility packages that generate puzzles. Word finds, crossword puzzles, scrambles, and cryptograms can be created instantly for any skill or content area. With word find packages such as *Wordsearch* and *The Puzzler*, teachers can tailor the size and format of the puzzle to students' developmental needs. While a primary teacher might choose a puzzle containing a few words in horizontal order on a small matrix (for example, eighteen letters across and down), a secondary teacher might select a puzzle with words arranged in horizontal, vertical, diagonal, and inverted order on a large matrix (for example, thirty letters across and down). Some might claim that activities like these do not teach reading; however, a case may be made for aiding spelling, because students must look at the words carefully and note internal letter arrangements. Generally, though, word find puzzles are most effective when organized around a theme, for instance, poetry terms, colors, or a science concept. In this way, you are helping learners to associate the terms with their cognitive structures.

Crossword puzzle packages such as *Crossword Magic* enable the teacher to create and edit puzzles in a matter of minutes. Recommended highly by Mangiapane (1983), *Crossword Magic* is formatted into a British non-symmetrical-style puzzle so that the filler words are not required to fit the puzzle. Unlike other drill-and-practice activities, crossword puzzles can be used to elicit and enrich students' background information. Since students need to manipulate their vocabulary in order to complete puzzles, higher-level thinking skills are used. Students must infer what the author means from the clues offered. Therefore, rather than simply offering synonyms or the denotative meanings of words, it might be more useful to provide clues that play on words or conjure up the connotative meanings of words. Crossword puzzles can be used to reinforce vocabulary in content-area instruction. Specifically, when teaching about paragraph structures in reading/language arts, you might create a puzzle including such terms as *cause-effect, comparison-contrast, chronological,* and *enumeration.* Since time need not be expended on the manipulation of words in the puzzle itself, you have more time to create better clues for any area of instruction.

Giving students opportunities to manipulate language is important for development. Scramble and cryptogram packages such as *Jabbertalky* and *Mystery Sentences* respectively also can be used as aids to reinforce learning in spelling, grammar, vocabulary, and problem solving. Challenged by the job of deciphering words or sentences, students must develop an awareness of the semantic, syntactic, and graphophonic cues of our language.

Presently, multipurpose utility packages exist that can be used to create a variety of puzzles and activities. Less sophisticated than most of the commercially prepared packages, *Teacher Utilities*, Volumes 1, 2, 3, and 4 (available from Minnesota Educational Computing Consortium [MECC]*), are convenient if your school district is a member. *Teacher Utilities*, Volume 1, contains four extremely useful programs for reading, "Crossword," "Word Find," "Review," and "Test Generator." It also includes two programs, "Block Letters" and "Posters," for creating signs. Since classroom signs are used to enhance the classroom environment while reflecting current events and holidays, their frequent and personalized changes can be accomplished readily with these two programs. However, as with the other programs on this disk, sophistication is forfeited for cost-effectiveness. More sophisticated programs such as *The Print Shop, Magic Slate* (see Chapter 2), and *The Professional Sign Maker* also are excellent aids for creating signs and posters. *Teacher Utilities*, Volumes 2, 3, and 4, contain programs for hangman, word unscrambling, and spelling.

With any of the aforementioned utility ideas, we recommend that you alternate the use of off-line print with computer activities. If, for exam-

---

*The Minnesota Educational Computing Consortium (MECC), an organization established in 1978, assists computer users and participating members in coordinating, obtaining, and using educational computing materials. Once school districts or state agencies pay a fee to become a MECC member, they are entitled to purchase software and supportive materials at a reduced rate. Several schools may join together for a MECC membership. MECC catalogs are available to describe the software programs available for the Apple, Atari, Commodore, IBM, and Radio Shack computers.

The MECC software described in this section is available for the Apple computer only, but different utility packages are compatible with other types of hardware. For more information, write to: MECC Distribution Center, 3490 Lexington Avenue North, St. Paul, MN 55126-8097.

ple, students have been assigned to read a novel, they can be guided through discussions beforehand or afterward by working through a computer activity related to the story parts, vocabulary, or concepts presented in the novel. Also, it is good to involve students in making exercises or puzzles on the utility package. For instance, students could be assigned the task of designing a crossword puzzle for a unit in a science or social studies book. (See Chapter 2 for Roberta Hart's use of *Crossword Magic* in her writing class.) In so doing, students are being asked to process the information presented in class as well as to use outside resources for creating clues. What better way to learn a body of knowledge than to have to use it for a creative purpose?

Authoring Languages

The concept of utility packages is one of the more viable approaches to tailoring Computer Assisted Instruction (CAI) to the classroom situation. Besides the tightly structured "authoring-systems" framework described above, there also are "authoring languages." More flexible than "authoring systems," "authoring languages" allow you to create your own lesson structure with a special set of commands that makes it easy to create an individualized lesson ("Computers As," 1984).

The most widely used authoring language is called PILOT (Programmed Inquiry Learning Or Teaching). PILOT was devised in the late 1960s to create dialogue for use with college students (Lathrop & Goodson, 1983). Many different PILOT programs exist on the market, each with its own particular features (Mason, 1984). For example, *E-Z Pilot* enables the user to quickly write lessons that tutor and to offer special help when the student is confused; *Apple SuperPILOT* has the ability to produce color graphics and sound effects; and *Appilot II* includes a built-in timer and voice output. *Vanilla Pilot*, recommended by George Mason (1984), is easy to use with its three sets of commands: the first for creating the exercises, the second for editing or modifying the first draft, and the third for adding pictures or enhancing the text. Since PILOT programs exist for different computers, research should be done to find the one that offers the best capabilities for your brand of computer.

Blanchard (1985) reported on the concept of Learning Strategies (LS) Textbases to help students learn from text. LS Textbases allow a student or teacher to enter any text from any content area. Furthermore, LS Textbases permit students to study a text using computer-based learning strategies, for example, reading/rereading, underlining, and sentence or paragraph reorganization. Teachers also can provide computer-based cues or prompts (coaching) to help students understand a particular learning strategy.

Recent developments in authoring packages have included interactive video capabilities. Students no longer need to be confined to responding with objective answers; they now can be encouraged to respond critically and creatively. Rather than asking a student to answer the "who," "what," "when," and "where" questions, the program can ask "why" questions. Students have the opportunity to interact with stories presented. Space can be provided at various points for them to draw and write about the story presented. They can be asked to predict what they believe will happen and to provide a rationale for their beliefs.

While capitalizing on the more sophisticated authoring languages, teachers can create adventure games, simulations, and problem-solving activities that branch appropriately to students' conceptual levels. Other than cost and time commitment factors, these authoring languages pose few obstacles. Rather, they invite teachers to write entire courses of study on the programs.

We often complain about the quality of software packages on the market. Utility packages provide us with the opportunity to design programs that reflect the needs of our students.

□   READABILITY ASSESSMENT   □

Readability refers to the ease with which a text can be read. It is determined by formulas that consider the two variables of sentence length and word difficulty. Usually, longer sentences are thought to be more difficult to comprehend because of the load on short-term memory; longer or less familiar words are thought to be harder to read than shorter, familiar words. Over the past fifty years numerous formulas have been developed. These formulas permit users to assign approximate grade levels to texts; for example, if a text is determined to be at the eighth-grade level, it can be assumed that a reader who reads at an eighth-grade level will be able to read it.

Traditionally, text difficulty has been a concern of teachers. We talk about pairing readers with texts to aid comprehension. If we were really "matching readers with texts" we would be looking at more than assigned readability levels. We would be concerned more about factors such as our students' background knowledge and interests versus the content of the text, the linguistic complexity of the text, and its overall coherence; we would look for texts that are "considerate" of our students (Armbruster,

1984). These are factors that readability formulas do not assess. In practice, when we use formulas, we are trying to locate texts that have readability levels consistent with 'the reading achievement levels of our students; we can get a "ballpark" estimate of how difficult a text may be for an idealized reader.

Davison (1984) says that readability formulas consider factors that *reflect* difficulty rather than *cause* difficulty. She points out that one of the main consequences of the formulas, the rewriting of texts with shorter sentences and words, leads to dull, stilted texts that often can be harder to comprehend than the originals.

Notwithstanding the controversy over the value of readability formulas, reading teachers are frequently called upon to determine the level of texts under consideration for adoption by a school system. When used as just *one* variable to be considered by textbook search committees, readability has some validity as a global assessment of general difficulty.

Some Widely Used Formulas

Two readability formulas widely used by publishers are the Spache (1974) for primary materials and the Dale-Chall (1984) for middle- and upper-grade materials. In both, words that are not on their lists of high-frequency/common words are deemed unfamiliar; the number of unfamiliar words and the average length of sentences determine the difficulty level.

To use these two methods, you have to check each word against the lists and do a number of calculations, a very time-consuming and tedious operation to do manually. It is a perfect application for a computer, which can do the whole procedure, searching the lists and doing the calculations, in a matter of minutes.

Because these two formulas were so complicated, others were developed to yield "quick and easy" estimates. The Fry (1977) formula, which can be used on materials for grade 1 through college, is popular with classroom teachers. You count the number of syllables and sentences per one hundred words (three passages are suggested) and go to a graph with averages of these two variables to locate a level.

Raygor (1977) developed a similar graph for secondary and postsecondary materials. For this method, instead of counting syllables, you count the number of words over six letters per one hundred words and use this variable, along with average sentence length, to make an estimate.

Rudolph Flesch formulated a way to estimate the difficulty of adult materials. Frequently used by advertising agencies to check the reading ease of advertising copy, this method is explained in *The Art of Readable*

Writing (Flesch, 1962). Again, the average number of syllables and sentences per one hundred words are the variables used.

The Gunning-Fog (Gunning, 1952) formula was developed for newspaper and magazine articles. The number of words with three or more syllables and the average sentence length per one hundred words are the factors calculated for the Fog Index.

While the last four formulas are less time-consuming than the Spache and Dale-Chall, they also are tedious to do by hand. Computers are ideally suited for quantitative tasks like counting syllables and words.

Software That Assesses Readability

There are many software programs that do readability analyses. Jamestown has produced a disk version of the Fry that allows you to type in three one-hundred-word passages and get a Fry estimate quickly and easily. *Micro Power and Light Readability* yields information from nine popular formulas.

One of the most popular packages is the Minnesota Educational Computer Consortium (MECC) *School Utilities*, Volume 2. Simple to use, it gives estimates from the six formulas discussed above: Spache, Dale-Chall, Fry, Raygor, Flesch, and Gunning-Fog. The directions for using the software are clear and require no special technical knowledge to follow. Of course, picking passages representative of the whole text is important: it is not good to use the first paragraph, sections with unusually long words or sentences, or parts with a great deal of direct discourse. Because of these concerns, it would be good for teachers or specialists to select the passages to be entered, but any good typist (teacher, student, or secretary) could type in the passages and execute the program.

The readability application is a valuable tool for classroom teachers and reading teachers who want to get a quantitative estimate for the difficulty level of a text. Content-area teachers, especially, may want to see if a proposed text is "in the ballpark" for the level of students (middle grades, junior high, senior high) they expect to teach. However, they should keep in mind the caveat of Duffelmeyer (1985) to "beware the aura of precision" that is communicated when computer programs are used to estimate readability. Just because a printout shows a text to be at a specific grade level does not mean that all readers at that ability will be able to read it with ease. In our interactive view of the reading process, other concerns such as background knowledge and format/writing styles that are "considerate" of readers in general may be even more important than a computer-assigned readability level.

☐   INFORMAL READING ASSESSMENT   ☐

Since standardized reading tests often yield questionable scores, teachers need to administer informal reading inventories (IRIs) to better understand their students' reading abilities. These IRIs usually contain passages at each grade level for the students to read orally and/or silently before responding to literal and higher-level questions. The scores are generally used to estimate students' independent, instructional, and frustration reading levels. This helps you to know which texts can be used without your assistance (independent level), with your assistance (instructional level), or not at all (frustration level).

While informal tests supply valuable information for accurate student placement, they take a great deal of time to administer, particularly if administered orally to each student. The time factor alone has dissuaded many teachers from interrupting their class routine to use informal reading inventories.

With the recent interest of educators in developing useful software packages for classroom use, there also has evolved a cadre of reading professionals concerned about developing reading assessment software. While not yet capable of replacing some of the more comprehensive assessment tools in print, they have the potential for yielding information on various aspects of students' reading skills.

Informal Assessment Software

One noteworthy software package is the *Informal Reading Placement Test*. Written by two reading professionals, this program can be used with developmental students (grades 1–6), remedial students (grades 7–12), and special education students. Totally administered and scored on the microcomputer, this test estimates the independent, instructional, and frustration levels of students from prereadiness through eighth grade in word comprehension and passage comprehension. According to the authors, they validated the test by administering it to three thousand students in grades 1–6 over ten years in the Baldwin, New York, public schools. Other information concerning the origin, reliability, and validity of the test components was not available.

The "Word Comprehension" test contains sixty-four analogies, eight examples at each of the eight grade levels. Analogies, according to Vacca (1981), require students to manipulate words in relation to other words. They go beyond the understanding of definitions; they foster conceptualization. This philosophy is reflected in the "Word Comprehension" test. By having to select the appropriate word for each analogy, students must understand and think about each word. The following analogy format is used throughout the test:

```
ride-car
fly-_____
    A) airplane
    B) train
_____

Type A or B
```

Since it is a test, students do not know whether or not they have responded correctly. However, if they get fewer than six correct (fewer than 75 percent), the test automatically stops and goes on to the "Passage Comprehension" section. Two nice features of the test are its randomization of items and choices within levels and its option to start students at either Level 1 or Level 4. This helps to accommodate individual differences from the start.

The "Passage Comprehension" test presents graded reading passages, controlled for vocabulary and sentence length, followed by four comprehension questions. The questions test main ideas, details, inference, and vocabulary. Presented with whole text, students must use graphophonic, syntactic, and semantic clues in search of the answers. Although, as with many informal assessments, the higher-level thinking skills of analysis and prediction are forfeited for an estimate of how well students assimilate facts and identify details and main ideas, this test can be used as one indicator of comprehension.

Procedures similar to those of the "Word Comprehension" test are followed for beginning and ending the test; specifically, you can start students at Level 1 or Level 4, and the test ends automatically if a student gets fewer than three of the four questions correct (75 percent). It should be noted that students have the option of reviewing the text after each question is displayed, obviously indicating that a student's recall ability is not being measured. While it is an excellent idea to have the test stop automatically before the student reaches his or her frustration level, this feature should be regarded cautiously since the story itself, rather than the student's ability level, could be interfering with comprehension. Also, the two-level passage placement option is not as accurate as the one-grade-level-below passage placement of most printed informal reading assessments.

Along with this testing package comes a solid management system for keeping student records on both tests. The instructional-, independent-, and frustration-level scores for each student can be presented on the screen or printer, reflecting a composite of both word-comprehension and passage-comprehension scores. An example of the format appears in Figure 3.1.

Even though this test measures silent reading comprehension only, it can provide you with a quick, fairly accurate, informal reading assessment. Particularly appealing is the autonomous situation created; while each student is taking the test (provided that directions can be followed), you are free to work with other students.

The *Computer-Based Reading Assessment Instrument* (CRAI) also can be used to gain diagnostic information. Consisting of two forms of eight graded passages with probed recall questions, this package offers another computerized instrument to explore reading behavior informally.

If the assessment of oral reading is desired, we recommend that you use a tape recorder. Whenever a new passage appears on the screen, students would know to read it aloud. A student's reading then could be analyzed for the quality of miscues (deviations from the printed text). Do the miscues interfere with the overall meaning of the passage? Do they indicate difficulties with sound-symbol relationships or syntactical patterns in sentences? Do they indicate dialectical differences? While more time-consuming, this type of analysis, coupled with comprehension performance, does give a more thorough understanding of why some students may be showing signs of frustration with reading.

Another test package, *The O'Brien Vocabulary Placement Test*, purports to estimate students' independent reading levels by assessing their knowledge of word opposites, an approach also used in the "Word Opposites" test of the *Botel Reading Inventory* (1968). The author claims that this instrument avoids some of the pitfalls of the norm-referenced stand-

Figure 3.1. *Example of a student's placement record from the* Informal Reading Placement Test.

WORD PASSAGE COMPREHENSION
READING PLACEMENT LEVEL RESULTS
STUDENT: Frank, Marilyn

Word Comprehension: 7
Passage Comprehension: 6
Total Instructional Level: 6
Total Independent Level: 5
Total Frustration Level: 7–8

ardized tests and time-consuming informal reading inventories. Intended as a quick and accurate tool for teachers, this test contains sixty questions, ten at each grade level from first through sixth. Each test item contains the following format:

What is opposite of <u>come</u>?
(1) go
(2) green
(3) goose
(4) game

As can be seen above, each of the distractors contains the same initial consonant so that students use the first letter as a clue. Students continue with the test until they score fewer than five correct in a section. The points given for each section are totaled and converted to an independent reading level.

Although containing a less sophisticated management system than the *Informal Reading Placement Test* for reporting and maintaining students' scores, this test provides another means of assessing one aspect of reading.

Cloze Software

Cloze generators also are available for assessment purposes. Passages can be typed with every *n*th word deleted. Students are to supply a word that fits into the sentence framework. This aids the teacher in assessing a student's ability to respond to the semantic and syntactic cues within the sentence. It is important to recognize that many cloze tests seek one correct answer, which may or may not be the only suitable choice. If students obtain low scores, you should take the time to analyze whether the students' responses do indicate an understanding of the passage.

Cloze Generator, created by Giles Fortier and Serge Berthelot (1984), enables you to choose the cloze format and deletion pattern desired for any piece of text. For example, you could choose to delete every sixth word with a standard blank or every ninth word with the first letter intact followed by a standard blank (T_____ for TREE). This type of program provides a flexible yet easy way to format cloze assessments.

Since cloze tests are simple to prepare, albeit without management systems, you can prepare them with a word processing package. This option provides another simple way of deleting every fifth, seventh, or tenth word in selected passages in order to obtain a quick assessment of students' reading ability.

While inroads have been made with informal reading assessments, we visualize the creation of assessment software packages that will allow the student to read orally information from the screen. Miscues and related comprehension skills might be assessed on the microcomputer for a more comprehensive understanding of students' reading patterns. Voice-entry systems, if properly developed, could monitor the accuracy of student's word pronunciations during oral reading. With the emergence of more sophisticated voice-entry systems, this expectation will be realized.

☐   DATA BASES: FILING SYSTEMS FOR INFORMATION MANAGEMENT   ☐

The need to cope with information overload and excessive paperwork has caused most computer users to investigate computerized filing systems for home and professional purposes. While initially time-consuming to prepare, these filing systems have become an efficient means for retrieving the most obscure information. There are programs available for just about every computer. One such system, *Personal Filing System* (PFS: FILE), produced by Software Publishing Corporation for the Apple and IBM PC computers, is easy to learn, and we have used it with the Apple to design several files for classroom teachers and reading teachers. Any filing system can be used in a similar fashion.

PFS: FILE has two main functions, storing information and retrieving it. Files can be designed, edited, and updated on numerous disks to reflect current classroom needs and endeavors. The PFS menu indicates the available options: (1) Design File, (2) Add, (3) Copy, (4) Search/Update, (5) Print, and (6) Remove.

Initially, the Design File option is used to create a file on a separate data disk. The example in Figure 3.2 is a class file we created for a primary class.

Once the file was created, the Add option allowed us to create multiple forms of the same file; for example, every student in the class had a separate form of the same file. A sample of one student's file appears in Figure 3.3.

The Search/Update option allows the teacher to retrieve all forms or, with certain specifications, particular facts about students on the form. Specifically, if, for grouping purposes, you wanted to find out which students had below 2.8 on the standardized test, you would type <2.8 next to the standardized test scores on the blank form, and all forms with less than a 2.8 would appear. Or, if you were planning to devise an interest group on baseball, you would type ..Baseball.. to find out who had this interest, and the appropriate forms would appear. Once all forms

Figure 3.2. *Example of a class file done on* PFS:FILE.

CLASS FILE

NAME: BIRTHDAY:

INSTRUCTIONAL LEVEL:

CALIFORNIA ACHIEVEMENT TEST (CAT):

BASALS READ:

BOOKS READ:

BOOKS WRITTEN:

INTERESTS:

were retrieved, a total number of the retrieved forms would appear on the screen, indicating the number of students below 2.8 on the standardized test or the number of students with an interest in baseball, respectively. Any information on the forms, if appropriately sought, could be retrieved.

With the Print option, any filed information can be printed for off-line access. It is simply a matter of deciding what information to print and the format in which to print it. There also is an option for sorting the

Figure 3.3. *Example of a student's record in a class file.*

FORM ON CLASS FILE

NAME: ROBERT DOVE   BIRTHDAY: 3/15/78

INSTRUCTIONAL LEVEL: ORAL IRI—2, SILENT IRI—2

CALIFORNIA ACHIEVEMENT TEST (CAT): 2.6

BASALS READ: SCOTT, FORESMAN—RISE AND SHINE, AWAY WE GO,
TAKING OFF, GOING UP, ON OUR OWN, HANG ON TO YOUR HATS,
KICK UP YOUR HEELS

BOOKS READ: CURIOUS GEORGE, WHERE THE WILD THINGS ARE,
GOGGLES, MAKE WAY FOR DUCKLINGS, THE MOUSE AND THE
MOTORCYCLE, BLUEBERRIES FOR SAL, THE SNOWY DAY

BOOKS WRITTEN: NONE

INTERESTS: BASEBALL, ADVENTURE

information so that you can print out your students' forms in alphabetical order.

Student Applications

Data disks can be created for any number of purposes. Book files can be created for students, reflecting their opinions of self-selected or assigned readings. The book file in Figure 3.4 represents one file style that was designed for middle-grade students. The teacher or a student committee could type in the informational sections. As students read the book, they can add their personal responses (see Andy G. and Ellen H.).

Students also can create files for any content-area topic. In social studies, for instance, students could be assigned the task of locating biographical information about United States presidents. Each student

Figure 3.4. *Sample of a computerized book file.*

BOOK FILE

NAME: A FROST IN THE NIGHT

AUTHOR: EDITH BAER

PUBLISHER: PANTHEON

DATE: 1980

INTEREST LEVEL: 10–15

READING LEVEL: 7–8 GRADE

SUMMARY: THIS STORY OF EVA BENTHEIM, A YOUNG JEWISH GIRL, WHO GREW UP IN GERMANY IN THE 1930s AT THE BEGINNING OF THE NAZI REGIME. WE SEE THE WARM, MEMORABLE DAYS OF HER FAMILY LIFE TURN COLD AS HITLER COMES INTO POWER. SHE MUST LEAVE HER BELOVED GERMANY FOR HER OWN SAFETY.

STUDENT RESPONSE:

ANDY G.: IT WAS O.K. I LIKED THE PART ABOUT THEIR SUMMERS IN THE COUNTRY. I'M NOT JEWISH BUT I UNDERSTAND WHAT HAPPENED TO THEM NOW BECAUSE OF EVA'S STORY.

ELLEN H.: I LOVED EVA. ALL THE THINGS THAT HAPPENED TO HER IN SCHOOL WERE VERY REAL. SHE HAD A GREAT FAMILY—HER MOTHER, FATHER, AND TWO GRANDFATHERS. I FELT FRIGHTENED WHEN EVA WAS CAUGHT IN THE NAZI BOOK-BURNING DEMONSTRATION.

would enter information about the dates and number of terms in office, political party affiliation, major events while in office, familial background, and so forth. Students would use these files to compare and contrast the different facets of each president's public and private life. Specifically, students could find out which Democratic presidents served one term during wartime or which Democratic presidents, during the latter part of the 1900s, served while the country was in the midst of a recession.

Another example would be the classification of birds for a science unit. Students could create a file including the class, subclass, order, family, genus, and species of modern birds. Once students had entered the necessary information for various birds, they could begin to search for birds in the same genus or the same species. Similar procedures could be used for any unit of study in a content area.

Also useful is the creation of content-area resource banks. If students are assigned a research topic in any area, they can use a filing system for citing the references and resources available for a specific topic. They would identify the people, places, and print sources used in accessing information. For example, in seeking information about the four basic food groups, a student might list the school nurse, dietician, and health teacher as human resources, two health books and four periodicals in the library as good reference books, and the three current health magazines in Mr. B's class as easy-to-read articles for learning more about this topic. These files could be used continually as springboards for research with the idea that periodic alterations should be made to keep abreast of changes. If possible, these files should be made available to students in different classes and at different grade levels, particularly if files include an array of topics with sources at various readability levels.

Students could use files for extracurricular activities. Information about yearbooks, newsletters, and athletic clubs could be filed to keep abreast of student data and student initiatives. Records of subscriptions and students would be especially useful for the yearbook; organized files about circulation and the types of articles written would be helpful for a newsletter. Similarly, if athletic clubs had records organized, they could use the information to track down patterns in successful games, for example, characteristics of players, teams, and playing conditions.

Another student application is the use of filing systems for note taking (Geoffrion & Geoffrion, 1983). Students can create a note-taking file to expedite cross-referencing and the organization of material. By having each reference listed for any area of a particular topic, students can save an enormous amount of time in coalescing the information. Obviously, these applications are not limited to students. As teachers, we know the frustration of trying to sift through piles of paper to find the one piece of information needed to complete a thought or support an argument. Suggestions for organizing various classroom situations are offered below.

Teacher Applications

Besides the file we designed for the primary class above, we can think of several other filing situations in which teachers may be able to use this tool advantageously. Since a large number of students usually are assigned to one teacher in middle-grade and junior high school reading/language arts classes, record keeping can be a problem. The file in Figure 3.5 demonstrates an easy way to keep abreast of student assignments.

Remedial reading teachers, particularly if assigned to more than one school, also would benefit from some type of filing system. Given the constant shuffle of students into and out of these classes, records are apt to get disorganized. The file in Figure 3.6 represents one kind that can be designed.

J. W. Miller (1985) of Wichita State University used his computerized filing system in the reading center to keep track of his students' scores. Categorizing the scores into perceptual, intellectual, and reading areas made it easier for him to coalesce the information into his reports.

Teachers also can create school- or districtwide files that provide instructional ideas, teaching material suggestions, or formal and informal test descriptions. With an instructional idea file, teachers can provide a description of the idea, the assigned grade level(s), ability level(s), materials, and content area(s) for which the idea applies. If possible, stu-

Figure 3.5. Sample file for use in middle or junior high school.

MIDDLE/JR. HIGH FILE

NAME OF STUDENT: CLASS:

AGE:

ADDRESS:

TELEPHONE NUMBER:

READING INTERESTS:

READING ASSIGNMENT: DATE ASSIGNED: DATE ACCOMPLISHED:

Figure 3.6. *Sample file for reading teachers.*

NAME OF STUDENT: AGE:

SCHOOL: YEAR:

DATE OF BIRTH: TEACHER:

YEARS IN REMEDIATION: GRADE:

PARENTS' ADDRESS:

PARENTS' TELEPHONE:

STANDARDIZED TEST SCORES:

INFORMAL TEST SCORES:

INTERESTS:

READING STRENGTHS:

READING WEAKNESSES:

OTHER ACADEMIC STRENGTHS:

CLASSROOM MATERIALS USED:

GOALS:

dent reactions to the ideas or materials on the files should be included
to help teachers make informed decisions. With teaching material suggestions, teachers can identify publishers, skills developed, content-area
applications, and readability levels. The teaching material file could be
cross-referenced to the instructional idea file. With the test description
files, teachers could list the purpose of each test and how it should be
used in a classroom setting (Casteel, 1984).

Librarians can become involved in creating files of print materials
housed in the library as well as in teachers' classrooms. Organized with

such categories as topic, interest level, and grade level, these files can be used by students, teachers, and parents to make appropriate selections. McKenna (1985) has developed a library retrieval system called *Fiction Finder* for thousands of trade books, listing the title, author, type of fiction, length, main character, readability, and interest level. Students can use his data base to identify books for any number of categories. For example, if a student liked a particular author, a description of all books written by this author would be listed immediately.

Since software is appearing in schools at an ever-increasing rate, a school- or districtwide file of software packages should become commonplace. This type of file should include a description of the software, the publisher, technical/educational qualities of the package, suggestions for instructional applications, and teacher/student/parent reactions. We have developed this type of file for the software in our college curriculum materials center. Used not only to avoid duplications in purchasing but also to inform teachers of software applicability, this type of filing system can assist teachers in identifying appropriate software packages for different instructional purposes.

The aforementioned suggestions serve to demonstrate the many ways in which data can be organized for student and teacher purposes. Student files can be used to enhance the learning process; teacher files can be used to tap into students' needs and help teachers organize for instruction. Once filed electronically, information about any student, assignment, or resource is at your fingertips momentarily for parent conferences, supervision, consultations, and lesson planning. Eventually, with the diligent creation of numerous files, the onus of shuffling papers can be replaced with the opportunity to spend more time helping students to think critically and creatively.

☐   DATA BASES: INFORMATION RETRIEVAL   ☐

College and university students are used to thinking of the computer as a tool to help them find information for research papers. These days no undergraduate or graduate student in education gets through a program without meeting ERIC (Educational Resources Information Clearinghouse) in the college library. This is a broad data base that references and abstracts articles published in over seven hundred journals and other important documents such as convention papers, research reports, and curriculum descriptions not published in journals. Given a good set of delimiting descriptors, for example, "teaching reading through the arts in the elementary school from 1980 to 1986," the computer can search the ERIC data base and find in minutes sources that might take you hours to locate manually.

Data Base Systems

Too often teachers forget about the computer as an information retriever when they finish their coursework. But the computer can continue to serve them as a valuable tool.

For instance, a participant in a recent college workshop on computers and reading was bemoaning the quality and utility of current software packages available for her students. A reading teacher in a comprehensive high school in southern Jersey, she had just been given a computer lab with twenty Apples to use strictly for reading. Her targeted students were secondary school remedial readers who were reading at the fourth-, fifth-, and sixth-grade levels. Most of the software she had seen for middle-grade readers was inappropriate in content and format for these students.

We suggested she do a computer search of two comprehensive data base systems that were on line in our college library, DIALOG and Bibliographic Retrieval Services (BRS). These systems are like "information department stores" or "delivery mechanisms" for many specialized data bases supplied by individual information producers (Glossbrenner, 1983). DIALOG offers over two hundred data bases and BRS over eighty. While there is some overlap (ERIC is included in both), many specialized data bases are found in only one system.

Microcomputer Index, available on DIALOG, seemed to be a perfect source for our search. This subject and index guide to articles from more than fifty microcomputer journals includes digests of software reviews as well as articles. Using the terms "Reading," "Remedial," "Secondary," "Software," and "Reviews," the search produced several citations. Figure 3.7 shows a sample printout.

This printout told us that Michael Shelly favorably reviewed a Random House program called *Word Blaster* in the journal *Educational Technology.* According to the review digest, this program was a motivating drill-and-practice package suitable for secondary school remedial readers. We suggested the teacher read the entire review and preview the software herself before buying.

Resources in Computer Education (RICE) is another specialized data base in BRS. Compiled by the Northwest Regional Educational Lab (NWREL), in Portland, Oregon, RICE contains information on educational software packages, software producers, and research projects. Also included are hundreds of evaluations done by teachers all over the country

Figure 3.7. A Microcomputer Index *citation.*

```
047882   8307453
   Word Blaster
   Shelly, Michael
   Educational Technology,  Jan 1983,  v23  n1  p48-49,  2 pages
ISSN: 0013-1962
   Languages: English
   Document Type: Software Review
   Geographic Location: United States
   A  favorable  review  for  a  remedial reading program drill-
and-practice  program  for  the  Apple  II  ($150).  The reviewer
describes the  program as being a  motivating and "fun" approach
to the improvement of reading skills.
   Descriptors:   *Software   Review;   *Reading;   *Apple  II;
*Elementary  Education;   Remediation;   Courseware;   Secondary
Education; TRS-80 Model I; TRS-80 Model III; Atari 800
   Identifiers: Word Blaster; Random House, Inc.
```

through MicroSIFT (Microcomputer Software and Information for Teachers), a clearinghouse established by the National Institute of Education. Besides very complete bibliographic and ordering information, MicroSIFT also gives an abstract of the courseware's content and suggests potential uses. In response to the same search descriptors used with *Microcomputer Index* above, RICE turned up the following printout (see Figure 3.8).

We can see from the RICE abstract that Milliken's *Comprehension Power* also would be suitable for remedial readers in high school. From the evaluation we learn that the content is intrinsically interesting, that students have control over the rate with which it is delivered, and that the management system is excellent. Another prospect for our high school reading teacher!

This teacher went back to her computerized reading lab with several leads to software appropriate for her targeted student population. Instead of searching through hundreds of catalogs, which tend to overstate their products' utility, quality, and versatility, she can look directly at these preselected and objectively reviewed packages before ordering. By using the computer as an information retrieval tool, she can do her job more effectively and efficiently.

Another BRS data base of interest to teachers who are looking for specific information about software is the Texas Education Computer Cooperative (TECC). Developed by the Statewide Microcomputer Courseware Evaluation Network of the Region IV Education Center in Houston, Texas, TECC gives information similar to that found in RICE but also contains teacher and student evaluations of software.

Figure 3.8. Sample printout from RICE.

```
AN ACCESSION NUMBER: 000444. 8506.
RT RESOURCE TYPE: Software Package.
TI TITLE: Comprehension Power Program (Level B, Level H).
PD ORGANIZATION: Instructional/Communications Technology (Milliken
   Publishing Co.).
CI CONTACT INFORMATION ADDRESS: 10 Stepar Place, Huntington Station,
   NY 11746.
   CONTACT PERSON: Suzanne Berger.
   COST: $425.00.
HT HARDWARE TYPE: Apple II.
SR SYSTEM REQUIREMENTS HARDWARE: 48K, single disk drive, monitor.
   SOFTWARE: Applesoft, DOS 3.2/3.3.
   MEDIUM OF TRANSFER: 5 1/4 in. disk.
DE DESCRIPTORS: Instruction. Language-Arts. Reading. Basic-Skills.
   Computer-Managed-Instruction. Elementary-Education.
   Junior-High-Schools. Intermediate-Grades. Middle-Schools.
   High-Schools. Secondary-Education.
ID IDENTIFIERS: CMI. Eval. SIFT.
GL GRADE LEVEL: 4, 5, 6, 7, 8, 9, 10, 11, 12.
MI MODE OF INSTRUCTION: standard instruction, remediation, enrichment,
   assessment.
   INSTRUCTIONAL TECHNIQUES: drill and practice, learning management,
   tutorial.
II INSTRUCTIONAL OBJECTIVES: To develop ability to follow directions,
   to provide extensive and varied reading experiences, to improve
   vocabulary, to preview effectively, to read more rapidly with
   comprehension and to practice 25 major comprehension skills.
   INSTRUCTIONAL PREREQUISITES: Reading comprehension at fourth grade
   level and familiarity with computer keyboard.
   STUDENT TIME: June 1982 by the Portland Public Schools, Portland,
   Oregon.
AB ABSTRACT: DOCUMENTATION AVAILABLE: Program operating instructions
   and student instructions are in the computer program. Suggested
   grade and ability level, instructional objectives, prerequisite
   skills or activities, sample program output, program operating
   instructions, teacher's information, student's instructions, student
   worksheets and material defining comprehension skills are included
   in the supplementary materials. POTENTIAL USES This package could
   be used as an individualized course in effective reading, as a
   supplementary reading program in a language arts class, or as part
   of a remedial reading class for middle and high school students.
   The package would also be appropriate in ESL and literacy courses.
   The package could be used to provide objectives for targeted
   instruction and to provide feedback both to students and to parents.
EV EVALUATION MAJOR STRENGTHS: Content is of high interest, students
   can select their own reading rate, students may vary the reading
   rate with reading level, vocabulary is introduced in context and the
   content varies with each choice of reading rate. The student
   management program was judged to be excellent. Evaluators also
   rated the list of comprehension skills as comprehensive and
   well-chosen. Information in the program was described as relevant,
   up-to-date and written in the style of magazine articles.
   Evaluators felt students would learn from the content of the
   articles, in addition to developing the intended reading skills.
   SITE AND DATE: June 1982 by the Portland Public Schools, Portland,
   Oregon.
   OTHER DATA: Electronic Education Feb 82; Electronic Learning
   Jan/Feb 82.

   RECOMMENDATION: Evaluators indicate they would use or recommend use
   of package with little or no change. Refer to Evaluator's Guide
   ED206330 for interpretation of evaluative criteria.
```

Also available through DIALOG is *Menu — The International Software Directory (Menu — ISD)*. This data base lists all commercially produced software on the market and is updated monthly. Along with applications and purchasing information, this directory lists a brief description of each item and permits you to actually order while on line.

Besides these information sources on software, there are other data bases of interest to reading/language arts educators on BRS and DIALOG. *The Academic American Encyclopedia*, a product of Grolier Electronic Publishing, is available on both. A special feature of this data base is that it allows you to select and view only the parts of the article that you really want if you specify this option in your keyword. This eliminates the need to read the entire article yet permits you to get your portion "in context."

Magazine Index and *Book Review Index* are available on DIALOG. Updated monthly, *Magazine Index* includes many citations from the *Readers' Guide to Periodical Literature* and most of those found in *Popular Periodicals Index*. Accessible on both DIALOG and BRS is *Books in Print*. This data base offers all R. R. Bowker's guides to *Books in Print*. These guides give subject, author, title, and publisher information for all adult and children's books presently in print or forthcoming.

While these data base systems are readily accessible in most college and university libraries for nominal search fees, they are also available to computer users who have a modem with access to telecommunications systems such as Telenet and Tymnet. School systems or individuals can open accounts directly for little more than the cost of a user's manual. An excellent source of information about the scope and costs of the encyclopedic data bases is Chapter 6 of Alfred Glossbrenner's *The Complete Handbook of Personal Computer Communications: Everything You Need to Know to Go On Line with the World*.

Another information source that is of interest to educators is *CompuServe Information System* (CIS), a division of CompuServe, Inc., a large time-sharing service for business and government that has idle time at night which it makes available to personal computer users at nominal fees. Glossbrenner calls it the "nighttime utility."

Some features of interest to teachers on this data base are *Electronic Mail* (EMAIL) and *The Academic American Encyclopedia*, the same resource carried on DIALOG and BRS. EMAIL allows you to send and receive mail from any other CIS user. Updated semiannually, *The Academic American Encyclopedia* contains over 30,000 articles and is a good starting point for young researchers.

Just recently, *The Educational Software Selector* (TESS) was added to CompuServe. Created from the Educational Products Information Exchange (EPIE) data base, which will be discussed in Chapter 7, TESS is a

comprehensive and in-depth source of information about educational
software.

Students' Uses of Information Retrieval

Students also are beginning to use the computer to find information. In
Mamaroneck, Phil Restaino has added a modem and access to DIALOG
to his computer writing lab. With Phil, his assistant, or some specially
trained seniors to help them search, students can now use the computer
to find facts or reference sources for research projects in all curricular
areas. Besides *The Academic American Encyclopedia*, students working
on social studies reports have found *Facts on File* (news summaries),
Newsearch (a daily index of news stories and articles from over 1,700 important newspapers and magazines), and *National Newspaper Index* (a
front-to-back index of the *New York Times, Wall Street Journal*, and *Chris-
tian Science Monitor*) extremely helpful. This latter index is particularly
useful for answering general questions on current events. Students engaged in their senior English project, an in-depth research paper in the
humanities, have found *MLA Bibliography* invaluable. This data base in-
dexes books and journal articles on literature and linguistics. By searching
this source, students can support their critiques of major authors or
specific works with those found in the professional literature. As a result
of this new tool, Mamaroneck High School students find research easier
and produce papers of a higher quality than when they were doing their
reference work by hand.

Less expensive than a modem to access general information data bases
is a cable TV hookup. Instead of paying for on-line hours, you pay the
cable company a nominal monthly fee; for example, Vision Cable charges
about thirty dollars a month. *Dow Jones News/Retrieval* has been made
available by Vision Cable to school districts in its sending area. We visited
Palisades Park, one of the first districts to take advantage of this service.

Students at Palisades Park High School use several data bases in this
system. Besides the encyclopedia (once again, it's *Academic American*),
they come to the library to read news reports, sports results, and weather
predictions, all important in their everyday lives and updated on the
system within minutes of access! Business classes call up *Current Quotes*
and *Historical Quotes* for stock and bond prices; they also read *Disclosure*,
which carries profiles on 8,500 publicly held companies, when they need
information on corporate structures and earnings per year.

Science and health classes use *Medx* to get information on current
medical news and both prescription and over-the-counter drugs. We
checked out ADVIL, which came up as its generic term, ibuprofen, and

learned that it should not be taken with a diuretic, information that sent one of us to check with her doctor.

Social studies classes assign one student a day to access important news, print it out, and then organize it into a current-events report to be presented in class. Librarian Rosalie Pagano is in school at 7:00 A.M. to help the students who will be reporting on any given day. She sees the system as especially beneficial for limited-English-proficient and special education students. One Korean boy she was working with learns best through print, once he has been introduced to important concepts and vocabulary in oral-aural sessions. Understanding a social studies unit on the Hitler years was much easier for him when he could walk away from a session with a printout of the encyclopedia article entitled "Hitler." Special education students who never "did research" before learn to use an index and access an entry in the encyclopedia, thrilled that they can read the screen in the library and take home a printed copy to read to their parents and friends.

At the Lindbergh Elementary School in Palisades Park, *Dow Jones* is situated among other reference tools. Predictably, the younger children use it mainly for the encyclopedia, but we also observed them reading the movie reviews. While their purpose was mainly to find out about current movies, they were also internalizing how a review is structured. We could see an excellent reading-writing activity emerging from this specialized use: children writing group-composed and individual reviews of favorite movies after sharing those read from the *Dow Jones Cinema Movie Reviews*.

Rosalie Pagano says that the best thing about having the service is that it gets students into the library and gets them reading. They read the weather, news, and sports from the screen, sometimes taking notes if needed; they print out the longer reports from the encyclopedia, disclosure, and medical services so that they can reread the information and restructure it for various assignments; they read the index to *Academic American* to be able to access the exact entry they want, and this often leads them to search other standard print encyclopedias in the library.

Because of its low cost, cable hookup may be the best way for school districts to offer computerized information retrieval to their students. Presently, cable companies are bringing *Dow Jones* to schools in Clearwater, Florida, Quincy, Massachusetts, and Princeton, New Jersey. Because of its business-world name, schools may not think of *Dow Jones* as a facility useful in education, but, as the Palisades Park experience shows, it offers many services that can promote realistic reading, writing, and research opportunities for students at all levels.

Each of the computer "tool" applications has tremendous potential for enhancing the reading/language arts environment. Word processing has revolutionized the way in which people approach writing tasks. Teacher utility packages are giving teachers the latitude so desperately needed with CAI software. Readability packages are alleviating the tedium traditionally associated with calculating a text's approximate grade level. Assessment packages are providing teachers with the opportunity to quickly substantiate their impressions of students' class performance. Computerized filing systems are giving students and teachers options for organizing and managing large quantities of data, while information-retrieval systems are opening up huge warehouses of information to students and teachers within minutes.

As each tool becomes accessible and understood, it needs to be examined in terms of its usefulness when combined with other tools. For example, the information gleaned from informal assessment packages can be stored on a computerized filing system to be later retrieved for developing a CAI program with an authoring language. Or, in another situation, while studying about dinosaurs, one group of students may be slotting in dinosaur characteristics on a class-created computerized filing system while another group is word-processing their dinosaur paragraphs. To enliven the learning process, a third group could be creating computer-generated word finds or crossword puzzles of the "dinosaur" vocabulary.

By using these tools collectively, a rich, supportive, integrated reading environment is created that invites students to use their schemata in creative ways. Judy Vihonski and Chris Chakmakian, gifted-and-talented teachers in Oakland, New Jersey, have been quite successful with their instructional applications of these tools. In studying about historic homes in the Oakland vicinity, their seventh- and eighth-grade students were responsible for reading literature about architectural designs and doing research in the community about these homes. They interviewed owners of interesting old homes, taking notes on such information as dates built, materials used, type of architecture, and families who lived there. After jointly designing a file that would contain the necessary main headings, these students used the computerized filing system to record the data accumulated. Then they were able to write reports from their pooled information. Also, since photographs were taken of the homes, the students included pictures with their reports, using *The Print Shop* to surround the photographs with borders and three-dimensional captions (see Figure 3.9). In studying one facet of their cultural heritage, these students used the

Figure 3.9. Booklet published by seventh-grade students
for an architectural project.

computer to develop their own data base, word processing to write their reports, and a graphics program to decorate their finished product.

☐   **SUMMARY**   ☐

We firmly believe that, if nothing else, the computer is quickly becoming a valuable tool for all of us. We speak from our hearts, since each of us wrote this text with her own word processing program. We did not panic every time a change had to be made, as in previous years. We knew that we could boot up our disk, make the changes rapidly, and save our modified text for future alterations. Similarly, as you and your students explore the vast "tool" applications available to you, you will come to realize the tremendous contributions the computer as tool can make to your classroom situations.

□4□

The Computer as Tutor
Drill and Practice

The reading resource center in Elmwood School is a cheerfully decorated, inviting place in which to teach and learn. Students' pictures, stories, and poems are artfully displayed on the walls. Numerous plants and interesting displays can be found amid the many games, puzzles, paperback books, and specialized materials for reading instruction.

When visitors enter the room, a bright green area rug immediately catches their eyes. A small round table sits on the rug in front of a couch, just big enough for two. On the table are several magazines and books. Two of the books have been placed standing on end as if waiting to be noticed. On the opposite wall, two study carrels stand back to back. Each has been cleverly made by cutting off one side of two cardboard boxes and placing it on top of a desk, thus assuring the user a private area in which to work, free of distractions. At one end of the room, there is a mini-computer center. It consists of three computers, a printer, and a small software library.

On the day that we arrived, the reading teacher, Mrs. Bailey, sat at a large table near the entrance as seven students from the fifth and sixth grades arrived for special help in reading. Mrs. Bailey began with a whole-group activity in which one student shared a piece of writing in progress from the previous session. It had been composed on the computer, and now the student read from a printout and elicited suggestions for revision from the group. After the writing conference, another student shared a book that she had just finished reading. After the group discussed the book, the student selected a brief excerpt to read aloud.

After the whole group activity, Mrs. Bailey assigned individual tasks based on student needs. Two students went to the library cor-

ner. One set about finishing a paperback that she had been reading
for nearly a week. The other read a magazine article and selected
two new books to check out for independent reading. A third student
revised his written retelling of a story that Mrs. Bailey had read aloud
to the group. He worked at one of the carrels, adding information
that had been omitted and reworking parts that were not clear. The
remaining students worked in pairs or individually on assignments at
the computer. One continued the writing that had been discussed
earlier. The others were assigned programs designed to provide practice on reading for meaning. The programs, *Tutorial Comprehension*
and *The Puzzler*, had been selected for use that day. (These programs
will be discussed in Chapters 4 and 5 respectively.) Mrs. Bailey cir-
culated among the students to help them get started and to confer
with them about their work. As she conferred with them, she made
notes about their progress.

•   •   •

It is obvious that the computer has been successfully integrated into the
instructional program in this classroom. Rather than allow the computer
to stand apart as an end in itself, Mrs. Bailey has effectively put it to use
as a supporting tool for the existing curriculum. The computer is used
in a variety of ways and in conjunction with a variety of other instructional materials. Although it is used sparingly for drill and practice, Mrs.
Bailey has found that there are times when the computer as tutor is an
application that is well suited to her students' needs.

After expressing her disappointment with the overall quality of software programs, Mrs. Bailey told us that she works hard to find the very
best available. She looks for programs that are motivational and allow for
student collaboration. Especially desirable are interactive programs that
encourage language manipulation, experimentation, and invention.
Chapters 4 and 5 discuss ways that teachers like Mrs. Bailey are making
use of the computer as tutor.

In the tutor mode, the computer user works with software that already
has been programmed to provide instructional assistance. Often referred
to as Computer Assisted Instruction (CAI) or Computer Assisted Learning (CAL), this computer mode reflects the state of the art in educational
software. Because computers emerged from the field of mathematics, early CAI/CAL software was designed for the traditional math-teaching
model: teach one step, drill and practice that step, test until it is mastered.
This same model was applied to the development of early software for
reading/language arts. Since the model works best for drill and practice

on isolated skills, a plethora of packages at the letter, word, or sentence level was produced.

Reinking (1985) searched the *MicroSIFT* data base (Northeast Regional Lab) for software packages developed for reading/language arts. He found that 70 percent offered drill and practice on single-letter/single-word skills. Of 105 packages, only 7 dealt with whole text. Rubin and Bruce (1984) found that only 21 of 317 packages required students to read connected text. This situation developed, not because reading people saw this as the best use for computers, but because this type of workbook-style lesson was the easiest to program.

Since a great deal of drill-and-practice software is presently available, Chapter 4 is devoted to describing selected examples of this type. Often denigrated as an animated workbook, this type of software can be useful, especially if integrated holistically into a reading situation. Drill-and-practice software, as defined in this book, supplements previous instruction or teaches rules and concepts so that students develop an understanding of the skill or concept provided. Whether presented as an instructional unit or in a gamelike format, the software's objective should be to facilitate learning as an outgrowth of or a prelude to teacher instruction. We firmly believe that the teacher should be an integral part of the learning situation, either in initiating instruction or in reinforcing the skills and concepts presented in the software package.

Recently, the combined effects of sophisticated programming techniques and reading educators' demands for better software have led to the production of software packages that offer whole text and promote more active student participation. We call these interactive. Interactive software is designed to elicit student reactions to the text presented. Unlike drill-and-practice software, it encourages divergent thinking. Chapter 5 discusses selected software packages that provide students with opportunities to respond to the ideas presented on each program. Also described will be those software packages which encourage students to compose discourse related to the topics at hand.

The onus of selecting and applying quality software from the burgeoning array of commercially prepared reading/language arts packages is on the teacher. We are highlighting representative software so that you will have a framework from which to work. To select the programs, we did informal surveys of classroom teachers and ran a computer search for the most highly rated in the RICE, TECC, EPIE, and *Microcomputer Index* data bases (see Chapter 3). We also culled the best-rated from the EPIE* read-

---

*EPIE (Educational Products Information Exchange) is a consumers' review service that does in-depth evaluations of computer software and hardware. See Chapter 7.

ing and language arts files. Most software packages can be used on the Apple computer systems and, when specified, other computer systems. Whether supplementing previous instruction or providing interactive text, the software selected reflects our interest in providing a medium for promoting total language development through active student participation.

☐   PREKINDERGARTEN / PRIMARY   ☐

Helping young children get started with computer learning involves a great deal of planning and decision making. Most teachers of children in the kindergarten and primary grades stress active learning through concrete experiences and exploration. They may wonder how the computer fits with their notions of active participation in the learning process. They may be afraid that computers will take time away from book reading, discussions, and small-group activities. Their fears may be well founded if the computer is introduced into the classroom with no attempt to coordinate its use with the existing curriculum.

Many classroom teachers have used the learning center concept as a viable way to organize and coordinate computer instruction within the daily program. A computer center such as those established for science, art, and library books can be set up in the room. To minimize distractions, the computer can be mounted on a rolling cart and placed with the screen facing away from other members of the class. Many teachers like to place computers near or adjacent to the writing center. Charts with reminders about the care and use of the computer may be on display as well as any special instructions for specific activities. At various times during the day, students may be assigned or may volunteer to work at the computer. During the reading period, work at the computer may be assigned as part of the independent activities that some students do while others work in small groups with the teacher. As each piece of software is added to the classroom collection, it is introduced to the group as a whole and again in small groups before it is assigned for independent work.

The center concept helps teachers integrate the computer with other learning tools. Finding the appropriate software for use in the computer center presents an additional challenge. We have identified four key objectives for selecting software for this age group: (1) the program must allow the learner to manipulate language symbols in meaningful ways, (2) it must stimulate thinking along with language skills, (3) it must be interesting and entertaining enough to inspire practice, and (4) the instructions must be clear enough for a child at the designated developmental level to follow independently with ease. Following are descriptions of software that teachers in self-contained classrooms and reading resource centers tell us meet these criteria to a sufficient extent to be useful in their programs.

Single Purpose Packages: Readiness

Sticky Bear ABC is a simple-to-operate and entertaining program designed to assist young children in learning the alphabet and in making associations between letters and pictures of objects and words that begin with those letters. When a child presses a letter on the keyboard, that letter and a related picture and word appear simultaneously on the screen. The process is randomized so that children cannot predict what combination of word and picture will appear with the letter they have pressed. There are over 250 picture combinations in the program, which help keep children interested in playing the game over and over again. The use of a bear as a central character has natural child appeal. High-resolution graphics, music, and lively animation also help to make this a successful program.

Although it is geared primarily to the home market, teachers have used *Sticky Bear ABC* effectively with small groups or individual children in the classroom. Teacher preparation time is minimal. Four- to six-year-olds can use the program independently after only a brief introduction. Teachers and evaluators have expressed concern about some of the objects used to represent certain sound-symbol correspondences. In cases such as *a* for *airplane* and *w* for *whistle*, the objects do not reflect the sound-symbol correspondence that would normally be found for those letters in beginning phonics books (Doyle, 1985). Our experience indicates that the interaction stimulated between child and adult and among children working together with *Sticky Bear ABC* is an important outcome of this program and one that tends to keep it lively and interesting.

Juggles' Rainbow is designed to develop directional concepts: left, right, above, and below. Included are a brief program to introduce the game and three instructional programs. The programs make use of paper strips placed vertically and horizontally on the keys to form two or four sectors. What appears on the screen corresponds to the sectors on the keyboard. For example, in the game "Rainbow," first the child presses any key above or below the strip, and a block appears on the screen to correspond with the sectors on the keyboard. The child presses keys to correspond with the directional cues on the screen. After a succession of correct responses, a rainbow is gradually formed. "Butterfly" follows the same principle for teaching right and left, with the formation of a butterfly as the learner's reward. "Windmill" makes use of four quadrants and allows children to practice all four directions as they build a windmill.

Among the positive features of this program are its clear and colorful graphics, its ease of use, the optional use of sound, and the fact that when a child experiences difficulty the program automatically goes back to the first portion of each program. The games are short, and they progress in a logical manner that is largely learner-controlled.

Adults wishing to introduce *Juggles' Rainbow* to young children are cautioned to review the instructions thoroughly in advance. Our experience has been that children four to six years of age are quite capable of using this program independently, even though they may experience some initial confusion. Teachers will be concerned that the program uses only uppercase letters. Nevertheless, we suggest that they place signs on the keyboard to match the words on the screen. This serves as a good way to reinforce the association of word to concept.

Pick-a-Dilly is another software package designed to strengthen concepts and develop thinking skills rather than to teach reading specifically. Playing a game similar to Concentration, children sharpen their abilities to make sound, motion, and object associations and to remember bits of information for short periods of time. The various program options in the menu allow *Pick-a-Dilly* to be adjusted for use by younger and older children. For example, while younger children might work with the "Standard Program," older children might use the more advanced "Pick 3," "Pick 4," or "Music Only" programs. Because many children are not acquainted with the game format used in *Pick-a-Dilly*, it may require more time to learn than most programs for this age group. Once it is learned, however, children really enjoy the challenge.

Multipurpose Packages: Readiness

Kindercomp consists of six games of increasing difficulty designed for children between the ages of three and eight. The first three games, "Scribble," "Names," and "Sequence," sometimes referred to as electronic doodling, are entertaining ways to help preschool children locate keys on the keyboard and recognize letters. The "Letters" game helps reinforce letter recognition and is better suited to kindergarteners than it is to older youngsters. According to *Key Notes: The High/Scope Early Childhood Computer Learning Report* the pattern-matching game "Match" offers challenges to a wide range of players' skills and may be used with preschool and kindergarten children to develop attribute, direction, and number discriminations (High/Scope Educational Research Foundation, 1985).

Children need adult help in interpreting the menu and selecting a game; however, in a very short time they are able to recognize and choose the game they want from the menu whether or not they can actually read the choices. While most teachers are positive about their use of the *Kindercomp* programs, some have criticized them because they seem to lack a "real" purpose in terms of the school curriculum and because very often the letters displayed on the screen do not look as they would on a printed page. Others report another less troublesome problem in the game "Names," in which all the letters are displayed in uppercase form. Teachers are quick to add, however, that despite this drawback, children enjoy practicing typing their names and are fascinated by having them flashed on the screen in various sizes and patterns.

Teachers using *Kindercomp* in the High/Scope early childhood program recommend that a cardboard keyboard with upper- and lowercase letters be placed on each key to help children match letters on the screen with those on the keyboard. They recommend *Kindercomp* as a program offering a good deal of entertainment for young children and a feeling of comfort working with a computer.

Children's Carrousel is similar to *Kindercomp* in that it is a software package with a variety of different programs. The nine programs included range from "Alphabet Song" and "Shooting Stars," which do little more than acquaint children with the computer, to more advanced games involving the identification of same and different shapes, colors, and letters and the sequencing of letters and numbers. Although many teachers report it to be a useful addition to their software libraries, some are critical of certain aspects of *Children's Carrousel.* Doyle (1985) summarizes some of these criticisms as poor graphics, directions that must be read to children, and content that is more entertaining than educational (p. 29).

In addition to programs designed to promote aspects of prereading and concept development, a number of programs have been developed to introduce the keyboard along with prereading skills. *Muppet Learning Keys* is a program of this type. It has received good reviews from teachers and parents. The program makes use of a separate keyboard with oversized, alphabetically arranged letters. The accompanying software includes three programs that allow children to explore colors, numbers, and letters. Certain keys allow children to change the color and number of objects on the screen and to add motion and sound. Teachers using the program report that children have no difficulty transferring from this to the regular keyboard.

A Beginning Reading Program

The computer programs described so far are quite representative of those available for developing language and concept development in young children. The final program that we will describe is not so typical, yet its name is more likely to be recognized by teachers and parents alike. *The Writing to Read System* is a multimedia literacy program for young children. It has received widespread national publicity. The program uses computers, tape recorders, and typewriters along with printed materials to teach children to read and write. Children are taught for one hour each day in a separate computer center rather than in the regular classroom. Fifteen minutes of that time is given to instruction at the computer. Color images on the computer screen are accompanied by spoken words to help children recognize and type forty-two phonemes (sounds) of the English language. After each computer session, children listen to the same lesson at a tape recorder as they enter responses in a work journal. They then listen to a tape-recorded story as they follow along in a book. The fourth fifteen-minute stop is at a typewriter, on which they may type whatever they wish. The children learn to type narratives, stories, and poems.

The creation of John Henry Martin (a retired teacher, principal, and school superintendent), the program was underwritten by International Business Machines, and it makes use of their computers and Selectric typewriters. The favorable results of two years of experimental testing by the Educational Testing Service encouraged IBM to market the program in districts nationwide. It should be noted, however, that although the results were highly favorable for the kindergarteners using the program, no differences were revealed between those pupils and others in comparison groups at the end of first grade, leaving open the question of whether the results are sustained over time (Howitt, 1984).

We have observed and talked with a number of teachers in various school districts using the *Writing to Read* System. The reviews among these teachers and our own opinions of the program are mixed. We feel that it is important to share what we have learned, largely because this program has been given so much national publicity that it usually provokes more questions and attention than any other single program designed to teach reading. We chose to discuss it here because the computer portion of the program makes use of the tutorial mode. Ohanian (1984), a critic of the program, describes a typical *Writing to Read* lesson using the computer:

On the day I visited the classroom, the computer was drilling a youngster on the word chair. The voice output repeated "This is a chair. Say chair. Say ch. Type ch. Say air. Type air. Say chair. Type chair." As the phoneme was pronounced the appropriate letters made their way from the border of the screen to the center. The child was instructed to say the word, then say each phoneme sound, and then say the whole word again. And then the child was to type the word. (p. 30)

In the final step, if the word is typed correctly it will appear on the screen. If not, the learner will be taken through the same procedure again. Ohanian's criticisms of the program are not unlike those of some of the teachers we interviewed. She complains that the division of learning into tiny pieces divorced from content fails to give the child a sense of the purpose of reading, that the work journals are indistinguishable from basal workbooks, and that the writing instruction is inconsistent with current research in the writing process (p. 30).

Pam Smith (1985), of the Willard School in Ridgewood, New Jersey, reports similar concerns among teachers there; however, she reports many positive comments as well. According to the teachers at Willard, the children's interest in writing increased as a result of *Writing to Read*. Children were writing stories at home and in class and bringing them to the *Writing to Read* lab to type. Not only were the children highly motivated to write, they could read everything they wrote. "Special needs" children were more attentive than usual in this program and were able to retain what they had learned. The teachers also thought that learning the concept of left to right was one of the primary benefits of the program (p. 6).

Like many of the teachers with whom we have worked, the teachers at Willard are very clever at adapting materials to meet their own standards for what is appropriate. For example, *Writing to Read* calls for the children to move from the computer to the work journal station and on to the listen-and-read station. One first-grade teacher thought that this forty-five-minute period was too long for children of this age to sit wearing headphones. She changed the sequence, inserting a puzzle activity between the required stations. Other teachers felt that some of the work journal activities needed additional directions, and so they developed their own materials for that purpose (P. Smith, 1985, p. 7).

Writing to Read is a very expensive program to purchase and manage. In many ways it is inconsistent with what was said in Chapter 1 about the reading process. It is, however, definitely a program that parents and administrators are likely to inquire about. For that reason alone, it is an important program for teachers of reading to know about. Anyone considering its purchase would do well to observe it in operation and to talk to teachers and administrators who have been using it for at least two years. As with all the programs described here or elsewhere, a consideration of how the materials fit into your framework of reading instruction is of utmost importance.

☐ ──────────────── **ELEMENTARY** ──────────────── ☐

Computer software at the elementary level should focus on meaningful text, whether at the word, sentence, or paragraph level. Students need to recognize how words can be used to alter the meaning of text structures. They need to use the language cue systems to help them derive meaning from the passage. It is therefore important that reading/language arts computer software packages be used with this framework in mind. Although gaps exist between the kind of software published and the type of instruction sought, there are ways of adapting the software to the students' instructional needs. Until software is produced to reflect current practices and theories in reading, we need to do two things: select only the best software available and generate ideas for modifying existing software packages.

Software at the Word Level

The Hinky Pinky Game provides students with practice in rhyming pairs of words from definitions, formulas, and hints. Designed for anyone aged nine or above, this software package can be used for vocabulary development, deductive reasoning, context analysis, and dictionary skills. The object of the game is to guess a pair of one-syllable (hink pink), two-syllable (hinky pinky), or three-syllable (hinkety pinkety) words that not only rhyme but also reflect the definition offered on the computer screen. An example of a two-syllable rhyme would be "lunar schooner" for a sailing vessel on a voyage to the earth's satellite. Although an old idea in a new package, the concept still is good. Students are engaged in the development and manipulation of vocabulary. They need to draw upon previous experiences and background information in order to respond accurately.

The most appealing aspect of this program is its versatility with content-area instruction. Since an editor component is included, students can create their own hinky pinky for any unit of study. In fact, ideas are included in the documentation for integrating hinky pinkys into art, language arts, science, and social studies. In so doing, students must create definitions and hints for helping others solve their problems. Having worked with hinky pinkys without the computer, we recognize their motivational appeal. Putting this idea into a computerized word game makes the creation and presentation process easier for students and teachers.

Software programs such as *Homonyms I* and *Homonyms II* can reinforce or extend an understanding of word differences. When confused about spelling and meaning differences in sound-alike words, students can benefit from well-prepared programs of this nature. Like other Milliken software programs, this package provides the teacher with a sound management system to monitor students' progress. Although not recommended for all students, this program can benefit those who need to practice the use of homonyms in context.

Individual student assignments can be made, extending from grades 3 through 9. Homonym lists are presented for each lesson so that the teacher can make assignments to accommodate individual differences. This option, according to Geoffrion and Geoffrion (1983), is an important feature to consider when evaluating software packages. A twenty-item preassessment test is used for each level to determine which, if any, homonym pairs are causing confusion. Similar to the practice exercises, each test item requires the student to select the correct homonym for the sentence presented. If a student gets all items correct, the student can automatically progress to the next level. The option to practice only with those items causing difficulty prevents unnecessary repetition; it also provides for greater individualization.

This type of program can be used as a teacher supplement for skill development. Because students are exposed to words in context, they have the opportunity to fine-tune developmental reading skills that might otherwise not be mastered during class instruction.

We recommend that teachers provide creative outlets for reading and writing with homonyms. A program such as *The Hinky Pinky Game* can be a vehicle for developing homonym pairs. Students could create definitions such as "approaching the second year of life" for the homonym pair *to/two*. Also, having students use utility packages for creating cryptograms or crossword puzzles (see Chapter 2) on different homonym pairs may help them to apply their skills to other contexts. On- or off-line writing activities for selected homonym pairs (for example, important schoolwide "principles" for a "principal" to consider) also are suggested for helping students to communicate the extent of their skill acquisition.

Similarly, software packages created to hone students' understanding of word differences should be used to supplement, not supplant, language activities in the classroom. Whether used in conjunction with basals, newspapers, novels, or other print sources, such software packages can assist in vocabulary development.

Another interesting drill-and-practice software program for reading skill development, conceptualized by Bill Martin, Jr., is *Word Blaster* (see *MicroSIFT* review in Chapter 3). Designed for students in grades 2 through 6, this program presents single sentences with blanks on a colorful Cape Canaveral–like screen under a missile. Four distractors go across the top of the screen; students send the missile to shoot the appropriate word. If the correct word is selected, a parachutist places the word in the blank for students to see the complete sentence. If the incorrect word is selected, the student has another chance before scoring a miss.

As described by the authors of the program, its clozelike format requires students to use the graphophonic, syntactic, and semantic cue systems to select the correct word. Also, to help teachers understand which cue system may be causing difficulty, a simple management system is built into the program to assess the number and type of errors.

Recommended by Michael Shelly (1983), this program is a motivating and "fun" approach to the improvement of reading skills. Joseph Lanni, reading teacher in Caldwell–West Caldwell, New Jersey, concurs with Shelly's review. Lanni has seen his typically unmotivated students eager to use this program as they develop contextual analysis skills. Since level-of-difficulty and rate-of-presentation options are provided, students at varying reading levels can profit from this program. Its colorful graphics and gamelike format challenge students to deal with the contextual analysis of sentences. If used along with more developed text on or off the computer (see M-SS-NG L-NKS and *Cloze-Plus* for cloze practice with more developed text), this program has a place in the language arts classroom.

Software with More Developed Text

If effectively programmed, software programs with more developed text (more than the word and sentence level) can be extremely effective for promoting reading comprehension, particularly if reader options are provided. David Reinking at the University of Georgia has created a reading comprehension program, soon to be released by Milliken, in which students can opt to review the vocabulary or develop the background information necessary to process the passage's content. For example, if students need more information about a passage on hailstones, they can select the option that graphically describes the formation of hailstones. Students also can elect to review the vocabulary presented in the same passage, see the main ideas of each paragraph highlighted, or read the passage at a lower readability level. (The software is programmed to present all the passages at lower readability levels, with alterations in sentence length and vocabulary.) These options are significant aids when reading computerized text. Having originally used the program for his dissertation to see whether students' comprehension would be significantly improved, Reinking found that intermediate-grade students who read his interactive text scored significantly higher on the comprehension than those who read the passages on the computer without the text-help option. He also found that readers readily selected the help options, especially the supplemental background information. Thus, this program framework should serve as a prototype for developing reading software. When students were given control over the amount of information needed to process the text's meaning they become aware of their level of understanding for any given passage. This promotes a more active, holistic approach to reading development (Reinking & Schreiner, 1985).

A current software program that provides some of the features of Reinking's program is *Comprehension Power*. Even though students cannot build on their schemata for a topic, they can preview text and read it at an appropriate rate. *Comprehension Power* is designed for average students, grades 4 through 12, and remedial students with mature interests and primary-level reading abilities. Passages at each level are presented with questions following each reading segment. Verbal feedback is immediate; however, branching is not incorporated into the program. Individualization of instruction is difficult since students have to go through passages sequentially.

The program does have an excellent management system for evaluating student progress and diagnosing specific student difficulties. When used in conjunction with other materials, this program can be a useful diagnostic tool.

Another program, *Tutorial Comprehension*, approaches reading by developing five comprehension areas: main ideas, details, sequence, inference, and critical reading. Although intended for students in grades 2 through 4, this comprehension series can be used effectively with older remedial students who could benefit from skill development in these areas.

Each of the five comprehension packages has three components: pretest and posttest evaluations, instructional or tutorial lessons, and graded practice lessons. The paper and pencil pretest and posttest evaluations are keyed to a specific skill and provide the teacher with a quick, informal assessment of the student's knowledge. The results are used as a basis for placing students into the tutorial or practice lessons. The tutorial lessons provide instructions on different aspects of a specific skill and present exercises to assess a student's level of understanding of that skill. For example, the inference tutorial presents three different lessons: making an inference, cause and effect, and what happens next.

This first lesson lists four steps for making an inference. Subsequently, exercises such as the following are presented:

> The puppy jumped for the ball. He rolled in the grass after he caught it.
> The puppy was:
> lazy
> excited
> playful

Depending on the type of exercise, different objective formats are used. At the end of each lesson, scores are provided to help the teacher determine the student's next step. If successful with each lesson, the student proceeds to the practice lessons on the other disks. The practice lessons reinforce the skills presented on the tutorial. A separate set of thirty to forty examples is provided for each grade from 2 through 4. An example from the "making an inference" lesson, grade 3, would be:

> The bright sun glistened off the frozen surface of the pond. It was very cold but I was too excited to feel it. We had been practicing ever since the pond froze. The Rangers were ready to skate.
> What kind of team were the Rangers?
> a hockey team
> a basketball team
> a soccer team

Once all practice lessons have been completed, a posttest can be used for further analysis of skill acquisition. Along with the three components are lesson planners, record-keeping systems, and scope and sequence charts. Comprehensive in design, this series aids the teacher in individualizing instruction for comprehension development. Janet Forer, Chapter I teacher, Fair Lawn, New Jersey, in using this entire series with selected second-, third-, and fourth-graders, found that the detailed description of lesson-planning and record-keeping procedures helped her keep abreast of students' needs while providing them with appropriate skill exercises. She observed that her students were motivated to do the lessons because of the challenging yet nonthreatening presentations of each skill. She also found that the immediate feedback gave students a stronger feeling of accomplishment and more lasting retention, two major problems among remedial readers. Since this series does emphasize a subskill approach to reading instruction, it should be used only for certain students as a supplement to a total reading program. Even selected students need to use other materials that emphasize the use of a multitude of skills simultaneously so that the processing of meaning, as opposed to the development of isolated skills, is seen as the goal of purposeful reading. Since pretest evaluations are provided, we recommend that they be used along with other standardized and informal assessments to determine which students might benefit from this type of program.

Cloze formats have become a popular means of developing reading comprehension. Because students need to apply their syntactic and semantic awareness of language, this format has appeared in standardized and informal tests, commercially prepared print sources, and computer software programs. Kibby (1981) predicted that this format would be widely used for nearly all tests of reading ability by the end of the 1980s. Two widely acclaimed clozelike software packages are M-SS-NG L-NKS and *Cloze-Plus*.

M-SS-NG L-NKS, written for students in grades 4 and up, is designed to help students reconstruct literary passages by having them fill in missing letters one at a time. Created by Carol Chomsky and Judah Schwartz, this program enables students to use their existing reading-comprehension and problem-solving skills to fill in the blanks created with one to nine available patterns. For example, a sentence from *The Cricket in Times Square* (written by George Seldon) would be displayed in one of the following selected forms:

> Level 1: -t w-s th- t-m- -f y--r th-t cr-ck-ts l-k- m-st.
> [consonants only with vowels omitted]
> Level 2: l- w-s -h- t-m- o- y-a- t-a- c-i-k-t- l-k- m-s-.
> [every other letter]
> Level 3: l- w-- t-- t--- o- y--- t--- c------- l--- m---.
> [first letter of each word]
> Level 4: It --- the ---- of ---- that -------- like ----.
> [every other word]
> Level 5: l- -a- --e -i-e o- -ea- --a- --i--e-- -i-e -o--.
> [vowels only with consonants omitted]
> Level 6: -t --s --e ---e -f ---r ---t -------s ---e ---t.
> [last letter of each word]
> Level 7: It --- --- ---- -- ---- ---- -------- ---- ----.
> [blanks representing the letters]
> Level 8: -- --- --- ---- -- ---- ---- -------- ---- ----.
> [blanks representing the letters]
> Level 9: [nothing but the title and author at the top of the screen]

Considered to be an enjoyable word puzzle by EPIE evaluators, it can be a challenging vocabulary development exercise for good readers; however, it may be frustrating for poor readers who do not have an adequate sight vocabulary or stored knowledge about standard spellings. We recommend that when poorer readers use the program they be paired with more adept readers. In fact, it may be better to allow students to read the whole, unmutilated text on paper before presenting them with computer screenfuls of deleted text. Also, since a game in progress cannot be stored, time for completing the exercise is necessary.

Because the program uses excerpts from children's classics like *Charlie and the Chocolate Factory* (Roald Dahl) and *My Side of the Mountain* (Jean Craighead George), excerpts from literary classics like *Moby Dick* (Herman Melville) and *The Old Man and the Sea* (Ernest Hemingway), and passages on nonfiction encyclopedia topics, students are exposed to a variety of good writing. If students have the opportunity to work through the nine difficulty levels for any passage, they become extremely familiar with an author's style, a desired outcome of literacy development (May, 1982). By level 9, students supposedly can rewrite the passages verbatim. This demonstrates their facility in recalling the graphophonic, syntactic, and semantic structure of the passage, requiring an eidetic memory.

While a good memory can serve one well at times, students still need to examine the passage critically and creatively. Teachers should use the passages to stimulate a discussion about the author's purpose and bias in writing. Since students become well versed with the passage structure by using the various clozelike formats, they can use their information about the textual structure as background for further analysis of the content.

M-SS-NG L-NKS also has a separate editor software program for including teacher- and student-selected passages with the same clozelike format. This provides a viable option for tailoring the passages to the students' ability and interest levels.

Success with Reading is another software package that offers cloze passages taken from children's books. Each story disk contains six selections from six different books. Students are presented with a full text with deletions cued by the first letter and dashes for the missing letters. For example, the first screenful of *If You Sailed on the Mayflower* begins like this:

What would you eat and d---- on the Mayflower? Day after day, you would eat the same kind of f---.

Users are encouraged to guess the missing letters. If they try a letter that is wrong, it will not appear on the screen. If they wait long enough without a successful choice (16 seconds), the computer will start filling in the letter. A score is kept on the lower left-hand portion of the screen. This is determined by the amount of time it takes to guess the missing letters and the number of wrong guesses made.

We tried the level C package (suggested for third grade) with eleven nine-year-olds. The books (*If You Grew Up with George Washington, Wanted Dead or Alive, If You Grew Up with Abraham Lincoln, Five True Horse Stories,* and *Rip Van Winkle*) were presented with the program, and the children were told they could read the books and then do the cloze program or vice versa. Although most of the students were eager to get at the package before reading the books, half the students decided afterwards that it would be easier to do the cloze exercise after reading the books. All the children were enthusiastic about using the software, saying that it was fun to try to figure out the words from the clues given—the story line, the first letter, and the "dots," as they called the dashes left in for the missing letters. They said it was like doing a puzzle and the timer motivated them to work as fast as they could.

For those teachers who want to write their own stories or use selections from books other than those that come with the package, the program offers a write/edit mode with a variety of cloze options. You can choose to omit all vowels, all but the first letters, or all the letters, with dashes appearing for all deleted letters. We think the best option is the one to omit individual letters as you are typing in the text. This will allow you to produce exercises similar to the sample supplied with the package; you can tailor your cloze for your intended uses, such as leaving more text in for less experienced readers. You may want to delete all verbs or all letters except the first in verbs, or you may want to delete content words like important nouns. This write/edit feature is easy to use and gives you complete control over the format of your cloze exercise.

Besides a management system, *Success with Reading* has a "tractor" option—a "beat the clock" game format—that allows the user to compete against a moving "tractor." The story disks are available in four levels, specified for grades 3, 4, 5, and 6. Because of its great versatility as a tool for creating your own cloze passages and its introduction as a program offering gamelike exercises over passages from popular trade books, this software is a valuable addition to any class or school collection.

Unlike M-SS-NG L-NKS and *Success with Reading, Cloze-Plus* does not emphasize the recall of words from selected passages. Rather, it provides predetermined cloze exercises for selecting words for every *n*th deletion. Reading passages (rated as interesting by EPIE) are presented with two types of activities. The "Structured Cloze" format requires students to use context to fill in a deleted word or phrase in a paragraph. Students either select the correct word/phrase from four or five choices or supply the omitted word. An example of this format from the Level E disk would be:

> Linnaeus, an eighteenth-century naturalist, called chocolate "food of the gods." Modern scientists give another reason for what makes it so heavenly. This is why people _____ it. Something in it makes the eater feel loved!
> a. leave   c. sell
> b. help   d. like

If the correct word is chosen, it is placed in the blank; if an incorrect word is chosen, the student gets another try before being shown the correct word. The "Vocabulary-in-Context" format requires students to use context to select, from four choices, the meaning of a difficult or unfamiliar word. An example of this format would be:

> These forests provide the moisture the cacao trees need. Wetness is very important to their growth.
> Moisture means about the same as:
> a. soil   c. paths
> b. dampness   d. leaves

Although designed for grades 3 through 8, the passages seem more appropriate for students in grades 4 and up. Besides the verbal feedback provided after each correct answer, a part of a picture, related to the passage's theme, is provided. This sequence continues until the entire seven- to twelve-paragraph lesson is presented. Mary Savino, basic skills teacher in a parochial school, Irvington, New Jersey, has used the Level E program with her sixth-grade students. She believes it is one of the better pieces of software available because her students find the stories interesting and they are motivated to solve the puzzles.

The comprehensive manager system provides an assessment of the students' performance with the type of context clues used (for example, synonyms, definition, categorization, and time order). Also appealing is the help option provided for discerning the correct word choice.

While exercises contained therein demand students' attention to contextual detail, limited use of applied comprehension is required. Besides the recognition of contextually appropriate words or word meanings, it would be useful to ask questions about the passage's content. We suggest that this be done to reinforce an understanding of the whole passage.

Because of their intrinsically interesting content, many of the reading-for-meaning packages described in the foregoing section can be used with older learners in remedial and developmental programs (*Comprehension Power, Cloze-Plus,* M-SS-NG L-NKS), but drill-and-practice software for this level can also serve very specific purposes. High school students find they must prepare for proficiency tests and SATs as well as improve rate and comprehension to keep up with their ever-increasing reading demands.

Software at the Word Level

At the word level there are programs that can help students take a direct approach to building vocabulary, one of the major components of the aptitude and achievement tests. While opinion is divided on the place of drill and practice on word lists as opposed to wide reading and experience, there is some evidence that any approach is better than none (Petty, Herold, & Stoll, 1968). The key to the effectiveness of explicit vocabulary improvement is the learner's intentions. Holbrook (1984) says that direct instruction offered to students who are interested in developing on their own can work very well.

Although it sounds like a phonics or structural analysis program, *Word Attack* is a highly recommended package (EPIE) that offers four separate activities for vocabulary words at nine levels of difficulty. While the publisher recommends this for "grade four through adult," it is probably best used in junior high and up, since older students see the value of such exercises for test preparation. Since there is an editing option, teachers can add their own word lists to expand and individualize the program.

The four activities are: word display (word, definition, and sentence are given), multiple-choice quiz (words or definitions are given), sentence completion (student must recall and spell the correct word with a help option), and finally, the word attack game (student "shoots" or "attacks" one of four words to match a given definition, hence the ubiquitous name, *Word Attack*). Less motivated students will work with this exercise because of its arcadelike format; highly motivated students will like the option of speeding up the game and competing with themselves. The editing feature and large word bank within the program make it a good choice for students preparing for high school proficiency tests or SATs. One teacher who runs an after-school tutoring center has found this program very effective for the high school students he prepares for the PSATs and SATs.

Another less comprehensive vocabulary builder is *Power of Words*, Volumes 1 and 2. Recommended for good junior high students and high school students, the words are at high school and college level. First the student selects a synonym for a target word. If correct, positive reinforcement is given; if wrong, the correct answer is displayed. Next, whether the answer was right or wrong, an instructional component appears. This didactic segment contains parts of speech, pronunciation, definition, a sentence with the word, and sometimes synonyms, antonyms, etymological information, words often confused, and humorous graphics.

For those older students who still need practice in a component of vocabulary building, namely structural analysis, there is a program that might be more motivating than the usual workbook approach. *Fundamental Word Focus* presents a game format for diagnosing and reinforcing structural analysis for grades 4 through 9. The teacher must place students at their appropriate levels and monitor results since no teaching or branching is provided. The teacher must do the direct teaching as needed, but there is plenty of help in the accompanying manuals. Nobil (1983) gave it a favorable review and praised Random House for its array of quality software.

Software at the Sentence Level

Some drill-and-practice work on the sentence level might be appropriate with older students. Sentence-combining exercises have been suggested to improve students' composing and comprehending abilities (O'Hare, 1973). Milliken has produced a tutorial program called *Sentence Combining*, which encourages students to combine short choppy sentences by using conjunctions, relative pronouns, and adverbial connectors such as *because, before,* and *after.* Although suggested for grades 4 to 8, these activities might be better used with junior high students or remedial secondary students. Close teacher monitoring can provide many opportunities for students to transfer the learning to real writing and reading activities, for example, noting *who* clauses when they are important in a text. Both J. Hall (1983) and Lombardi (1983) gave this program a favorable review. EPIE praises some of the thirteen tutorials but thinks some might be confusing, hence the caveat to monitor and teach along with the program.

Software with More Developed Text

Since older students need to read effectively and efficiently, comprehension and rate building are concerns at the junior-senior high level. One sure way of improving reading is to encourage wide reading of good literature. Combining book reading with computer-mediated responses is an option available through Media Basics' *Return to Reading Series.* Over one hundred books read by students in grades 4 through 12 are now in this computerized response library.

After students read a book, they engage in a thirty- to forty-minute exercise that is divided into three sections. Designed to help students express their feelings about the book, "Responding to the Book" contains five open-ended questions with no right or wrong answers. In "Understanding the Book," students answer questions that assess their literary appreciation, comprehension, critical thinking, and vocabulary. Enrichment activities such as games and puzzles are included in the section entitled "Going Beyond the Book." Some interesting activity sheets also are provided. For instance, Orwell's *1984* is to be read with a response journal, encouraging personal reaction through writing. Sentence combining and creating activities are examples of other postreading exercises.

It should be noted that the books do not come with the software. These must be in your library or purchased separately, but they are all well-known favorites and classics. You will have to select the packages that go with titles your junior-senior high school students might be reading. Many titles appropriate for the middle grades also are included in the collection.

Two other comprehension programs suitable for older students (college and adult as well as high school level) are *66 Passages* and *88 Passages.* The former contains selections from third- to eighth-grade level and the latter includes selections ranging in difficulty from sixth-grade to college level. The content is definitely designed to appeal to adults.

Students read the passage and then answer comprehension questions. If an answer is incorrect, the program responds with the reason why and instructs them to go back to the text. If an answer is correct, the program acknowledges it and also supports the answer with a reason. Selections are grouped around specific topics so that readers can choose an area that interests them. This also helps them to build up semantic connections that will aid text processing as they go through the cluster.

Myrna Erhlich of the Jersey City State College Reading Clinic and Dorothy Minkoff of the Trenton State College Clinic both highly recommend these packages for remedial and developmental readers at the college level. They especially like the record-keeping system and the degree of student control that the programs allow, keeping teacher intervention at a minimum.

Improving rate while maintaining comprehension is another concern of older readers. This is an area in which the computer can be especially helpful since it seems made to order for the necessary record keeping of words read per minute (WPM) and number of comprehension questions correct—definitely an improvement over a teacher-held stopwatch!

Speed Reader II is one program specified for use by junior-senior high school and college students. Consisting of five activities purported to promote reading speed, it is best suited for readers with well-developed comprehension abilities. Since the first three activities require you to recognize flashed letters and words and lines of text flashed half a line at a time on alternate sides of the screen, we would not recommend them. Recent research at the Center for the Study of Reading has raised questions about the value of tachistoscopic exercises like these to increase perception (McConkie, 1984). The "Column Reading Lesson" presents the text in column form and instructs the reader to "read each line with only one fixation." Again, this is questionable since it can make readers concentrate on the technique rather than on getting the meaning.

The one activity that we would recommend is the "Reading Passage Lesson," which presents continuous text by the screenful, with the reader controlling the rate by hitting the space bar. The computer accurately clocks your WPM and offers an optional eight-question comprehension check to encourage readers to temper their quest for speed with a concern for how well they understood the text.

The software also includes an editor option, which allows you to enter your own passages to expand the ten-session program.

Two other rate-improvement programs recommended by Dorothy Mulligan of the Jersey City State College Electronic Learning Lab are *Speed Reading . . . The Computer Course* (Bureau of Business Practice) and the Sack-Yourman courseware program *Speed Reading.* The first program includes a tutorial that introduces the principles of speed reading as part of its practice lessons. It also offers "Rapid-Perception Drills," which are, according to the manual, "designed to 'warm up' your eyes for the reading selections that follow. . . . Eye movement drills will train your eyes to fixate correctly." Again, while these activities are questionable, the "Practice Readings" section, which permits full text reading by the screenful, is very useful. It also offers the unique option of moving from reading on the computer to reading from printed materials while being timed by the computer. Ten-question comprehension checks are another feature.

The Sack-Yourman program *Speed Reading* does not contain perception or eye-movement drills; it focuses solely on improving comprehension and rate. This courseware, from the College Skills Center producers of *88/66 Passages,* offers interesting selections off the computer in conventionally printed formats with postreading questions on the computer screen. Reading rate and comprehension scores are tracked by the computer. Michael Labuda of the Jersey City State College Reading Department has used this program successfully in his college power-reading courses.

SAT Preparation

Another drill-and-practice application for the computer in the high school is SAT preparation. While this kind of practice does not teach reading, it is a valid concern of students who are college bound. In fact, Frank Smith (1982, p. 191) says that teachers should make it clear to students that drills to improve performance on a test may have little to do with learning to read; he says that students understand this kind of "ritual." Anyway, despite claims made by the College Board to the contrary, students who have "crammed" or "prepped" for these kinds of tests usually do better than those who do not.

Most of the computer programs designed for this purpose have an instruction mode and a test mode. When students choose instruction, they get test questions with possible multiple-choice answers, much as they appear on SAT exams. Instruction is provided in the form of explanations about why an answer is right or wrong. In the test mode, usually answers are just scored, and the student or computer keeps track of progress.

A popular package developed jointly by CBS Software and the National Association of Secondary School Principals is *Mastering the SAT*. Besides the usual explanations of answers and simulated tests (four), this courseware also includes test-taking strategies. Another package, for the verbal section only, that received a high rating from EPIE is *English SAT 1*. The main problem with this program is the limited practice it offers: for the reading subsections there are only thirty-six analogies, thirty-six antonyms, and three comprehension passages. This might be best used by sophomores or juniors as an introduction to the content of the PSAT.

Betsy Staples (1985), in reviewing four packages, noted this same deficiency, namely, a limited number of items in each subsection. One feature she liked in *The Perfect Score* was the answer-selection mechanism: you are forced to read all choices as you move the arrow to select, a good habit to promote in test-taking situations like this. On the negative side, this is one program in which you must do your own record keeping, a chore one would expect the computer to do for you.

The *Owlcat SAT Preparation Course* has some unique features. In the instruction mode, you can call for help from a dictionary when you are doing the verbal sections, and in an option called "Buddy Study," you can compete with a buddy, answering questions under timed conditions. A negative feature is that you cannot change an answer once it has been recorded. Another feature to beware of with this package is that the beginning diagnostic disk may be used only once, and this is not clearly stated in the documentation. If you purchased this for use by students in a study lab, you would need to make backups or instruct students not to answer the items on the screen.

Barron's Computer SAT *Study Program* is, according to Staples, "little more than an electronic answer sheet," since you read all the questions from the standard Barron's study books and use the computer to record your answers. In the instruction mode, you get only "a hint and a second chance." Again, you have to keep your own records. The Barron's print materials, which have been successfully used for a long time, seem to be a better buy than their computerized version.

Similar to Barron's, Harcourt Brace Jovanovich's *Computer Preparation for the* SAT requires you to use their book *How to Prepare for the* SAT along with the computer program. One positive feature of this package is the study plan it creates for you from the diagnostic information it garners from your answer patterns. You are told what areas should get high, medium, or low priority in your study-time allocation. Unlike Barron's slow and cumbersome courseware, in the instruction mode this courseware gives you speedy feedback and the option to call for explanations. Staples found the content of this course to be significantly more difficult than that of the other three packages.

The computer packages seem to be best used as adjuncts to courses or study groups in SAT preparation. If a few are housed in a high school resource center or library, students needing more practice in specific subsections could pursue these individually, outside of the course. Perhaps very bright, highly motivated students could use only a computer course to prepare for this test. But for the large majority of students, none of the packages available today would seem to be stand-alone replacements for teacher-guided review sessions in which students could ask their own questions and learn from those raised by others.

SUMMARY

In this chapter we have described and discussed applications for selected software designed to provide drill and practice in specific facets of a reading-instruction program. From exercises on the letter, word, and sentence level for the very young to materials providing word and whole-text comprehension practice for adult learners, these computer programs are offered as examples in the ever-proliferating pool of educational software for reading and language arts instruction.

In the next chapter, we will highlight software that is more interactive in nature. From programs requiring open-ended responses in reading and writing to those presenting simulations and problem-solving activities, these programs represent some innovative applications of the computer. These types of software, although still casting the computer in the tutor mode, feature the technology as a facilitator of divergent thinking, interactive reading, and creative writing activities rather than merely as an electronic drillmaster and record keeper.

□ 5 □

The Computer as Tutor
Interactive Learning

Chapter 4 described tutor-mode software that provides drill-and-practice materials for specific reading objectives at the word, sentence, and more developed text levels; Chapter 5 will introduce some representative tutor-mode software designed to present learning episodes in more interactive and open-ended ways. Rather than offering questions to be answered by just one "right" answer as did the packages in Chapter 4, these programs require users to participate actively in learning situations by testing hypotheses, chatting with the computer, creating with language, and engaging in problem solving. The computer often acts as a patient guide or coach, encouraging creative thinking and allowing for divergent responses. As in Chapter 4, the program descriptions have been categorized according to the level for which they are most appropriate, prekindergarten/primary, elementary, and secondary/postsecondary.

□   PREKINDERGARTEN / PRIMARY   □

The criteria for selecting interactive software at this level focus on the ability of computer programs to allow children to manipulate language symbols and to use language and thought creatively. Such software also must capture and maintain their interest and allow them to be independent learners. The programs described below are representative of those that meet most of these criteria. They have been used successfully with young children by teachers and parents.

Story Machine.   *Story Machine* is an engaging interactive program that involves young children in reading and writing activities. Using a dictionary of forty-five words, the program allows children to write sentences, paragraphs, and short stories, which are animated on the screen. The list of words includes articles, nouns, verbs, prepositions, adjectives, pronouns, and possessive pronouns. Although the vocabulary is limited, beginning readers enjoy experimenting with it. In the process, their reading vocabularies are extended, and an awareness of sentence grammar is developed.

Learners are offered four options: story, dictionary, disk, and choices. The story option allows for story creations. The dictionary presents the words in the program, according to parts of speech. The story option provides clear directions for saving stories onto separate disks, and the choice option offers the sound and color choices. If the child selects the story option, a split screen is presented; the upper portion is used for the animation of text while the bottom portion is used for the child's writing.

Although teachers are generally very positive about *Story Machine*, they do report some technical limitations. For example, objects need to be positioned correctly in order for certain verbs to be acted out. One object cannot "eat" or "zot" another object unless they are close together. The program will automatically erase any sentence that cannot be executed, however, so that children can immediately write a more acceptable sentence. The inclusion of only uppercase print also concerns teachers of beginning readers.

Teachers using *Story Machine* suggest the following ideas to extend the potential of this program. We pass them along as good recommendations for this and other programs of this type:

- Make certain that the *Story Machine* dictionary is readily available. Use the dictionary card provided by the publishers or create a large chart or handout. This will help children focus on the manipulation of language rather than on the memorization and recall of isolated words.
- Use the program with small or large groups of children so that one child's ideas can be a stimulus for other children. Also, by sharing typing responsibilities, children are freed to think of ideas for writing.
- Occasionally rewrite some of the stories on a word processor with appropriate upper- and lowercase print. This will help reinforce vocabulary included in the dictionary. Use the word processor to highlight words, replace words, and move sentences around.
- Use sentences written with *Story Machine* as a stimulus for writing more extensive stories. For example, the sentence "The cat runs to the tree" could be the beginning of a story involving a chase and rescue.

CARIS.   *Computer Animated Reading Instruction System* (CARIS), was designed to introduce reading skills to very young children or to those with learning disabilities or low readiness (CARIS *User's Manual*, 1983). The program uses a whole-word approach in which students form brief sentences using words selected from lists of nouns and verbs. The sentences are then animated on the screen.

According to teachers, one of the strengths of CARIS is that the pictures help reinforce the meanings of the words selected by the child and the sentences created. They also report that spelling skills are visually and kinesthetically reinforced and that the program has motivational appeal. Reported among the program's weaknesses is the limited set of thirteen nouns and fourteen verbs offered to form sentences. Teachers also say that some of the graphics are confusing for children. For example, the picture for BALL is a circle of dots. Some teachers are concerned that nonsense sentences such as THE BOAT FLIES can be created from the random noun-verb combinations. They worry that disabled or beginning readers may be confused and even be deterred from reading for meaning (Broida, 1985). Other teachers are less troubled by this, since most children enjoy the nonsense sentences and seem quite capable of separating the nonsense from what is possible. They suggest that this type of activity may even reinforce children's sense of reading for meaning.

Kidwriter and Questions and Story.   Two programs similar to *Story Machine* are *Kidwriter* and *Questions and Story*. *Kidwriter* allows children to create pictures and write stories to go with them. The picture stories may be saved. Children can create a directory of picture stories, which may be linked together to create a "storybook" of several pages. Unlike *Story Machine, Kidwriter* is not limited to a certain number of words, and although there is no animation, there is greater flexibility in the ninety-nine objects and five or more scenes that can be changed. Because children can create such varied combinations of scenes, objects, sizes, and colors, teachers consider *Kidwriter* to be more open-ended and more apt to stimulate creativity in children.

Questions and Story queries children about their name, favorite color, activity, and friend. The answers are then incorporated into a story. Although this program contains no graphics, students are captivated by its personal nature. We have observed its use in a reading clinic with children who were among the poorest readers. These children were known to have extremely short attention spans, yet they sat for very long periods of time manipulating language as they created and read a number of different versions of "their own stories."

Language Experience Recorder. Based on an approach to beginning reading that uses material dictated by students to launch children into reading, the *Language Experience Recorder* enables teachers to enter, save, and recall children's dictation for display on the screen or on a printout. The program can generate individual word lists for a particular story. Words are displayed alphabetically with their frequency of occurrence in the story. All the words used by an individual student or group may also be listed in this way.

Teachers using the *Language Experience Recorder* have an excellent opportunity to model revision and editing for children. Students can suggest changes in a story and test them out with ease. The collection of words generated by the writing can serve as a word bank for categorizing, alphabetizing, and spelling. Stories on a particular topic may be illustrated and grouped together to form class or individual books. This program is highly consistent with the framework for reading instruction established in Chapter 1. It makes good use of the special qualities of the computer and applies them in a sound approach to literacy development in young children.

Nucleus. *Nucleus* is a software product developed in England for the Acorn computer. It consists of eight programs, six of which are "content-free," allowing the teacher to enter a file for use in a variety of ways by one or more of the remaining programs. *Nucleus* uses a special keyboard called a "concept keyboard." This extra keyboard has a flat surface with an array of touch-sensitive key areas arranged in a grid pattern of eight rows by sixteen columns. To enter information, overlays are placed on this surface. The first program, "Litset," is used to make files. By placing its overlay on the keyboard, the user can assign any word to one or more of the underlying keys, thus permitting teachers to design and record their own files for language and topic (unit) work (*Nucleus Newsletter,* 1984).

Three *Nucleus* programs of particular interest to kindergarten and primary-grade teachers are "Pressword" (Infants), "Word Recognition," and "Character Formation." "Pressword" (Infants) is a twenty-column whole-word processor used for language development and topic work. This overlay has two bottom rows given over to special facilities, such as new words, word endings, and punctuation. Word spacing is automatic, as are capital letters after a full stop or question. The overlay may be used as a simple sentence maker or as a core file of "Names" to cover a particular topic under study. Some teachers have made overlays containing a core of words from their own reading programs, a theme topic (such as "friends"), while others have devised cloze procedures (text with deleted words) in which an asterisk (*) in a sentence must be replaced by an appropriate word.

"Word Recognition" is a program that accepts any data file containing letters only and displays words in lowercase letters one at a time in random order. The pupil's task is to match the display with the appropriate word, picture, number, color, or shape on the overlay. The major advantages to most of the *Nucleus* programs are their flexibility and their adaptability to content under study in a particular classroom.

Unlike "Pressword" (Infants) and "Word Recognition," the *Nucleus* program "Character Formation" has a fixed content to introduce children to manuscript writing. The overlay provided has large lowercase letters that are pressed by the teacher or child to produce even larger letters on the screen. Six major groups allow the user to "trace" the direction in which digits and lowercase letters are drawn.

Creatures of the Night.   Unlike the other programs described here, *Creatures of the Night* is a multimedia package. Developed by Troll Associates, it is aimed for children in grades 2 to 4. The package consists of a forty-eight-page "I Can Read" book, a matching read-along cassette, and a micro-software disk containing four learning games related to the story. This package represents a growing trend by developers to combine the use of books and technology around a theme or literary work. While the software program in itself is not interactive, it acts as a stimulus for students to become interactively involved with the book as a source of information for answering the questions in each of the computer games it includes.

Before using the computer program, children are instructed to read the book or listen to the audio cassette or use the two together as a read-along. When children have become familiar with the story, they may use the program disk. The four learning games are based on the story; successful completion of the games requires information found in the story. The games in *Creatures of the Night* are "Mouse House," "Word Catcher," "Make a Face," and "Nimble." "Mouse House" is a true-false question-and-answer game. Correct answers permit a mouse to travel through a maze. "Word Catcher" involves selecting the right word to complete sentences based on the story. Students receive points for speed and accuracy. In "Make a Face" students build faces of favorite characters as they correctly select the best meaning for underlined words from the story. Students receive points for selecting the correct synonyms, antonyms, and homonyms in the game "Nimble." *Creatures of the Night* is one of fifteen packages in this series. Other titles include "Dogs and Puppies," "Paul Bunyan," and "The First Thanksgiving."

We have described interactive software representative of some of the better available programs of this type. We are most enthusiastic about those programs that allow the greatest teacher and student input and flexibility and those that stimulate creativity. As developers continue to experiment with new techniques and as they speak to classroom teachers about their needs, we are confident that increasingly better software will be available for young children. Indeed, some of the programs discussed in the next section for elementary grade students hold promise for greater user control and flexibility.

□   **ELEMENTARY**   □

In response to reading educators' advocacy for an active approach to reading text, interactive software programs are beginning to emerge. At the elementary level, interactive software programs encourage skilled readers to apply their prior knowledge to the reading task, set goals for the task, and integrate the new material with existing schemata (Geoffrion & Geoffrion, 1985). The focus of these packages is the active cognitive participation of the reader.

Although the software industry has not been providing enough programs to satisfy those with a holistic orientation to reading instruction, Geoffrion and Geoffrion (1985) believe that software programs that focus on a dynamic approach to reading will be developed in the not too distant future. These "dynabooks" will enable readers to constantly monitor their reading by being able to select that portion of the program which relates to personal goals and needs.

As an example of how a "dynabook" would work, the Geoffrions present a page of text about reading readiness. At the top are the major options: OVERVIEW DEFINE NOTES EXPAND FILE HELP. At the bottom appear these direction options: BACK? WHERE? NEXT? If you were reading along, you could get an overview of the next section, ask for a definition of a word, write some notes, get more information on something, go to a file, go back or forward in the text, or ask where you are in the text.

For instance, if you came upon a reference to "Sesame Street" and wanted to know more about it, you could highlight the term and call for the EXPAND option; a piece of text describing the television show would then appear in another window, thus supplying you with background information without your having to leave the text.

Reinking's program (described in Chapter 4) contains some of the capabilities of the "dynabook" concept. However, since he was limited by the technology available at the time, he used a more linear approach

(Feeley, 1985). In other words, students would have to read a passage before deciding which "help" option to select. However, the idea of simulating printed-page reading on the computer has been and continues to be explored by reading educators. Yet, until enough programs of this nature appear on the market, we need to capitalize on existing programs that provide some comprehension monitoring and hypothesis testing (Miller & Burnett, 1985).

The Puzzler. One software package, *The Puzzler,* cooperatively developed by a team of teachers from Canada is based on the notions of Goodman and Burke (1980), which foster the reading strategies of predicting and confirming. Unlike traditional CAI programs, this program avoids elaborate graphics, offers no feedback, does not keep performance records, and considers teacher involvement as important as the disk-based lessons. Students alternate between reading a page of text and predicting the passage's main topic. With each new page come more clues about the topic to help students confirm or challenge their hypotheses.

For example, one of the passages, entitled "Zingles," presents this first page on the screen:

Zing, there it goes again!
Will people never stop rattling
my brains? All day long, zings
keep echoing throughout the malls
and supermarkets. Oh, it's a
trying life being a zingle.

Before students may go on to the next screen, they must make some predictions as to what they think a "zingle" is. Several predictions may be typed in, for example: (1) cash register, (2) computer game, (3) candy vendor.

Following the prediction page, which must be displayed before the presentation of the next page, comes this page:

People keep blocking my view
leaning on my head; little kids
shake me repeatedly, rattling
my colorful brains. They seem
to delight in watching my brains
become fewer and fewer.

Now students can delete predictions or add others, based on further clues received from the text. This procedure continues until all five pages of this passage are presented. Students are supposed to use the clues to predict who or what "zingles" are.

Although some may disagree, the beauty of this package is that there is no one correct answer; in fact, teachers are not privy to any more information than the students regarding the main topic. This avoids inadvertent prompting by the teacher to have the students converge on one right answer. Rather, the students are encouraged to openly share their ideas about their predictions, based on clues within the story.

Designed for large or small groups, this program encourages students to become quite involved in discussing their hypotheses. Having watched students engage in this program, we have been impressed with the high level of interaction among participants. Students use their schemata to prove or disprove a hypothesis; the sharing of their background knowledge provides others with alternate viewpoints about the topic.

As suggested by Larry Miller (1984), one of the authors of *The Puzzler*, once a whole group of students have been introduced to the process of confirming and predicting, they should "puzzle" through the series of computer-based exercises to apply these strategies. Smaller student groups then should assemble to share their predictions at each given part of the story. As a future step, students should become involved in writing original strategy lessons for inclusion on a special story-creation disk.

Again, this works well as a group activity. Groups then can put their "puzzles" on disk with a word processor, or they can read the segments aloud with the rest of the class writing down possible solutions. Any "puzzle" lesson can be augmented with transparencies or the overhead projector.

This last step helps students make the connection between reading for clues from the author and writing clues for the reader. This interactive process helps students to focus on the nature of text structure in order to accomplish their task goals.

Highly rated by Fay Wheeler (1983), *The Puzzler* sets the stage for engaging students in higher-level thinking skills as they interact with the computer. She considers this program to be "an exciting alternative" to the electronic page turners. Rather than determining the correct answer, students are encouraged to find as many plausible answers as possible. *The Puzzler* is representative of "the best" for our discipline.

Microzine.   Programs that offer story branching require students to interact with text. Typically, students read a section of a story and then must choose, from one of a few options, the direction of their story. The story continues until another set of options appears, at which time students must again choose how the particular plot will develop. This sequence of passage presentation and student selection continues until the story ends or comes to an impasse.

This notion of interactive text has popularized the "twistaplot" pro-grams from *Microzine,* a bimonthly computer-based periodical for stu-dents in grades 4 through 8. One of *Microzine'*s regular features, twista-plots usually are adventure stories that can change each time students read them (Newman, 1985). The plot of the story is determined by the choices a student makes at various points in the story. Although, as Julie Sickert (1983) has discerned, some of the potential paths are rather silly, students still are fascinated by the idea that the adventure can change every time. The attractive graphic and open-ended presentation of these stories encourages students to read with a critical and creative eye.

Story Tree.   Other programs also have been designed that include this twistaplot element in a more elaborate fashion. *Story Tree,* for one, has included word processing capabilities so that students can read and write stories that branch to different endings. Sometimes referred to as a mini-authoring program for students (Farstrup, 1985), *Story Tree* provides a well-designed format for writing adventures, mysteries, articles, and poems. Since stories already have been written on the disk, students are prepared for writing and understanding the different branching options by first reading some good examples.

In using *Story Tree,* students can create regular stories or super stories. With regular stories, students have two branching options: CONTINUE and CHOICE, with a limit of two choices per page of text on the computer screen for the story to branch. With super stories, students have three branching options: CONTINUE the story from one page of text on the com-puter screen to the next; CREATE four choices per page of text on the computer screen for the story to branch; or create a CHANCE option, with the story going to one page part of the time and another the rest of the time. The CHANCE option depends on the computer's random selection. A comprehensive tutorial, "The Checkmate Mystery," with an accom-panying flowchart in the documentation, is included to help students understand step-by-step procedures for developing a story.

Designed for writing with and without the computer, *Story Tree'*s documentation also includes organizational ideas for implementing the process of writing and editing story branches with small and large groups of students. The concept of using a flowchart or map (see Chapter 6) is mentioned to aid students in visualizing the story's flow in branches. Its multidimensional uses for writing in different genres and for different curriculum areas also are explained in the documentation.

Because the stories can be saved and printed, teachers do not have to be concerned about scheduling constraints. Students can work on dif-ferent parts of their story at any time. This feature is excellent for encouraging teachers to use this program as an accompaniment to the total reading/language arts curriculum.

Highly rated by Patti Littlefield (1984), a reading and writing specialist in California, *Story Tree* is one of the more flexible creative writing programs available today.

Story Maker. Another software program inviting students to make choices about the direction of their story is *Story Maker.* As with *Microzine*'s twistaplots and *Story Tree*, this program makes explicit use of the story grammar components. An initial story segment is presented. The student then has to select, from a number of choices, the way in which the story should branch. This format continues until the story concludes in some way. Certain stories on the disk allow students to create their own branches, thus giving them more opportunities to internalize the structure of the text.

When the story cannot be modified, students can set a goal to reach with respect to the story's resolution. Randomly provided, these goals encourage students to predict whether their choices will lead to the desired goal. To further clarify the direction of their choices, they can view the tree branch provided in the program. For example, one of the goals for the story "The Haunted House" is "Lace gets a lion and Lace meets catwoman." The story opens with the statement "Lace opened the Front Door and . . . " The student must select one of three options: (1) "saw the Joker"; (2) "slipped into what looked like a big bowl of spaghetti"; (3) "stepped on a mouse." Since only one of these options ultimately leads to the chosen goal, the student must select the correct one. If not, within a few frames, the story ends with the option to print the story and try again with the same goal.

Considered by the Geoffrions (1985) to exemplify the dynamic storybook concept, this disk has been a wonderful prototype for other interactive programs. Since the stories are relatively short (see below), students can continue predicting until they reach their goal.

Paul's Story
With Goal Reached

LACE OPENED THE FRONT DOOR
AND SAW THE JOKER. HE PICKED
UP HIS CAN AND SPRAYED LACE
WITH WHIPPED CREAM. LACE
SLIPPED ON THE WHIPPED CREAM.
THE RIDDLER AND THE CROWMAN

BOTH RAN INTO THE ROOM. ALL
THREE BAD GUYS CARRIED LACE
TO CATWOMAN'S BEDROOM IN THE
HAUNTED HOUSE. CATWOMAN LIKED
LACE AND GAVE HER A PET LION
TO TAKE HOME.

That's My Story.   Many software packages with word processing components are interactive in that they provide story prompts and story starters for students to consider in composing text. One package, *That's My Story*, provides twelve different kinds of story starters with "what if" statements to encourage students to think creatively about the story's direction. Ranging from the second- to the eighth-grade level, these story starters are imaginative introductions to a variety of fictitious events. One story starter, for instance, discusses how Ralph, the smallest dragon in the land of dragons, feels about his size problem and his need to do something about it. Once this five-line story is read, students are presented with two "what if" statements:

What if:
1. Ralph decides to ask a friendly dragon named Harry to help;
or
2. Ralph changes the way he looks.

Students have the option of writing down their thoughts about either of the two "what if" statements, as long as another student has not yet composed a response. Students then compose two of their own "what if" statements for their own or other students' responses. Since each story starter must be on a separate disk, the stories and their branches can be as long as desired.

Although, as EPIE notes, the word processing capabilities are very limited, the interactive component of this program is quite useful. Teachers and students have the option of using the stories on the disk, creating their own stories, or designing curriculum-oriented problem-solving activities. Since the "what if" statement is an integral part of this software framework, students constantly are prompted to predict outcomes for real or fictional events.

As the documentation suggests, story starters can be generated in all content areas so that students are given the opportunity to think critically and creatively. Math problems fall naturally into this pattern. For example, "what if" the cost of peaches goes up fifteen cents and you have only one dollar? Science experiments can be simulated so that students can predict, for instance, "what if" sodium is combined with chloride? Exercises in moral development also can be created with students discussing alternatives for dealing with such problems as petty thievery.

Especially helpful is the formation of small groups of students to discuss and defend their rationale for responding to the "what if" statements. Even though the computer does not "talk back" with a response, the text on the screen can be the impetus for provocative discussions among the students.

Play Writer: Tales of Me.   Creating books as a result of interacting with computer text is easily done with *Play Writer: Tales of Me*. Part of a series of other *Play Writer* packages with word processing features, this program creates an autobiographical or biographical sketch of the student's choice. With initial teacher assistance, the well-organized directions and simple questions help to elicit fairly straightforward, accurate responses from the student. Questions appear on the screen in either multiple-choice or sentence-completion format. Initially, the student is asked about whom he or she would like to write. If, for instance, the student chose to write about Jason, the following questions would be asked:

What day was Jason born?

Jason had:
a. brown eyes
b. blue eyes
c. hazel eyes
d. green eyes
e. other

These questions are used in the beginning portion of the story to introduce background information about Jason. As the text evolves, the following types of questions appear to help in the creation of Jason's tale.

Summer is over and Jason has to start a new year of school. He has a new homeroom, a new teacher, and a new desk. What are the names of the kids whose desks are next to Jason's?

Jason decides to leave school and go exploring. As the first thing, he discovers a(n):
1. old woman
2. hairy ogre
3. dark cave

Although four chapters' worth of questions are presented for the completion of the book, students can stop at varying points in the program. The information is stored so that students can continue from where they stopped. Once students have responded to all of the questions, they can edit or print their stories. Since the responses may or may not fit syntactically with the text structure, it behooves students to view the approximately ten-page story creation before printing it on the *Play Writer* paper. As the publishers explain, this paper is for the masterpiece, the one with which the storybook is made. Once the story reads smoothly, students are encouraged to use the stickers and hardcover binding provided with the software package to make a book.

A more elaborate form of *Questions and Story* (see "Primary" in this chapter), this package uses students' responses to create a personalized story about the students' interests. After responding to the questions, students get to read an enlightening tale about a selected student that interweaves the writer's responses into the story framework. Although, as stated previously, the students' responses may not fit into the preprogrammed text structure, the word processing capabilities include editing procedures for making changes readily.

Elementary school students of varying ability levels can begin to compose with this program, especially if the teacher provides the necessary assistance. Lucille Van Eck, Chapter I teacher in Mahwah, New Jersey, has used this program with her students. As seen in the excerpt below, one of her third-grade students, a boy with spelling and writing anxieties, was delighted to create an entertaining tale about himself using invented spellings (see Figure 5.1).

Adventure Games and Simulations

Adventure games and simulations are other avenues for encouraging thoughtful student responses. In fact, software programs categorized as adventure games also are interactive in that they encourage students to discover the cause-effect elements in the mysterious or adventurous story line. The same goes for simulations. With simulations, students are taken to some environment remote from the classroom where they have to make decisions about complex events or conditions. Although they may not be writing as much text as with some of the reading-writing packages described above, they do have to make decisions and monitor their progress accordingly. This thinking process, according to Willis and Kuchinskas (1983), involves the higher-level reading skills of prediction, generalization, and hypothesis testing. Also, students are actively involved in reading to learn about the content or topic presented. And, as most computer

Figure 5.1. Sample of an autobiographical tale created with Play Writer: Tales of Me *by a remedial third-grade student.*

The Adventures of Me
by
JASON HARSCHE
For MY DAD HE HELPED ME IN BASEBALL

On MAY 5, 1972, at 2:30 P.M., a very amazing thing happened: a blue-eyed, brown-haired baby named JASON ANTHONY was born. JASON weighed 7 POUNDS and was 19 INCHES tall. This historical event took place in a hospital in PALM BICH, FLORIDA. Needless to say, JASON's parents were very happy.

At first, JASON seemed pretty ordinary, until everyone noticed how much he loved to sleep all the time. All day and all night, SNORE, SNORE, SNORE! The only time he woke up or cried was when he wanted something to eat. "What a great kid," JASON's parents said.

By the time JASON was ONE YEAR OLD, he had learned to say a few words. The first words he said were MOM, GOOD, DAD, BOTLE, and JUSE. By the time JASON was TWO YEARS OLD, his favorite question was "WEY DO I GET IN TRUBL".

When JASON was TWO YERSOLD, after he had learned to walk and talk pretty well, a very important event occurred.

---

enthusiasts would agree, adventure games and simulations make excellent use of the computer's capabilities.

Even though many of these programs are designed to be used with an older student population, there still are many programs available for elementary students. In highlighting a few of the programs available, we will describe important considerations in using these programs.

Typically, many adventure game topics include mysteries, war games, romances, science fiction, and fantasy. The user generally gives commands to the computer so that a means of escape, survival, resolution, or discovery becomes available. Obviously, as students spend days or even months trying to resolve their dilemma, they are learning serious problem-solving strategies. However, since many educators are questioning the transfer value of these packages to academic tasks, it may be more advantageous to use adventure games that supplement topics presented in class. One recently developed series by Windham Classics uses literary classics as a basis for the adventure series. Presently, packages are available for *The Swiss Family Robinson, Below the Root* (based on the Green Sky Trilogy), *Treasure Island, Alice in Wonderland, Robin Hood,* and *The*

Wizard of Oz. Students aged ten and up assume the role of the hero or heroine to experience the challenges of each adventure.

For instance, with the *Alice in Wonderland* software package, the student becomes Alice. While meeting the famous Wonderland characters, the student playing Alice is challenged to get out of Wonderland safely. In using the keyboard or joystick, the student can assume different sizes to perform various movements in Wonderland (for example, jumping, running, crawling, climbing) and can communicate with the characters (for example, Tweedledee, Tweedledum, the Queen of Hearts, the Cheshire Cat) to seek her destination. Cleverly designed and easily understood, this type of adventure series adds another dimension to literary studies. Even though restricted to the programmed responses between characters, students still are highly motivated to respond analytically to the situation at hand. They must use the cues insightfully to figure out which moves will lead them to their next successful encounter.

Simulations create the same challenge. Every decision made not only involves the ability to think critically but also assumes that the student can read carefully and follow directions. The appeal of using simulations is that important concepts are conveyed with minimum classroom disruption (Balajthy, 1984). Also, students can be presented with an entirely new dimension to any content area being explored in the classroom. In exploring, for example, the various battles of the Civil War with MECC's *Civil — Elementary, Volume 3* program, students need to use their math and reading skills to win a battle. While memorizing facts and figures about each battle may be enough to pass a social studies test on the Civil War, it is not enough to be successful with the Civil War simulation. They must use this information, coupled with their understanding of the costs and strategic war efforts involved in winning battles, to beat the other side. This, in fact, prepares them more for real-life situations than the absorption and regurgitation of facts so prevalent in social studies classrooms.

Searching for appropriate simulation disks involves more than looking at its age-appropriate presentation of material. Simulations should dovetail with content area learning. For example, if studying about aquatic life, MECC's *Odell Lake* would help students learn about or reinforce the survival patterns of fish. Or if studying about wild animals, MECC's *Odell Woods* would complement classroom learning about the characteristics of wild animals. And the widely used *Oregon* simulation is a useful program for chronicling one's experiences along the Oregon Trail if this period of history or this part of the United States is being studied.

MECC's *Lemonade* and *Apple* programs and the more involved *Bicy-*

cle program, while enjoyable as isolated computer experiences, become more effective if provided as an extension to the study of our free-enterprise system. In addition to using important math skills with these programs, students can become more sophisticated in appreciating entrepreneurial responsibilities if their attempts with the programs are preceded by pertinent classroom discussions or activities. Even though simulations are thought of as the best of computer games and traditional class lessons (Willis & Kuchinskas, 1983), they still should be used within the context of the learning situation.

With any of the programs discussed in this elementary section, a common thread appears. These programs attempt to involve the student in an active exchange between the student's background knowledge and the information provided on the screen. When interacting with the material, students are asking themselves "what if" in order to make the appropriate response. This predictive, hypothetical thinking framework should be the essence of computer involvement. A similar theme prevails with the software discussed in the next section for secondary students.

☐   **SECONDARY AND POSTSECONDARY**   ☐

Most of the interactive or divergent-response software now available for adolescent and adult students may be globally classified as prompt programs that involve reading-writing-thinking skills and adventure games/simulations that require problem solving.

Prompt Programs

The prompt programs are written to engage users in a dialogue as they compose text, guiding them through the writing of prose patterns such as essays, character sketches, and narratives.

An early program called *Topoi* or *Aristotle's Topics* was developed by U.S. Army captain Hugh Burns and George Culp of the University of Texas at Austin to help college students write persuasive essays. It begins by taking the writer through an exploration process to clarify the purpose of the piece. Here are some excerpts from a college student's attempts to write about computers and reading:

> COMPUTER: Computers and reading. Will you be amazed by the recent scholarship in this area! Be sure to ask the librarian in the reference area.
>
> So now will you briefly describe the purpose of your paper by com-

pleting this statement: The purpose of this paper is to . . .

STUDENT: The purpose of this paper is to show how computers can be used in the teaching of reading.

COMPUTER: Any more? (If so, type in; if not, type *no*) [Student types response.]

Fine, Chris, you and I will talk again about your purpose. What are the good consequences of computers and reading?

STUDENT: Computers are affecting how people use language. They make writing physically easier and reading more spontaneous. You can compose, delete, move text around, check spelling, and add graphics as you write. When reading, you can scroll backwards and forwards easily.

COMPUTER: Terrific, Chris. Anything else? You can add more information, ask a question, or give a command. Try explaining a little more.

And so it goes, with some of the subsequent prompts being: Does public opinion about computers and reading differ from private? What would be a result of using computers and reading? If nothing else I want my reader to know . . .

Best regarded as a brainstorming session to get users writing expository, persuasive prose, *Topoi* makes them think about a subject in terms of rhetorical devices such as definition, cause and effect, and consequences. The early 1980 version that we used had technical limitations like permitting only a three-word title and restricted editing features, but the idea of having questions to answer as she began her paper seemed to help Chris organize her thoughts.

Prompt programs also have been developed for other kinds of writing. MECC has produced *Writing a Narrative* for grades 7 through 9 and *Writing a Character Sketch* for high school. *Writing a Narrative* has two interactive tutorials, one on brainstorming and the other on drafting a story. It also contains a straight tutorial on point of view in writing.

The first tutorial, "Idea Storming One-Two-Three," is a prewriting activity that presents students with two objects on a screen that they have to name. All answers are accepted, and then the screen shows several less predictable possible names. Viewers must select one name for each object and use their imaginations to find a relationship between the two. For example, a twelve-year-old Boy Scout selected HAWK for a birdlike object and COOP for the other that could be a type of cage with a door ajar. Next, he was asked to list action words for HAWK and sensory words (sight, sound, touch) for COOP. Finally, he was given the option of seeing his word lists on the screen or having them printed out (the documentation includes a handout for copying these lists if there is no printer). Also given was a list of words like *then, later,* and *next* to be used when ordering his story. It was suggested that he write a story about the objects with his word lists as a starting point. He wrote:

> The park ranger placed the large, red-tailed hawk that he had captured into a wire-mesh coop, only half-closing the latch. After the ranger had walked away, the wily hawk started to work the unsteady latch. Snap! The latch broke open and out flew the proud bird to his usual haunts.

The second interactive tutorial, "Catch the Moments," encourages students to write about real experiences. First, they are asked to list some experiences that have changed their opinions or beliefs; then they select one of these to write about. Next, they respond to questions about setting, characters, main actions, and the high point. Finally, they list their opinions/beliefs before and after the experience. A sample printout of the response of a ninth-grade girl appears in Figure 5.2.

According to Jenes (1984a), while this program can help students develop a plot for their own narratives and introduce them to the main story elements, activities do not provide student feedback. We tend to agree with him but can see a place for something like this (especially "Catch the Moments") if students work in pairs or small groups and use the prompts as stimulation to compose and talk about the story elements as they go along. The adolescent who wrote the responses in Figure 5.2 liked using the software. Although we did not see her finished narrative, she felt it would be easy to write with this beginning.

The third activity in this package, called "Point of View," explains the differences between first person as actor, first person as observer, and third person reporting. Just as the other two activities follow the writing-as-process approach in encouraging prewriting, drafting, and revising, this one develops the ideas of voice and audience, two important components of a holistic approach to writing.

The other MECC software program, *Writing a Character Sketch*, is described as a structured, interactive prewriting activity designed to guide older students to analyze a character from literature, history, or their own lives. After they have selected a character, they have to type in two words to describe him or her. Next, they are encouraged to explore why they think these words seem to fit by supporting them from (a) External Characteristics, (b) Behavior, (c) Others' Reactions, and (d) Comparing or Contrasting. A group of college freshmen used the program to begin a sketch of Lincoln. The printout of their work looked like the example in Figure 5.3.

Jenes (1984b) gave this program an excellent review. While we agree that it presents a good way to involve students in character analysis, which is important for both reading and writing, we would like to point out that some may find the routine too structured, something that could be said about all the prompt programs for older students. Our group of college students found it useful in helping them to think of ways to support their

Figure 5.2. *Sample printout from "Catch the Moment," a tutorial from* Writing a Narrative.

You have chosen to write about:
    OVERCOMING FEAR OF COMPUTERS
Here is what you have for your Setting:
    When—LAST TERM; THIS TERM
    Where—EIGHTH-GRADE COURSE IN BASIC; NINTH-GRADE
        ENGLISH
Here are the Main Characters:
    ME
    MRS. WRIGHT, ENGLISH TEACHER
    THE COMPUTER
Here are the Main Objects:
    THE COMPUTER
    WORD PROCESSING
    BASIC
Here are the Main Actions:
    REMEMBERING HOW POORLY I DID IN BASIC IN JUNIOR HIGH
    AFRAID OF MORE COMPUTER COURSES
    MRS. WRIGHT SUGGESTS WE WRITE OUT POEMS ON THE WORD
        PROCESSOR IN THE COMPUTER LAB
    WORRYING OVER THE FATEFUL DAY
    THE DAY ARRIVES
    WORD PROCESSING IS SO EASY. YOU TYPE AND CORRECT AND
        MOVE WORDS AROUND. I DID FINE.
    I WORKED AND REWORKED MY POEM. I LOVE THE COMPUTER.
Here is the Key Event:
    USING WORD PROCESSING ON THE COMPUTER WITH PLEASURE
Your opinion or belief before your experience occurred:
    FEARED COMPUTERS
Your opinion or belief after your experience occurred:
    LOVED COMPUTERS AND LOOKED FORWARD TO OUR NEXT LAB

---

ideas about the character. Also, they liked working together. It appears that these kinds of activities work best when used with groups of students for prewriting or for discussing a character from fiction or the real world. They can serve as well-developed guides for teachers or group leaders.

Another prompt program designed to develop narrative writing is *Composition Strategy: Your Creative Blockbuster.* This program uses keywords and cues to direct writers' thought processes as they work. After a sentence is typed in, the program will insert a keyword such as *because,*

Figure 5.3. *Sample printout from* Writing a Character Sketch.

Chosen Character   ABRAHAM LINCOLN
You have examined why LINCOLN is SERIOUS AND BROODING by looking at
the following characteristics:

EXTERNAL CHARACTERISTICS

   1. Appearance:
      LINCOLN USUALLY WORE A PLAIN BLACK WAISTCOAT AND
      STOVEPIPE HAT PECULIAR TO THE 1800s. HIS DARK BLACK BEARD,
      PIERCING EYES UNDER HEAVY BROWS, AND FURROWED
      FOREHEAD MADE HIM GIVE A SERIOUS AND BROODING IMPRES-
      SION. THERE WAS AN AIR OF FOREBODING ABOUT HIM.
   2. Physical traits:
      BECAUSE HE WAS TALL AND LANKY, HE WOULD THROW HIS LEGS
      OVER THE ARM OF THE CHAIR WHEN HE WAS SITTING AROUND
      INFORMALLY WITH MARY AND THE BOYS OR WITH HIS CLOSE
      ADVISORS. RATHER THAN WALK OR RUN, IT COULD BE SAID THAT
      HE AMBLED OR LOPED AROUND WASHINGTON DURING THE WAR
      YEARS.
   3. Speech:
      HIS VOICE WAS STRONG AND RESONANT AND COULD MOVE
      AUDIENCES. THAT'S WHY HE CHOSE TO GIVE HIS OWN SPEECHES
      TO CONGRESS RATHER THAN TO HAVE THEM READ BY THE CLERK
      AS WAS DONE BY HIS PREDECESSOR.

before, or *while* that will prompt what should come next. When the piece is completed, all the prompt words are stripped away, and only the student's text is left.

There are six prompt modes to choose from: (1) Beginner, which uses a single, connective word prompt (*because, after*) of your choice that remains the same throughout the paragraph; (2) Changing Connectives, which uses different, single-word prompts in a set sequence of connectives; (3) Choosing Connectives, which allows you to select connectives or none at all; (4) Changing Perspectives, which uses groups of words like *because they saw that* and *whenever I say that* and allows you to change point of view (person and number) and sensory orientation (seeing, hearing, saying); (5) Composition Strategies, which is similar to Changing Perspectives except that the computer chooses the point of view and sensory orientation for you to encourage your own distinctive style; and (6) Expert, which assumes that you have become a good writer, sensitive to voice, point of view, connectives, and sensory style, and thus permits you to choose any of the prompts or none as you write on your own.

We tried out the program to see how it might work. After selecting a topic, "Lunch at Malibu," we were engaged in some prewriting activities such as picturing the scene and our audience in our mind's eye, deciding on a point of view, and talking to ourselves about what our characters might be saying. Next, the actual drafting began with the following question:

> As you think about Lunch at Malibu, which part of the experience is strongest for you?
> 1. THE PICTURE(S)
> 2. THE SOUND(S)
> 3. THE FEELING(S)
> 4. WHAT YOU SAY

Selecting PICTURES, we were then asked to choose a mode. Being somewhat humbled by all this scientific pedagogy (Behavioral Engineering puts this out), we chose BEGINNER and then selected BECAUSE as our connective. Here is a sample of what we wrote (prompts are in parentheses and are deleted when the piece is printed out):

> (THIS COMPOSITION IS ABOUT LUNCH AT MALIBU BECAUSE) We all had a great day and wanted to remember it for a long time. (BECAUSE) Wanting to get out on the Pacific Palisades, we rented a brand new Buick Regal and headed north on Highway One. (BECAUSE) We knew there were some good restaurants, frequented by the local luminaries, nestled in dugouts along the road. (BECAUSE) Helen and Frank told us they had seen Robert Redford dining at a place called The Sea Shell just last week, and we thought we'd try our luck.

We won't go any further with our narrative, since this should give you an idea of how the program works. Because this program encourages active prewriting and makes the writer focus on connecting sentences, point of view/audience, and sensory writing, it might prove helpful to adolescent and mature writers who have difficulty getting started and developing a consistent style. However, there is one aspect of the program that we found questionable. Throughout, users are directed to move their eyes to various positions while they are thinking about what to write. The developers point to research in Neuro-Linguistic Programming to support this technique for improving composing. The references given appear to be written by the same group of authors and published mainly by one unknown publisher in California. We would suggest trying the program without the eye-movement activities.

A new prompt program designed to encourage your students to read their text as they are composing is Colette Daiute's *Catch*. Besides questions that focus the writer-reader on content and revision like "Does this paragraph have a clear point?" the program contains several pattern-matching options that require a focus on form. For instance, "Empty Words" identifies such terms as *sort of* and *you know* with the accompanying prompt "The highlighted words may not be necessary. Do you need to make changes?" "Vague Words" highlights words like *stuff* and *thing* with the prompt "Can you use more specific words?" Other options include checks for clarity (coherence, reference) organization (guide words, summary), sentence structure (long/short sentences), and punctuation (commas).

A nice feature about *Catch* is that is can be used within the word processing program with which students are writing. The prompts appear at the bottom of the screen containing their piece so that students can interact with the text as they go along.

To test the effectiveness of *Catch* on the composing-reading-revising strategies of young writers, Daiute (1985b) conducted an experiment with fifty-seven seventh- and ninth-grade students in a New York City public school. Both the experimental and the control group learned to type and to use word processing, but only the experimental group added the prompt program as they composed. Several writing samples of drafts and revised texts were collected at various points throughout the school year and were subjected to statistical analyses. The pre- and postwriting samples were written in pen to see if learning would carry over to writing with conventional tools.

Although all subjects wrote more words on their final drafts, the experimental group added more words when they revised than did the controls. According to a measure of syntactic complexity (words per *t*-unit), sentences written by the experimental group increased in complexity over the year and, by the end of the year, were more complex than those of the control group. While the control group, which was using the word processor alone, revised mainly by adding on to their pieces and by making superficial changes, the prompt group made more meaningful revisions both within and at the end of their texts. It appears that they were reading their work more closely and revising the content as they thought about the questions raised by the prompt program.

This study also shed some light on the effects of writing with the computer. While classroom teachers generally observe that students write more and revise more when composing with a word processor, such was not the case with these junior high school students. When their midyear writing samples (composed on the computer) were compared with the samples drafted and revised by pen, it was found that they wrote less and revised less when using the computer. Daiute wonders whether this might have happened because these students were more comfortable using familiar tools like pencils and pens. She suggests that it may take a long time for students at this level to become fluent with the computer as tool; revision may suffer because they have not mastered the word processing commands. Again, as hardware and software become more "transparent," that is, more automatic and easier to manipulate, students will write longer pieces and revise more. The Apple Macintosh and Commodore Amiga offer relatively "transparent" word processing right now. Daiute notes that students who can type well or young children who have not yet mastered fluent handwriting might write more with the computer. (This is one reason why we think children should learn keyboarding early and maintain practice throughout their school years.)

Daiute concluded that the *Catch* program was successful in engaging students in reading their texts. While the experimental subjects made revisions that showed they had read and interpreted the prompts and then made changes accordingly, the control subjects made changes that did not indicate a close reading of their texts.

Without the intervention of teacher conferences, peer conferences, or prompt programs that cause writers to read their pieces with specific points in mind, word processing is just another writing tool, albeit one with great potential for making the physical act of writing easier. That is why we recommend that teachers provide environments that encourage interaction, whether it be between teacher and student, student and student, or students and a prompt program to guide them as they read what they have written with a focus on revision and audience.

Adventure Games

Adventure games can provide stimulating and challenging ways for students to develop problem-solving and organizational abilities while engaging in reading and writing activities (Jarchow & Montgomery, 1985). Many of these games are appropriate for high school and adult populations.

Sharyn Kost, who runs the English Workshop in Bridgewater-Raritan High School East, allows her basic English students to work on adventure games, either singly or with partners, when they finish reading and writing activities that they have contracted to do. Referring to her students' favorite game, *Cranston Manor,* she illustrated why she uses adventure games in her program.

The object of the game is for a pair of players to get into Cranston Manor and collect sixteen treasures, which will be among other objects they can "take" as they go through the house. Sharyn has one student type commands (keyboarding skills are required) while the other edits (correct spelling is necessary for the commands to work). As the partners explore, they must keep detailed maps, note where they got each object, and write a list of their treasures. While helping these students add to their reading/writing vocabularies, these activities promote logical thinking and organizational skills. As for the maps, Sharyn finds that most of her students prefer to keep a simple, linear record of their moves, which helps to give them a sense of sequence and an adequate way to retrace their steps.

To give commands, they must use two-word verb-object strings like look room, take crowbar, and drop crowbar. This feature gives Sharyn the opportunity to review the subject-verb-object syntax convention; they also explore the notion of synonyms, since if their typed command — for example, get book — doesn't work, they must try a synonymous term like take book.

Players are instructed to take along objects they meet on the way since these may come in handy later on. This feature encourages planning ahead and anticipating outcomes. They must type in the direction in which they are proceeding, for example, North or West; hence, they develop a sense of location and sequence.

If at any time they want to review what they have done, players can request to see their last few commands and take an "inventory" of what they are carrying. This feature encourages self-checking and strategy planning in terms of what has already happened.

Players are cautioned to beware of pitfalls that could lead to disaster and to look for clues to avoid these dangers. According to Kost, they begin to think creatively and to read purposefully so as not to miss hints and suggestions.

Another game used in this high school workshop class is *Death in the Caribbean*. With this game, you are lost on a tropical island and must find buried treasures while surviving unspeakable terrors. Students again practice directional skills as they deal with information such as: You are facing east. Path goes to your left. Players must position themselves mentally to face east and then to go north. Again, they must type in verb-object commands and spell accurately to progress. One feature of this game that really makes it fun to play is that it has a ghost that "steals back" from you! Sharyn Kost thinks the games teach many language and thinking skills in an amusing and adventuresome context.

A new program from the producers of *Rocky's Boots, Robot Odyssey* is a creative problem-solving game appropriate for the scientific-minded. You may choose to explore either "Robotopolis" or "Innovation Lab." In the former, you travel through an underground robotic city, and the only way to return to civilization is to get some robots to help you. In the lab, you can actually program some robots to help you get around in the strange, underground city.

Through a tutorial, you can learn to move the robots, build simple circuits, and design circuit chips. While model circuits and chips are supplied, designing your own models calls for diagram reading, following directions, and checking for failure points. This game does offer a real challenge and is definitely best for those who like to build from the bottom up.

Teachers who plan to use adventure games in classroom settings should be sure that the games may be stored on disk. Most adventure or problem-solving games take many hours to solve, and students have to be able to store what they have done and return to it at another period. All of the above games have this feature. We suggest that student disks and accompanying print-support notes and maps be kept in file folders so that students can easily resume their game during subsequent periods.

☐   SUMMARY   ☐

Chapter 5 has presented software designed to teach in an interactive way. These programs encourage active participation as they model reading strategies (as with *The Puzzler*), engage students in creating with language (as with the beginning writing software and prompt programs), and present problems to be solved (as in adventure games and simulations).

This chapter concludes our treatment of the computer as tutor. Chapter 6 will concern the computer as tutee. In this mode students can "teach" the computer by learning simple programming strategies and languages like Logo and BASIC while concomitantly reinforcing their reading and writing abilities.

☐6☐

The Computer as Tutee

Marcia Stewart, a kindergarten student, has a "compooter" in school. She always wants to use her favorite software package, *Facemaker*, so that she can select features of a face and then program the face to make all types of funny contortions. She knows how to press corresponding keys on the keyboard to make the face's ear "wiggle" or its eye "wink." Marcia's teacher, Mrs. Tebbetts, uses the faces as a catalyst for Marcia's language-experience stories. Marcia loves to talk and write about her creations.

•　　　　•　　　　•

Marcia is using the computer in the tutee mode. She gives the computer certain commands and sees it respond according to her wishes. Using the computer in the tutee mode implies that the computer is being taught, usually by a compatible programming language, to respond according to the computer user's commands. If the user communicates intelligibly with the computer, the computer responds sensibly; if not, the computer's output is usually unintelligible information.

Either with creative software packages or with simple programming languages, students can tell the computer what to do. This mode enables students to determine the kind of information to be processed by the computer. It involves thinking about and organizing ideas so that the output reflects the student's intent. Because most educators have viewed this mode as a way to teach programming languages rather than a way to explore the concept of thinking, its use as an instructional mode has been relegated to those with a flair for mathematical thinking. However, because literal, inferential, critical, and creative thinking are involved, students tend to use the same skills needed for reading comprehension. It is for this reason that we believe in the utility of the tutee mode for developing reading/thinking skills.

This chapter explains how and why the tutee mode can be used in the reading/language arts classroom.

☐   SOFTWARE PROGRAMS FOR THE TUTEE MODE   ☐

Any software program that permits young students to create simple programs or designs can be considered useful in the tutee mode. As described
above, *Facemaker*, with its built-in program to allow students to create
simple sequences of facial expressions, exemplifies this type of software.
Also useful for beginning readers are programs such as *Children's Carrousel, Kindercomp,* and *The Friendly Computer.* These programs provide
students with varied opportunities to use the keyboard to create designs.

Children's Carrousel is essentially a drill-and-practice/tutorial program.
It does, however, contain one program, "Shooting Stars," that gives the
learner initial exposure to the concept of controlling the computer while
developing keyboard familiarity. With the press of any key, colorful snow-
flakelike stars appear randomly on the screen. We remember watching,
in a preschool situation, the delighted faces of two three-year-old computer novices as they created a screenful of stars. Not surprisingly, of all
the programs on the disk, they insisted on playing with "Shooting Stars."

Kindercomp has one program entitled "Draw" that presents a blank
screen for students to draw multicolored designs in low-resolution graphics (tiny blocks rather than dots appear on the screen). Selected keys are
programmed to respond in a certain direction: U (up diagonally to left),
I (up), O (up diagonally to right), J (left), K (right), M (down), N (down
diagonally to left), and comma [,] (down diagonally to right). The C
button changes the color of the block automatically to one of approximately sixteen colors. The F key is used to fill in any closed area with the
color appearing on the screen. Although the low-resolution graphics
preclude young students from designing exact replicas of everyday objects, students still have the opportunity to discover how to create graphic displays on the screen.

The program "Picture" on *The Friendly Computer* allows students to
draw pictures while discovering some of the capabilities of the computer.
Inside a personalized picture frame, children have the option to draw freely or place preprogrammed shapes (square, circle, rectangle, diamond,
triangle) and pictures (house, person, car, sun, tree) on the screen in a
variety of colors. Their pictures can be saved on the disk, viewed in the
"Picture Show" program, and printed with any compatible printer.

Older students may enjoy *Mr. Pixel's Programming Paint Set.* Part of
a series of six interrelated disks in the Mr. Pixel series, this program provides a creative vehicle for designing pictures on the screen while developing a foundation for programming. Icons (pictures or images representing objects) are given on the bottom of the screen so that students can

select easily what they want to draw on the screen; they can draw freely, use preprogrammed shapes, change colors, repeat drawings in different parts of the screen, or change a drawing's size. The well-developed documentation and easy-to-follow directions help in getting started with this program.

After initial trial-and-error stumbling with any of these prototypes, students discover the cause-effect relationships between the keys on the keyboard and the resultant lines on the screen. Because students love to create a picture or design on the screen, the computer becomes a powerful vehicle for self-expression. Creative use of these programs in the primary classroom can affect literacy development. Specifically, programs such as *The Friendly Computer* or *Mr. Pixel's Programming Paint Set*, which allow the designs to be printed, can be used for reading and writing activities. Students can create simple picture books with or without themes describing or telling about their picture creations. These books can be exchanged with other students so that student authors have a chance to share their thoughts with an audience. It is also instructive for students to describe the procedures used to make the design. This helps to prepare students for the sequential nature of programming. Teachers can translate the sequential description into simple flowcharts so that students become familiarized with flowcharting procedures.

☐   **FLOWCHARTING**   ☐

Flowcharts are pictorial representations of computer programs that use special symbols and arrows to create a "map" of what the computer will do (Dwyer & Kaufman, 1973). Flowcharting, like programming, requires knowledge of a particular subject and an understanding of how to process the information. Unlike programming, it does not require mastery of a computer language.

If, for instance, a student drew the letter *T* on the "Draw" program of *Kindercomp*, a simple flowchart such as the one shown in Figure 6.1 could be created.

The figure demonstrates that Susan pressed the K key nine times to move to the right, the J key four times to move left and back to the middle, and the M key eight times to move down. This flowchart could serve as a guide to the student using the program or as a reminder to Susan for her next experience.

As teachers of reading, we can provide students with a series of steps for developing competent flowcharting strategies. Once students know

Figure 6.1. Susan's
Kindercomp *program.*

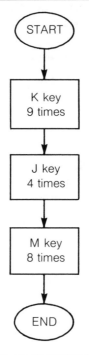

Figure 6.2. *Description of basic shapes used for flowcharting.*

Oval signifies START or END of program.

Parallelogram signifies INPUT or OUTPUT box.

Rectangle signifies any PROCESSING operation except a decision.

Diamond signifies a DECISION box. The lines leaving the decision box are labeled with the result (YES or NO) that causes each path to be followed.

Arrows signifiy the DIRECTION of flow through the flowchart.

when and how to connect the four basic shapes with arrows (see Figure 6.2), they can design a respectable flowchart as an outgrowth of their thinking about "tutee" type software programs, programming languages, or everyday events.

As creative vehicles for expressing their thoughts about daily events, flowcharts can vary in complexity to reflect students' developmental readiness. For instance, a flowchart to describe getting ready for school may include as many steps and as many decisions as students can handle. Compare Figure 6.3 with Figure 6.4.

In working with flowcharts, students strengthen many reading skills that would otherwise go unnoticed (Wepner, 1983). One skill, sequencing, is critical for representing the flow of events. Students also need to think in terms of identifying the main idea, supporting details, keywords, and symbols for creating an organized flow of events. They also must make critical decisions about the relevance of each step included and synthesize this information into the total flow. Any software program or programming language that demands this kind of procedural thinking can be expressed in a flowchart format. To further reinforce the organized, sequential thinking process, we recommend that you use flowcharts on occasion to supplement and graphically represent students' thought processes.

□   **PRIMARY PROGRAMMING PACKAGES**   □

Delta Drawing. Another useful software package in the tutee mode is *Delta Drawing.* Considered a precursor to the programming language Logo, *Delta Drawing* also enables primary students to create their own colorful drawings on the computer screen by pressing a few keys on the computer keyboard. Basically, students draw on the computer screen with the Delta cursor, similar in appearance to the "turtle" in Logo. Students control its movements by giving it commands. The screen is used in two ways, for graphics and for text. In the graphics mode, the screen displays the picture. In the text mode, the screen shows the program. While conceptually similar to Logo, the commands in *Delta Drawing* are easier for young and inexperienced students to remember. Not only is it already programmed to move x number of steps on the screen and to turn x number of degrees in either direction, but also its one finger commands on the keyboard coincide alphabetically with the commands built into the program. Creating colorful scenes and designs becomes very manageable once a few of the following commands are tried:

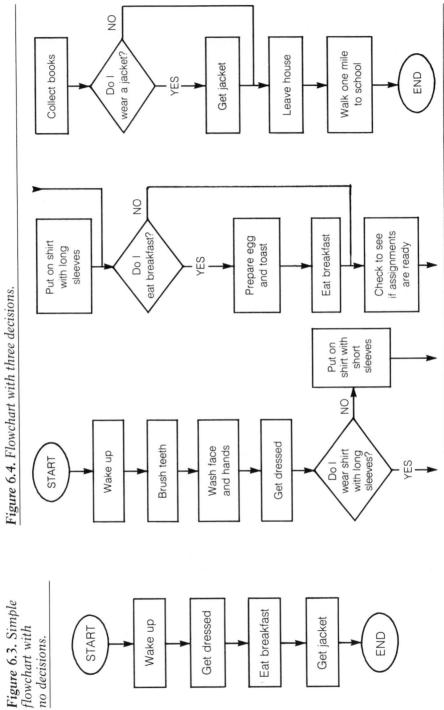

Figure 6.3. Simple flowchart with no decisions.

Figure 6.4. Flowchart with three decisions.

Command	Key	Function
Draw	D	Delta cursor goes forward one step and draws a line
Right Turn	R	Delta cursor turns right 30 degrees
Left Turn	L	Delta cursor turns left 30 degrees
Move	M	Delta cursor goes forward one step without drawing a line
U-Turn	U	Delta cursor turns 180 degrees

Therefore, if a student wanted to draw a simple two-inch square, the following commands would be registered in the text mode: 4D 3R 4D 3R 4D 3R 4D 3R. This means the Delta cursor repeated four times the pattern of moving four steps and turning 30 degrees right three times (right angle) in order to design the closed figure of a square.

Since any closed figure can be filled in easily with color, the student could simply type C for color, select one of five numbers (1 = white, 2 = orange, etc.) and press the CONTROL key and F key simultaneously to fill in the square with the desired color. Erasing mistakes and "misdraws" is done easily by pressing the E key. What makes this program so intriguing is its simplified design for creating structured programs. A simple square can be used as the first program for a more elaborate design. Once the square was drawn, the student could type the 1 key so that this first program, a square, was stored. Then, at any time, the student could type a 1 and the square would be drawn again. For example, if the student wanted to draw a simple house, the following could be tried:

1< . . . 4D . . 3R . . 4D . . 3R . . 4D . . 3R . . 4D . . 3R . . . . . >1 [closes first program of square]

By typing 2, the first program and the second program are drawn automatically:

2< . . . <1> . . 4M . . 1R . . 4D . . 4R . . 4D . . . . . >2

Delta Drawing's appeal for the reading/language arts classroom flows out of the kind of thinking involved and the infinite applications to reading and writing. In planning designs to be created, students need to think of a main idea for their design (for example, a flower, a fish pond, a tree, a country scene). They then decide on the details needed to create their design. It is the sequencing of these details that helps them to create their simple programs, which, ultimately, evolve into their main idea. For example, if they wanted to create a simple scene, they might create the program shown in Figure 6.5.

Figure 6.5. *Display of graphics and text created for a simple scene from* Delta Drawing.

```
I< ...      U  ..   3M ..   3R  ..  2ID ..   3L ..   M  ..   C:3 ..   ^F .....>I

2<...    <I>..   U  ..   M  ..   3R ..   C:I..   D  ..   M  ..   3R ..   U  ..
  6D ..   R  ..   5D ..   4R ..   5D ..   4R ..   5D ..   U  ..   2M ..   R  ..
  4L ..   M  ..   C:4..   ^F ..   U  ..   M  ..   R  ..   4L ..   C:I ..  3M ..
  3R ..   6D ..   3R ..   3M ..   3R ..   2D ..   3R ..   D  ..   3R ..   2D ..
  U  ..   4M ..   D  ..   3R ..   0  ..   3R ..   D  ..   3R ..   D  ..   2M ..
  3R ..   D  ..   3R ..   D  ..   3R ..   D  ..   3R ..   U  ..   3L ..   M  ..
  C:4..   ^F ..... >2

3<...    <2>..   2M ..   C:I ..  3R ..   IOM ..   4R ..   L  ..   6M ..   R  ..
  L  ..   M  ..   D  ..   R  ..   D  ..   R  ..   D  ..   R  ..   D  ..   R  ..
  D  ..   R  ..   D  ..   R  ..   D  ..   R  ..   D  ..   R  ..   D  ..   R  ..
  D  ..   R  ..   D  ..   R  ..   D  ..   3R ..   M  ..   C:2..   ^F .....>3

4<...    <3>.....>4
```

Before becoming involved with a programming language, students can begin to understand the kind of thinking involved in creating a program. As with flowcharting principles and reading demands, students must develop the ability to understand and communicate the organizational patterns inherent in the author's graphic or typewritten representation of ideas.

Other intriguing ideas for this type of program involve the LEA approach. Since *Delta Drawing* designs can be printed with a print program such as *Zoom Grafix*, any picture can be printed on a compatible dot matrix printer. Once printed, any word processing program can be inserted. Either the teacher or student can type any thoughts generated about the picture. These thoughts can be printed beneath the picture and read to the teacher. They can be used as a basis for a reading lesson. Imagine the sense of accomplishment felt when students get to read what they wrote about their picture.

These printed creations could be used to compile a class picture book or individual storybooks for each child. Obviously, the possibilities for working with these student-generated illustrations and descriptions are infinite.

E-Z Logo. Since *Delta Drawing* has its limitations, particularly as a programming language, it should be thought of as one of many avenues for utilizing the tutee mode. Another transitional type of program for primary students, *E-Z Logo*, gives students the ability to explore many aspects of turtle graphics while preparing them for using the Apple Logo language (Giblin & Giblin, 1985). Suggested for students through grade 3, this program has two parts: "E-Z Logo 1" and "E-Z Logo 2." "E-Z Logo 1" includes twenty-four predetermined activities, each of which introduces a new turtle graphics skill to be used in a challenging Logo activity. "E-Z Logo 2" extends the skills taught in "E-Z Logo 1" by challenging students to explore and create their own graphics.

The *E-Z Logo* commands have the primary-level aura; each command can be executed with one keystroke, representing the first letter or associated letter of the command.

Key	Command
F	Forward
B	Back
R	Right 30 Degrees
L	Left 30 Degrees
U	Pen Up (like Move in *Delta Drawing*)
D	Pen Down (to resume drawing)

Its simplistic, ready-made array of worksheet and computer activities enables the teacher to use it readily in the classroom. Students can follow the prescribed sequence of activities, experimenting with mazes, patterns, shapes, and letters so that by the time they are using "E-Z Logo 2" they have enough Logo experiences to create complex designs.

Introducing Logo to Primary Children. One kit, *Introducing Logo to Primary Children,* uses a combination of one-key Logo commands, concrete learning experiences with the Tasman Turtle, activities for the program *Delta Drawing,* and simple Logo applications to provide a gradual introduction to Logo programming. Packaged with activity cards, posters, and a teacher's manual of activities, this kit is a multifaceted resource for introducing primary children to the fundamentals of Logo. Since the program disk does not contain *Delta Drawing* or the Tasman Turtle commands, teachers must be aware that the kit alone is not enough to explore fully all that is recommended in the teacher's manual. However, the combined purchase of the recommended resources provides teachers with a comprehensive and well-organized idea package for the rudiments of Logo instruction. Gaye Carabillo, second-grade teacher, Boonton, New Jersey, currently is using this kit with her students. Since some of the keys will draw a perfect square (the S key), rectangle (the H key), triangle (the T key), or curve (the C key), her students get very excited by the geometric pictures that they can design so quickly. She feels this package is a godsend for any teacher who is uneasy about programming with Logo.

☐   **LOGO**   ☐

For those ready to embark on learning a full-fledged programming language that enables students to draw complicated computer graphics with a minimal number of commands, Logo is recommended. Aside from the numerous books available on using Logo in the classroom (Bitter & Watson, 1983; Moore, 1985a, 1985b; Poirot, 1983; Thornburg, 1985; Watt, 1983, 1984), there also are kits such as *Getting Started with Logo* or *Learning Through Logo* that prescribe computer activities. Such kits usually provide teachers with manuals, activity sheets, and posters that are carefully sequenced for teaching Logo to students at any level. However, we believe that students should not be introduced to Logo until they are developmentally ready, usually not until at least third or fourth grade.

Developed by Seymour Papert at MIT, Logo enables the student to control the learning environment and explore mathematical concepts. Logo is called a procedural language since programs are built by combining commands. It also is an interactive language in that any command may be executed by simply typing the command. Turtle graphics is part of Logo; this allows a person to draw geometric figures on the screen by placing simple words and numbers together in logical order.

Once the following commands in Logo are understood, this knowledge creates endless possibilities for exploring Logo's powerful capabilities.

Keys	Command
FD	Forward
BK	Backward
RT	Right turn
LT	Left turn
PU	Pen Up
PD	Pen Down

Each command must be followed by a space and then a number. For example, FD 40 will move the turtle straight forty "turtle" steps.

With Logo, the student must determine the number of turtle spaces to move and the number of degrees to turn. To draw the two-inch square described in *Delta Drawing* would require the following commands: FD 60 RT 90 FD 60 RT 90 FD 60 RT 90 FD 60 RT 90. As each new command is learned, programming becomes easier and quicker. An example would be Logo's REPEAT command. Any set of commands can recur as many times as specified. The simple square could be drawn with the following: REPEAT [FD 60 RT 90]. With this statement, the student is telling the turtle to repeat the process of moving sixty turtle steps and turning right 90 degrees four times.

The development of procedures also expands the student's programming horizons. Once students know how to create a simple procedure, they can use it as part of a supraprocedure or program. Referred to as nesting, simple procedures can be used as building blocks for more patterns. Herein lies the infinite potential of Logo; any set of procedures can evolve into graphic works of art, limited only by the programmer's imagination.

A procedure is defined by the command TO followed by a space and then a title of no more than thirty characters. Students know they are in the procedure mode when the immediate Logo prompt ? is replaced by the deferred prompt >. A simple procedure for a square with the REPEAT command would look like the following:

```
? TO SQUARE
> REPEAT 4[FD 60 RT 90]
> END
```

After typing END, the word needed on the last line of the procedure, the message SQUARE DEFINED would appear on the monitor. Once this procedure has been defined, it now can be used as a command to draw another figure, for example:

```
? TO STARSQUARE
> REPEAT 8 [SQUARE RT 45]
> END
```

This would draw a series of squares, rotating around an axis, that would resemble a star.

Editing features ease any programming anxieties; color features enhance any programmed creation. Also, the ability to include variables

within procedures opens up all kinds of possibilities for procedural variations in size and format. Given our simple square procedure, students
would know that every time they wrote SQUARE, a two-inch square would
appear on the screen. To create a three-inch square, they would have to
write another procedure unless they used the variable option. This option would allow a square of any size to be drawn. The following procedure represents a square with the variable included:

```
? TO SQUARE :LENGTH
> REPEAT 4[FD :LENGTH RT 90]
> END
```

If a student wanted a two-inch square, the student would type
SQUARE 60; if a student wanted a three-inch square, the student would
type SQUARE 90.

The more students learn about Logo, the more creative they become
as programmers. Logo's structured design helps students to develop the
kind of thinking they do when they read. In reading, we talk about thinking on the literal, inferential, critical, and creative levels. Consider how
students employ the same thinking strategies when they work with Logo.

Literal Thinking

When working with Logo, students must attend to significant details,
follow a sequence, and follow certain sentence patterns, all literal-level
thinking. In attending to significant details, they must know what commands to use to turn the turtle left 45 degrees (LT 45). They also must
be precise in writing procedures; that is, they must know to begin a procedure with the word TO, and the name of the procedure defined (TO
STAR) as well as know to end the procedure with the word END. In following a sequence to get a desired outcome, as described for flowcharting
or any programming language, students must know that to build a procedure, they cannot make an array of squares before making an initial
square first. Finally, in following certain sentence patterns, students need
to know, for example, when to use brackets and the REPEAT command.
These are all examples of literal-level thinking.

Inferential Thinking

Inferential thinking skills (such as determining the main idea, recognizing
details that support the main idea, making predictions, and understand-

ing cause-effect relationships) also come into play as students learn Logo. In determining the main idea and supporting details for a set of Logo procedures, students' thought processes often are similar to those used when composing with words. Initially an idea germinates with thoughts about the procedures needed to execute the idea. For example, to make a simple drawing of a house, students need to identify which procedure to include to draw it (Wepner, 1986).

```
TO HOUSE
SQUARE
FD 30 RT 30
TENT
END
```

(TENT refers to a triangle positioned to go on top of a house.) Students constantly are making predictions in Logo. Each time a set of commands or procedures is written, the student anticipates what will happen and how its use and/or modification would affect another procedure. Devout Logoists often are found at the computer spending many hours in predicting the effects of their latest procedural alteration. Concomitantly, Logo lends itself to understanding cause-effect relationships. Because students direct the turtle's movements by their written commands, students begin to see the relationship between what they write (cause) and what the turtle does (effect).

Critical Thinking

Two critical thinking skills also come into play: evaluation according to criteria and evaluation according to logic. In evaluating a procedural design, students consider specific criteria such as size, color, and shape. A set of unstated standards usually play a major role in deciding the value of a design. Logical thinking is used to determine which changes, if any, are needed in the commands or procedures. This involves a subtlety of judgmental thinking that comes with age and practice.

Creative Thinking

Logo is a catalyst for creative thinking. Any command or set of procedures can be a springboard for a new creation. For example, the drawing of a trapezoid (RT 35 FD 50 RT 60 FD 50 RT 60 FD 50 RT 120 FD 95) may lead to the design of a pinwheel.

```
TO PINWHEEL
REPEAT 8 [TRAPEZOID]
END
```

Logo in the Reading/Language Arts Curriculum

As shown above, the kind of thinking considered important in teaching children to communicate with written text also is necessary for communicating with Logo. Students learn another vocabulary to manipulate the language. The more proficient students become with the language of Logo, the more control they have over their learning environment. Students become self-directed and self-controlled through creative experimentation. They begin to add to and restructure their own schemata, which, as psycholinguists have pointed out, is critical for comprehension. Although they are not reading pages of text per se, students learn how to think, write, and read their procedures analytically and critically. They learn the importance of organizing thoughts in order for their goals to be realized.

While primarily thought of as a graphics programming language, Logo also has text capabilities that extend easily into the reading/language arts curriculum. For instance, with the text capabilities of the computer, students can learn to write poetry, riddles, and songs. Bitter and Watson (1983) show how the song "Happy Birthday" can be personalized to include a student's name.

```
TO SONG :NAME
PR [HAPPY BIRTHDAY TO YOU]
PR [HAPPY BIRTHDAY TO YOU]
PR SE [HAPPY BIRTHDAY DEAR] :NAME
PR [HAPPY BIRTHDAY TO YOU!]
END
SONG "MICHAEL
```

In demonstrating how students can play with language and its structure, Judi Mathis (1985) shows how Logo can be used to generate sentences, play word games, rearrange parts of words, and create specific writing products. In designing activities with Logo's list-processing capabilities, Mathis has become convinced that students will explore new learning frontiers while developing the rudiments of good programming habits. One of her favorite activities, "Fractured," takes a familiar nursery rhyme, generates new twists, and helps students explore parts of speech, meter, and rhyme.

```
TO CREATE.ADULT.JACK.JILL
CLEARTEXT
PRINT [WHAT IS YOUR NAME?]
MAKE "NAME READLIST
PRINT [WHAT IS THE NAME OF YOUR SECRET LOVE?]
MAKE "LOVER READLIST
PRINT [TO WHERE WOULD YOU LIKE TO TRAVEL?]
MAKE "PLACE READLIST
PRINT [MY FAVORITE PASTIME IS TO _____]
MAKE "FUN READLIST
PRINT [NAME A PORTION OF THE HUMAN ANATOMY]
MAKE "BODY.PART READLIST
PRINT [NAME AN AEROBIC EXERCISE]
MAKE "ACTION READLIST
JACK.JILL
END


TO JACK. JILL
CLEARTEXT
PRINT [WELCOME TO THE ADULT VERSION OF]
PRINT ['JACK AND JILL']
PRINT []
PRINT SENTENCE [BY] :NAME
PRINT []
PRINT []
PRINT SENTENCE :NAME SENTENCE [AND] :LOVER
PRINT SENTENCE [WENT TO] :PLACE
PRINT SENTENCE [TO] :FUN
PRINT SENTENCE :LOVER [FELL DOWN AND BROKE]
PRINT SENTENCE :BODY.PART [AND]
PRINT SENTENCE :NAME [CAME]
PRINT :ACTION
END
```

When the program is run, the following questions are asked:

```
?CREATE.ADULT.JACK.JILL
WHAT IS YOUR NAME?
JEAN
WHAT IS THE NAME OF YOUR SECRET LOVE?
SAM
TO WHERE WOULD YOU LIKE TO TRAVEL?
```

```
SWITZERLAND
MY FAVORITE PASTIME IS TO _____
READ
NAME A PORTION OF THE HUMAN ANATOMY
MY HEART
NAME AN AEROBIC EXERCISE
RUNNING
```

Based on the answers, a personalized nursery rhyme is created.

```
WELCOME TO THE ADULT VERSION OF
'JACK AND JILL'
BY JEAN

JEAN AND SAM
WENT TO SWITZERLAND
TO READ
SAM FELL DOWN AND BROKE
MY HEART AND
SAM CAME
RUNNING
```

Students also can use the split-screen capabilities to write captions, descriptions, or dialogues about any design created in the graphics mode. For example, any design can be printed with *Logo* printer programs or *Zoom Grafix*. Students can therefore begin to generate enough material to create books about any topic, from simple books about the size and color characteristics of a triangle to more complex books about the construction of a building. Students also can create *Logo* designs that depict different aspects of fairy tales. Fourth-grade students at Montclair-Kimberley Primary School, Montclair, New Jersey, have created pictures for such fairy tales as "Beauty and the Beast" and "Little Red Riding Hood." In telling the story, they used their *Logo* pictures to represent graphically the fairy tale's plot.

Logo also can be used to create autobiographical or biographical designs. Students can draw pictures that depict themselves physically, psychologically, and socially. When engaged in a biography about another classmate, students' socialization skills are naturally enhanced.

At Montclair-Kimberley Academy, we saw sixth-grade students using Logo to depict current social and athletic events. Teacher Roberta Hart has been instrumental in helping her students to create unique designs. With the aid of MIT Logo's animation capabilities, these students developed graphics with movement that brought to mind the Olympics, break dancing, and karate. While observing these students, we noticed that they thought of themselves as teams, challenged to fulfill their own Logo project requirements.

Another application of Logo is its use in beginning reading and writing. Moxley (1984) describes how teachers can use his programs or develop new programs to help students develop writing and reading skills. His varied programs can be used for such skills as letter recognition, word recognition, and sentence composition. Students and teachers also can create designs or scenes for language experience stories. Either Logo or a favorite word processing program can be used to write down students' thoughts about the picture (see Figure 6.6).

The possibilities are unlimited once the versatility of the language is understood. One of today's most popular computer languages, Logo can be applied easily to any curricular area across grade levels. B. Hunter (1983) describes how Logo was taught across grades in Montgomery County, Maryland, and Alexandria, Virginia. Her curriculum guidelines for its implementation provide an excellent framework for organizing Logo's instructional sequence (see Figure 7.4) Once the sequence is

Figure 6.6. *Winter scene created by Beva Eastman, William Paterson College of New Jersey, with Moxley's Logo program.*

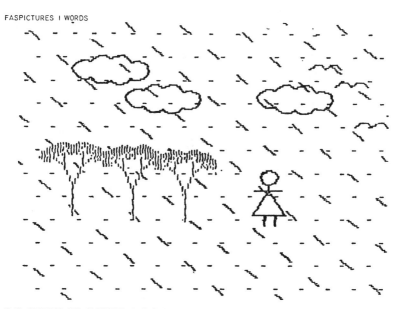

FASPICTURES I WORDS

IT IS SNOWING AND SLEETING. THE GIRL AND THE BIRDS ARE COLD!!!

planned, teachers simply need to think in terms of its applicability to the reading/language arts area.

Another popular programming language for the tutee mode is BASIC, an acronym for Beginner's All-Purpose Symbolic Instruction Code. Carlson (1982) believes that BASIC resembles block building and composition writing. Like a set of blocks, BASIC uses many copies of a small number of elements (commands) that are combined in rather standardized ways to achieve an original end result. Like an essay, a program is a finished product that fulfills a specified need. While young or inexperienced students may be concerned with the mechanics of writing or programming, older or more mature students will be involved with the overall form of their product. Thus, the analytical and synthetical thinking skills learned through BASIC, or any programming language, are the same skills valued in the reading/language arts classroom. We have found that the optimal time for teaching BASIC is when students are in junior high or high school. By this time, students understand the logic involved in manipulating BASIC commands to develop sensible programs.

As students explore the BASIC language commands, they can generate programs that get other students to "talk" about themselves. Programs asking them to share their favorite pets, colors, and friends can be developed within a few short lessons. For example, Mason (1985) has written a program in BASIC that asks students to write down the things they like. The Applesoft BASIC version could be written like this:

```
10 PRINT "THINGS I LIKE"
20 INPUT "I LIKE ";A$
30 INPUT "I LIKE TO ";B$
40 INPUT "I LIKE TO EAT ";C$
50 INPUT "IN SCHOOL I LIKE ";D$
60 INPUT "AT HOME I LIKE ";E$
70 INPUT "THE BEST THING IS ";F$
80 FND
```

Interestingly, some teachers have shifted their energies to designing CAI programs for their students. Modla (1984) used her knowledge of BASIC to write a program for teachers to use while teaching the difference between fact and opinion statements. Designed to reinforce second-graders' critical reading skills, this program contains a well-developed drill-

and-practice format. As described by Modla, students are to use the program after they have been instructed on the difference between fact and opinion statements. The program first describes characteristics of an opinion statement and then presents an array of opinion statements, which are to be analyzed in terms of their clue "opinion" words. For example, in the sentence BROWN BEARS ARE HANDSOME BUT WOLVES ARE NOT, students are asked to type the word that gives them a clue that the statement is an opinion. If they type in HANDSOME, the computer responds with THAT'S RIGHT!

Similarly, Schubert (1985) provides teachers with a program for dividing compound words, and Thomas (1985) offers teachers an analogy program. Although it is less costly to write one's own program than to purchase a commercially prepared drill-and-practice program, a great deal of time must be expended in the process.

Our inclination is to recommend that teachers use their programming expertise to help students develop and apply these skills to reading/language arts exercises. Once the following BASIC commands are covered (Wright & Forcier, 1985), students can write programs to reinforce reading/language arts skills and develop reading strategies for different content areas:

PRINT — outputs information to the screen.
LET — assigns values to variables.
INPUT — inputs information by gathering it from the keyboard.
END — terminates the program.
REM — inserts remarks into a program.
READ — reads information from data lines.
DATA — begins a data storage line.
GOTO — Absolute branch — directs the program to a specific point.
IF-THEN — Conditional branch — if a condition exists, then the program
    is directed to a point.
GOSUB — branches to the beginning of a subroutine at a specified line
    number.

Students need not create a program from scratch. The following simple multiple-choice framework can be used by students for any skill area. They need to provide the data to be used and shared with other students.

```
3 REM THIS IS A MULTIPLE CHOICE PROGRAM
7 HOME
20 READ Q$,A$,B$,C$,AN$
30 PRINT Q$
```

```
35 PRINT
40 PRINT "A) ";A$
45 PRINT
50 PRINT "B) ";B$
55 PRINT
60 PRINT "C) ";C$
65 PRINT
70 INPUT "CHOICE ";R$
80 IF R$ = AN$ THEN PRINT "CORRECT": GOTO 120
100 PRINT "TRY AGAIN": GOTO 30
120 INPUT "ANOTHER QUESTION?(Y/N)";N$
130 IF N$ = "Y" THEN 7
140 HOME : PRINT "THANK YOU"
150 DATA 1) A SYNONYM FOR APROPOS IS, PERTINENT, SUBJEC-
TIVE, INSTRUCTIVE, A
```

The program would generate the following:

```
1) A SYNONYM FOR APROPOS IS
   A) PERTINENT
   B) SUBJECTIVE
   C) INSTRUCTIVE
```

Students can insert as many data lines as needed to generate multiple-choice questions for any curriculum area.

Mason (1985) has written a simple spelling/visual discrimination program that students can modify to fit their classmates' interests and needs. Students also can write simple interactive programs that encourage students to converse with the computer. Flake, McClintock, and Turner (1985) wrote a simple *Counselor* program that uses the commands described above. This program is similar to the *Eliza* format. *Eliza* is a software program developed in the mid-1960s by Joseph Weizenbaum to encourage computer users ("patients") to converse with the computer ("doctor") in a simulated psychotherapeutic situation, using Carl Roger's approach. The computer was programmed to respond to the users' input by reflecting their thoughts back to them. *Counselor* also uses Rogerian therapy techniques to encourage students to describe their feelings. A typical computer-student interaction would be the computer asking the question How are you feeling today? to which the student responds Sad. This would be followed with the computer's response I would be surprised if you never felt sad. As Balajthy (1985) describes, this type of computer interaction is based on the "exact match" programming concept where certain keywords are matched to words in the program's memory so that a certain type of response can be given to the input. Once students understand the program's framework, they can use it to develop their own questions and responses.

Also, if students have the opportunity to explore BASIC graphic commands, they can pursue any of the activities mentioned throughout this chapter. Their graphic designs also could be used as part of their reinforcement for other types of activities.

Programming also can be used in remedial situations. Foley (1984) used her BASIC programming knowledge to develop her remedial students' interest in language. She collected four computers that were not being used and made them the focal point of her high school reading resource room. Students would come in groups of ten or twelve for basic reading and writing. After she introduced them to simple BASIC commands, she had them select poems to program. While they worked in pairs on the poems at the computer terminals, she could use regular texts with a small group of four or five students in a conventional reading group.

Instead of doing busy work (dittos or workbook pages), they were involved in a research and programming activity with real text. They had to find poems they liked enough to want to program. This brought them to the library and to various poetry collections. Next, they made the computer print their poems. The reading resource room was a special place where they learned something the other students were not exposed to, and they were working with language at the same time. The following is a program developed by one student for her favorite Robert Frost poem, "Stopping by Woods on a Snowy Eve":

```
10 PRINT "STOPPING BY WOODS ON"
15 PRINT "A SNOWY EVENING"
20 PRINT: PRINT
30 PRINT "A POEM BY ROBERT FROST"
40 PRINT "PROGRAMMED FOR YOU BY _____"
50 PRINTTAB(20); "JANE SMITH"
```

The printouts of the poems were displayed with pride by these remedial students who grew in stature because of their newly learned skill. Even though they could have typed these poems with a word processor, they were applying their BASIC knowledge to a reading/language arts activity. Foley's book *A Closet Is No Place for a Computer* (1985), is an outgrowth of her work with these students. Its innovative presentation of BASIC concepts, for students reading between the fourth- and fifth-grade levels, suggests ways to give remedial students a chance to learn BASIC readily without being frustrated with reading difficulties.

In analyzing the differences between Logo and BASIC, Flake, McClintock, and Turner (1985) demonstrate that each language has a different means of outputting the information to the screen. For example, the two programs below would produce the word HI down the screen ad infinitum until the computer user used CONTROL G to stop it in Logo and CONTROL C to stop it in BASIC.

Logo	*Basic*
TO HI	10 PRINT "HI"
PRINT [HI]	20 GOTO 10
HI	30 END
END	

These simple programs reflect the specific commands and programming details inherent in the language. Although any language is initially overwhelming for the novice, students eventually learn how to manipulate the commands. What appears critical is the exposure to programming concepts so that students can focus on critical ideas and modes of operation for the language being used.

□   **SUMMARY**   □

The tutee mode is another instructional dimension for using the computer in the reading/language arts classroom. Although traditionally regarded by reading teachers as ancillary to other modes of computer instruction, it can be considered as an integral component of computer utilization regardless of the content area or grade level.

In our observations of students, we have been awestruck by the high level of excitement generated by this mode. Because students are actively involved in eliciting desirable computer responses, they seem to spend an enormous amount of time and exert great effort in communicating with this technological tool. While adults' intimidation and fear of failure may stifle their level of productivity in the tutee mode, children appear intrigued by being in command. Their resilient and persistent approach to this mode is remarkable. As reading teachers interested in developing lifelong literacy with various instructional media, we need to seek software programs and instructional strategies that capitalize on this computer mode.

□7□

Organizing
the Computer Curriculum
A Process Approach

Awareness of the computer's uses as a tool, tutor, and tutee within the reading/language arts curriculum is one thing; integrating these uses into the total curriculum is quite another issue. Yet, in order for microcomputers to be used as a viable curriculum component, the "how" of integrating must be addressed. This requires a delicate balancing of what you consider to be important for your students and what the school district is willing to support for your general school population.

Since the computer should be used as a means to instruction within and between content areas, not as an end in itself, it is essential to think of computers as an avenue for facilitating learning. Although, as reported by Goldenberg et al. (1983), school districts typically have regarded computers as a separate body of knowledge to be taught as part of a computer curriculum (computer literacy, programming, applications), we strongly believe that its integrated use will serve students better in the long run.

This chapter is an attempt to help you get started or continue with your instructional computer plan, particularly for your reading/language arts curriculum. In so doing, it is important to consider how people in three roles—the computer coordinator/supervisor, the computer resource teacher, and the classroom teacher—can work together in effecting a cohesive computer curriculum.

□   COMPUTER COORDINATOR / SUPERVISOR   □

The computer coordinator/supervisor is responsible for coordinating and supervising districtwide computer efforts. One reason for the "growing pains" of school district initiatives with computer technology has been the lack of such coordination (Yin, 1985). The computer coordinator/supervisor is in a pivotal position for understanding district needs across disciplines and grade levels and within particular disciplines and grade levels. As more districts provide funding for this position, the fragmented efforts to "computerize" will coalesce into a coordinated plan for the district. While the coordinator's role has been delineated for the general school curriculum (Hoover & Gould, 1983), ideas still must be generated for reading/language arts (Wepner & Kramer, 1986).

☐   COMPUTER RESOURCE TEACHER   ☐

A new position in the schools, the computer resource teacher is establishing a visible role as the person responsible for establishing computer lab setups and overseeing schoolwide computer initiatives. Often hired from the ranks, this person usually has developed enough computer expertise to understand how to get students to enjoy the versatility of the machine. Orchestrating a lab situation for an entire school, however, is quite another task.

We remember one teacher, Jan Heiner, who was extremely eager about computers, enough so that his principal had pulled him out of his fifth-grade classroom to become the computer resource teacher. Although he had spent about one year learning all that he could about the computer, he had difficulty envisioning how to establish and subsequently maximize the use of the computer lab for reading/language arts. His courses, while providing an excellent overview of the technical aspects of computers, had not prepared him for using the computer as an integral part of the district's curricular goals. As with the computer coordinator/supervisor, the computer resource teacher needs guidelines.

☐   CLASSROOM TEACHER   ☐

The classroom teacher knows what students need, desire, and can handle with respect to computers. Although not in a position to make districtwide decisions, this person can provide valuable information to those overseeing any computer initiatives. Aside from having a direct effect on students' academic experiences, the classroom teacher's computer instruction can make or break the quality of the district's overall plan. The classroom teacher, in conjunction with the computer coordinator/supervisor and the computer resource teacher, can develop a coherent sequence of computer activities for each grade level.

While current financial, personnel, and time constraints may preclude many school districts from using professionals in supervisory or resource roles for this "ideal" coordination, we believe that these positions should be created eventually.

☐   QUESTIONS FOR THE PROCESS APPROACH   ☐

When we speak of a process approach, we refer to a systematic, continuous structure for effecting change. Usually in the form of a series of progressive, interdependent, and sometimes recursive steps, this structure is directed toward some end result, in this case, computer organization.

To create a structure that districts can shape to their own purposes, the following questions, borrowed from curricular planning guides, now will be addressed for each of these three roles:

1. Where do we want to be?
2. What do we have and what do we need?
3. How do we plan for what we want?
4. How do we know how well we are doing?

1. Where Do We Want to Be?

With this first question, you are asking yourself, "How do I want to incorporate microcomputers into the reading/language arts curriculum within the next five years?" The answer requires the formulation of goals that reflect the external and internal forces in your environment.

External forces include federal, state, and local government mandates. According to Slesnick (1984), these mandates are proliferating for students and teachers, sometimes appearing so quickly that their intent of achieving uniformity is frustrated by districtwide problems and misinterpretations. However, when developing goals, it is important to consider how these mandates will affect the instructional situation. If, in fact, all students must pass a test about computers before being graduated or promoted to the next grade, then this should be reflected in the goals. For example, instead of taking specific "computer literacy" courses, can students learn about computers and see positive applications by real experiences with word processing and tutorial courseware? Can these experiences help them pass a statewide test? Or, if computer training in the form of workshops or computer courses is mandated for all teachers, then courses or experiences in which teachers use computers should be written into the goals. By responding to external forces in this fashion, we are helping to shape computer education according to our teaching philosophies.

The internal forces include districtwide characteristics in terms of the student population, financial resources, community interests, administrative support, space allocations, and teacher preparation. Each must be considered so that the goals express realistic expectations for the district.

Consider the contrast between an overcrowded urban district with a 50 percent mobility rate and a wealthy suburban district with a 70 percent college acceptance rate. The urban district probably would be thinking in terms of using drill-and-practice programs to help students acquire some basic transferable reading and writing skills while the suburban district might be devising plans for exposing students to the use of information-retrieval systems for doing research reports. However, both might profit by exposure to word processing as a tool for communication.

While voices are heard from afar telling educators what students need in order to function in our "technological society," in many respects, they are not sensitized to the internal constraints of a given district. Only those living with the situation will know how to develop goals that make this form of technology work for their students.

The following discussion considers how the computer coordinator/ supervisor, computer resource teacher, and classroom teacher might address this first question ("Where do we want to be?"). The answers to this question will indicate where the district wants to be with regard to three modes of computer instruction (tool, tutor, and tutee); with regard to two levels of instruction (elementary and secondary); and within the confines of the forces (internal and external) impinging on the district. In addition, consideration should be given to how each mode (tool, tutor, and tutee) can be used to enhance reading/language arts instruction. This focus will help in making software recommendations that reflect well-integrated goals for a particular student population. Since instructional goals cannot be accomplished without certain district resources, goals should be simultaneously developed for acquiring hardware, establishing facilities, and developing staff proficiencies. Goals for garnering community and administrative support also are essential if the budget is to be endorsed.

Depending on the situation, the computer expectations of the district coordinator/supervisor, computer resource teacher, and classroom teacher will reflect different situational needs: coordinating district/school efforts, establishing a lab setup, and organizing a classroom, respectively. Each should research other school-related situations that parallel individual needs to help build a case for the goals set forth. Conferences, consortia, networks, workshops, courses, school visitations, and computer-related literature will help to prepare and defend one's goals.

For example, the computer resource teacher might want to observe existing labs in the district, labs in neighboring districts that service students of similar and different backgrounds, or model computer labs in the state that have been acclaimed for their cost-effective, exemplary service to students. Spence Hook, English teacher and computer resource teacher in Lounsberry Hollow Middle School, Vernon, New Jersey, visited other schools to see how they were integrating word processing into their writing programs. As a result of his findings, eight computers were placed in carrels in the library so that Mr. Hook could establish a drop-in writing center for his seventh- and eighth-grade students. By investigating what other schools in similar situations were doing, he was able to determine that he wanted to have a central spot for students to be able to come to write their final drafts and confer with peers and teachers about their writing projects.

Figure 7.1 lists factors to be considered for each role. Communication between these three roles is essential; otherwise computer goals operate in a vacuum of directionless aims. Once these goals are in place, the second question, "What do we have and what do we need?," should be addressed.

2. What Do We Have and What Do We Need?

Referred to as needs assessment, this part of the process is necessary in order to determine where computer initiatives currently stand in relation to stated goals. This needs assessment process is essentially a "discrepancy model," providing a status report on differences between the existing program and desired ideals. Knowledge of existing program status comes from teachers, students, administrators, and the community; it also comes from teacher/student observations, outside consultant evaluations, and any hard or soft data available. Through this step, those responsible for computer innovations will be aware of the areas that must be improved so that both short- and long-range goals can be accomplished. This step also helps to set the wheels in motion for establishing specific timetables for goal implementation.

Let's consider school no. 6 for a moment. The principal, Mrs. Hangston, decided that she wanted to incorporate word processing into the fourth- and fifth-grade writing curricula. Since her teachers were using a writing-as-process approach, she believed that word processing would be a useful instructional tool.

Figure 7.1. Considerations for answering question 1, "Where do we want to be?"

	COMPUTER SUPERVISOR/ COORDINATOR	COMPUTER RESOURCE TEACHER	CLASSROOM TEACHER
INSTRUCTIONAL MODES	*Tool* Use and selection of tool applications Scope and sequence for each grade level Coordination with reading/language arts instruction Selection of software packages Benefits *Tutor* Use and selection of tutor applications Scope and sequence for each grade level Selection of reading/language arts software Benefits *Tutee* Use and selection of tutee applications Scope and sequence for each grade level Coordination with reading/language arts instruction Selection of software packages Benefits	*Tool* Same as computer supervisor/coordinator but for lab situation *Tutor* Same as computer supervisor/coordinator but for lab situation *Tutee* Same as computer supervisor/coordinator but for lab situation	*Tool* Same as other two roles but for particular grade level *Tutor* Same as other two roles but for particular grade level *Tutee* Same as other two roles but for particular grade level
CONSIDERATIONS	Hardware—quality and quantity Districtwide staff development Facilities—labs and classrooms Budget—including funding alternatives Support systems—administrative and community involvement	Purpose of lab instruction Hardware—quality and quantity Schoolwide staff development Lab facility Networking options Security and hardware maintenance Budget—including funding alternatives Support systems—administrative and community involvement	Hardware—quality and quantity Individual in-service goals Budget Support systems—administrative and community

While undoubtedly appropriate, this idea created a number of additional questions to be resolved. Mrs. Hangston now had to take a hard look at the school in terms of space, equipment, personnel, and scheduling. She also realized that before her superintendent would budget for this project, she needed to assess her resources and delineate her needs. Many hours were spent with her teachers in analyzing the school's assets and deciding the school's needs.

Although initially hoping to have a few computers in every fourth- and fifth-grade classroom, she recognized, with the aid of her teachers, that a networked computer lab would be a better alternative for her school. It ultimately would service more students at less cost to the district. Since a few pieces of hardware already had been purchased (and, to her chagrin, were still not used extensively), they could be placed in the lab, a vacant classroom in the building.

As portrayed with school no. 6, good ideas need to be supported with background information about the situation at hand. For this reason, computer goals for any facet of reading/language arts instruction need to be viewed in light of school district realities so that the expressed needs account for existing physical, material, and personnel resources. How this is addressed in terms of answering the second question is considered below.

Once an inventory of existing practices and equipment has been taken, a clear picture of what is needed should emerge. Besides accounting for the availability of hardware and reading/language arts software, this inventory should be used to examine what exists in terms of curriculum, staff development, and facilities. Also, if budgetary allocations for computer initiatives, whether or not required by government mandates, are reviewed, an understanding of the level of administrative and community support should occur.

Figure 7.2 lists specific items to consider within each role; this may be used as a checklist to help you with this phase of the process.

In addition to identifying whether and how computers are part of the district's curricular plans, you need to find out what hardware has been purchased, where it is located, who is using it, and for what purposes it is used. The quantity and quality of software also needs to be identified in terms of its program applications and student use.

School districts have limited budgets for computer expenditures. Even with these limitations, many districts, in response to government mandates or community outcries, spend too much money too quickly before taking a hard look at program needs. Computers are purchased without thinking about facilities, staff development, or administrative know-how; software is purchased without assessing student needs or considering instructional benefits. One should first look at what has or has not been

(Continued on page 140)

Figure 7.2. Considerations for answering question 2, "What do we have and what do we need?"

Goals – Current Practices (or Equipment) = Needs

	COMPUTER SUPERVISOR/ COORDINATOR	COMPUTER RESOURCE TEACHER	CLASSROOM TEACHER
CURRICULUM	Existence and contents of computer curriculum guide (tool, tutor, tutee applications) Application and integration of computer curriculum guide to districtwide reading/language arts objectives, K–12 Teacher use of curriculum guide	Application and integration of computer curriculum guide to school's reading/language arts objectives Scope and sequence	Integration of computer guide/initiatives with reading/language arts objectives for classroom situation Previous student instruction Student ability and interest levels Previous instructional techniques
HARDWARE	Existing hardware, including peripherals (type and quantity) Location of hardware (in labs and classrooms) Hardware/software compatibility	Existing hardware including peripherals (type and quantity) Hardware/software compatibility	Existing hardware, including peripherals (type and quantity)
SOFTWARE FOR READING/ LANGUAGE ARTS	*District and school* Existing software Instructional use (tool, tutor, tutee) Instructional benefits Existence and use of Computer Managed Instruction (CMI)	*School* Existing software Instructional use (tool, tutor, tutee) Use of CMI	*Classroom* Existing software Instructional use (tool, tutor, tutee) Use of CMI
STAFF DEVELOPMENT	Number of teachers trained in the district Type of training (in and out of district) Teacher use of training Teacher proficiency levels Teacher training needed	Number of teachers trained in school Teacher proficiency and interest levels Teacher training needed for lab assistance	Individual in-service needs in terms of each instructional mode

FACILITIES	Suitability of space Student access (number and length of time) Adequacy of security and hardware maintenance	Suitability of space (including size, electrical outlets, ventilation, lighting) Adequacy of furniture for equipment and students Student access (number and length of time) Scheduling considerations Type and suitability of security and hardware maintenance Use and type of networking Availability of audiovisual equipment	Space availability and location (including outlets and lighting) Student access (number and length of time) Scheduling considerations Availability of audiovisual equipment for classroom demonstrations
GOVERNMENT MANDATES	District response to federal, state, and local mandates	Articulation of mandates	Awareness and implementation of mandates
BUDGET	Computer expenditures, allocations and needs for all of the above	Same as computer supervisor/coordinator	Same as other two roles
SUPPORT SYSTEMS	Degree of administrative support, proficiency, and initiatives Ongoing supervision and monitoring of computer instruction Level of support from board of education and community Community initiatives Communication	Degree of administrative support and assistance from building level administrators and district coordinator Level of support and input from board of education and community Community initiatives Communication	Parent involvement Teacher articulation between and across grade levels Administrative support Level of support from board of education and community Community initiatives Communication

done so that computer needs are identified in relation to computer goals.

The person in each role may, and indeed should, proceed differently in gathering this information. Since the computer coordinator/supervisor assesses the status of the entire school district, continual communication will occur with administrators, teachers, parents, students, and the board of education. Regular visitations to schools may be necessary in order to find out where and how the equipment and materials are being used. Also, in the event of conflicting perceptions, outside consultant reports also might be solicited to provide objective information about the use of existing resources.

Mrs. Kent, a newly hired computer supervisor in a suburban district outside Philadelphia, experienced this situation. The community, linked to the school through the district newsletter, thought that computer usage was widespread. Each monthly issue featured another classroom heavily involved in some form of CAI. The administrators, on the other hand, were, to put it mildly, totally baffled by the district's computer direction. Since no one had "taken charge," it became a catch-as-catch-can situation with the most outspoken teachers getting the computers for their classrooms. The teachers, of course, were frustrated by the injustice. Since staff development with computers occurred only two times in the district, most teachers were ill prepared for handling the technology, let alone ready to think in terms of curricular integration.

Once the computer supervisor realized what was happening, she called in an educational computer consultant to make a detailed report of existing conditions and provide recommendations for future efforts. This helped her to convince colleagues how to proceed.

The computer resource teacher, in contrast, is concerned primarily with a specific facility in one building. Therefore, this person's focus will be on current school conditions and teacher/administrator attitudes and efforts toward computer instruction. To establish or improve the computer lab and avoid duplication in instruction and expenditures, the computer resource teacher should communicate (via surveys or interviews) with teachers and the school building administrators.

The classroom teacher, while not responsible for schoolwide or districtwide practices, still needs to have a solid rationale for requesting enough of a budget to satisfy equipment and in-service needs. A comprehensive assessment of existing resources and computer proficiencies will help to convince the appropriate administrators to defend and support the teacher's requests.

Notwithstanding any defeatist attitudes, a determined person in any role should help to elevate the computer program to the level desired in the stated goals, with students' reading/language arts development included as the core to any computer pursuits.

3. How Do We Plan for What We Want?

Planning, the heart of any educational process, can save the district considerable time and money if well conceived and thoroughly researched (Wepner & Kramer, 1984). A plan to integrate computer instruction with reading/language arts must begin with the needs established in answering question 2 and proceed logically and sequentially to the goals expressed in response to question 1. Similar to Program Evaluation Review Techniques (PERT), a technique for helping planners to identify the necessary steps to be taken and the sequence in which to take them in order for a desired outcome to be reached, this plan accounts for and organizes how all the variables noted in answering the first two questions will be accomplished within a given time frame.

A sensible procedure for planning is to form a committee of teachers and administrators representing the district's different schools and grade levels. A committee plan would embody all the goals and needs for the entire district. The computer coordinator/supervisor, as committee chair, would be responsible for assigning tasks, reporting to the appropriate administrative levels, and stimulating interest beyond the planning committee. Even if a committee is not formed, certain factors need to be considered in any plan: curriculum, hardware, software, staff development, facilities, government mandates, and budget and support systems.

Figure 7.3 lists specific considerations for the computer supervisor/coordinator, computer resource teacher, and classroom teacher. Each factor now will be described separately.

Curriculum. Curriculum is listed first because without it the other items become superfluous. When we speak of curriculum, we are referring to the district's conceptualization of what should be provided for students. No matter how it is represented—whether in the form of curriculum guides, scope and sequence charts, lists of computer activities, or a series of goals and objectives—some type of guidelines should exist for helping teachers to know what they might be expected to teach.

Curricular plans evolve differently in every school. Some districts prefer to establish some type of scope and sequence before investing in staff development and equipment; other districts allow individual instructional pursuits to be the catalyst for developing a district guide.

Marlboro, New Jersey, is an example of the first option. Approximately eight years ago, when computers were beginning to appear in schools, the curriculum supervisor, in conjunction with a few classroom teachers who had computer expertise, developed a "computer literacy" guide. Containing objectives and activities (grades 1–8) for computer awareness, computer development, and computer systems, this guide was a mechanism

(*Continued on page 144*)

Figure 7.3. _Considerations for answering question 3, "How do we plan for what we want?"_

	COMPUTER SUPERVISOR/ COORDINATOR	COMPUTER RESOURCE TEACHER	CLASSROOM TEACHER
CURRICULUM	Design or refine computer curriculum guide Integration of districtwide reading/language arts curriculum Incorporation of three instructional modes (tool, tutor, tutee) Grade-level scope and sequence Plan for teacher implementation of curriculum guide	Plan program that coordinates computer instruction with the school's reading/language arts scope and sequence	Plan strategies that coordinate computer instruction with reading/language arts objectives for classroom situation Plan to assess previous student instruction, ability, and interest levels Incorporate previous instruction with computer into plan
HARDWARE	Consider type, quantity, features, peripherals, cost, software, compatibility, purchasing options	Consider same hardware features as computer supervisor/coordinator for developing new lab. If expanding lab, plan according to existing hardware	Plan for number of computers needed in classroom to accomplish curricular objectives
SOFTWARE FOR READING/ LANGUAGE ARTS	Select software that integrates reading/language arts and computer curriculum objectives Consider age, ability, and interest suitability Use software evaluation guides and resources (including CMI) Develop software inventory Investigate purchasing options	Use same considerations as computer supervisor/coordinator to plan for software library in lab	Use districtwide criteria to select grade-appropriate software If none exist, use suggestions outlined to select software
STAFF DEVELOPMENT	Plan individual and comprehensive staff development in and out of district Adhere to staff development procedures (needs, goals, resources, responsibilities, formats, scheduling, evaluation)	Plan on-site individual and comprehensive staff development to accommodate varying teacher needs and interests Use same staff development procedures as computer supervisor/coordinator on a smaller scale	List in-service needs to accomplish curricular plans Seek workshops that address these needs

FACILITIES	Decide on computer locations Make student/teacher assignments Consider physical conditions Plan for security and hardware maintenance	Plan and/or rearrange physical layout with appropriate furniture Arrange for security and hardware maintenance If appropriate, plan for purchase and installation of local area network Devise scheduling strategies with building level administrator to maximize student access across grade and ability levels	Plan for computers and audiovisual equipment in terms of space and location Coordinate computer instruction schedule with other curricular pursuits
GOVERNMENT MANDATES	Incorporate federal, state, and local mandates into plans for curriculum, hardware, software, staff development, and facilities	Same as computer supervisor/coordinator	Same as other two roles
BUDGET	Develop a 5-year budget to accommodate plans for curriculum, hardware, software, staff development, and facilities	Same as computer supervisor/coordinator	Same as other two roles
SUPPORT SYSTEMS	Design administrator in-service Incorporate administrative initiatives into plan Encourage administrators to include a computer component in their observations Plan communication strategies with board and community to elicit support and assistance	Include building level administrator and computer supervisor/coordinator in any lab plans Same as computer supervisor/coordinator	Plan strategies with other teachers to invite parents and community Involve teachers and administrators in plan Same as other two roles

for getting computers into the schools and establishing a districtwide staff development program. Besides identifying the initial focus of computer instruction, this guide created an awareness of district computer needs.

Ridgewood, New Jersey, fits into the second category. Because of the persistence and interest of a few faculty members, a generous computer budget was provided for one segment of the population. Once it became apparent that these faculty members were onto something big, the computer curriculum expanded across disciplines and grade levels.

As pointed out by Beverly Sangston (1983), curriculum guidelines offer teachers and administrators a framework for computer education. Its infusion into the regular curriculum involves an ongoing process of staff development, curricular revision, and instructional evaluation.

The following suggestions are offered for combining computer objectives with reading/language arts objectives:

- Decide on computer tool, tutor, and tutee objectives for each grade level.
- Identify the resources needed to meet these objectives.
- Determine how the computer objectives coordinate with the reading/language arts objectives. This involves thinking of the computer as one instructional medium for teaching reading/language arts.
- Use activity books, resource guides, and your own ideas to create activities that aid in coordinating objectives.

Figure 7.4 is a sample curriculum guide for fourth-grade students. It reflects a combination of ideas developed for fourth-grade students in Teaneck, New Jersey (Schweitzer, 1985), and Montgomery County, Maryland (Hunter, 1983). Although it deals specifically with reading/language arts, it can be adapted for any content area.

Hardware. Computer hardware has a dazzling array of features that must be considered before one purchases a hardware system. Critical features for any computer system include ease of use, durability, reliability, computer memory, documentation (teacher's guide), and expandability (ability to enlarge computer's memory and add on peripherals) (Patterson & Patterson, 1983).

Peripherals (input and output devices added onto the computer) are useful for enhancing computer-related activities and necessary for certain software packages. Examples of input devices are the joystick, graphics tablet, light pen, modem, card readers, and sense sheets. The joystick and graphics tablet (for example, the Koala Pad) can be used for games and drawings. The light pen enables the computer user to input infor-

(*Continued on page 148*)

Figure 7.4. Sample curriculum guide for fourth-grade students.

COMPUTER OBJECTIVES	READING/LANGUAGE ARTS OBJECTIVES	REPRESENTATIVE ACTIVITIES	RESOURCES
INSTRUCTIONAL MODE: TOOL			
The students will be able to: 1. understand various tool uses of computer	Compare and contrast ideas. Make inferences. Determine point of view.	Use pamphlets, magazines, and periodicals to see how the computer is used as a tool.	*Family Computing* (Scholastic) *Teaching and Computers* (Scholastic) *The Computing Teacher* (Scholastic)
2. understand advantages of using word processing	Compare and contrast ideas. Make inferences. Paraphrase stated information.	Introduce similarities and differences between typewriter and computer.	
3. understand commands in *Bank Street Writer* word processing program	Recognize meaning of computer terminology. Identify details. Identify sequence.	Introduce *Bank Street Writer* and various modes. Have students go through *Bank Street Writer* activity book.	*Bank Street Writer* program (Scholastic) *Bank Street Writer* activity book (Scholastic)
4. use *Bank Street Writer* commands to do simple writing activities	Recall meaning of computer terminology. Identify details. Follow sequence. Identify cause-effect relationships.	Provide simple writing activities to experiment with different *Bank Street Writer* commands.	
5. use *Bank Street Writer* to create "puzzler-type" stories for other students	Sequence sentences and paragraphs. Improve sensitivity to grammar and punctuation. Practice correct sentence structure and phrasing. Identify author's purpose. Develop interpretive reading strategies in order to make generalizations, draw conclusions, and predict outcomes.	Use *Bank Street Writer* for writing and printing "puzzler-type" stories. Use student-created stories for whole-group and small-group activities.	

(continued)

Figure 7.4 (*Continued*)

INSTRUCTIONAL MODE: TUTOR

The students will be able to:		*Comprehension Power* (Milliken)
1. follow oral and written instructions for operating a program	Recognize meaning of computer terminology. Identify sequence.	Introduce procedures for operating selected tutor programs. Discuss purpose for each tutor program.
2. operate drill-and-practice program without teacher's help	Recall meaning of computer terminology. Follow sequence.	Schedule students individually or in groups for selected tutor programs.
3. use drill-and-practice program independently to develop specific skills	Use of narrative and expository text to: a. extend vocabulary b. develop contextual analysis skills c. make inferences d. draw conclusions e. develop a sense of author's style	Use available record-keeping systems to tailor programs to students' needs. Show students how to keep their own records in skill development.
4. use interactive program for whole-group and small-groups to develop specific skills	Develop interpretive reading strategies in order to make generalizations, draw conclusions, and predict outcomes.	Introduce whole class to interactive program. Organize students into small groups to facilitate discussion of strategies used with program.
5. apply skills in using equipment and programs to develop stories for other students	Apply reading strategies to writing process.	Use small student groups to prepare stories.

MI-SS-ING L-INKS (Young People's Literature) (Sunburst)

The Puzzler (Sunburst)

INSTRUCTIONAL MODE: TUTEE

The students will be able to:

Objective	Reading/Comprehension Skills	Logo Activities	Resources
1. use simple commands in Logo	*Word Meaning* Identifies and uses: a. computer vocabulary b. general vocabulary c. acronyms d. antonyms Identifies key or direction words.	*Without computer* Role-play turtle commands. Write a set of instructions to execute a simple task. *With computer* Guide turtle through mazes. Practice steps for creating a simple Logo procedure.	*Apple Logo in the Classroom* (MECC) *Learning Through Logo* (Sunburst)
2. enter a Logo procedure into the computer and discover the result of executing the procedure	*Literal Comprehension* Follow a sequence. Follow certain sentence patterns. *Interpretive Comprehension* Predict outcomes.	Copy simple procedure. Use procedure's name to execute, save, and retrieve procedure.	*My Students Use Computers: Learning Activities for Computer Literacy* (Beverly Hunter, Reston Publishing)
3. use edit commands for modifying procedure	*Literal Comprehension* Attend to significant details. Use punctuation to obtain meaning. *Interpretive Comprehension* Compare and contrast ideas. Make inferences. *Critical Comprehension* Evaluate according to criteria (size, shape, and color).	Use Logo editor to modify a procedure so that simple modifications are made in size, color, and shape.	*Discovering Apple Logo: An Invitation to the Art and Pattern of Nature* (David Thornburg, Addison-Wesley Publishing) *Exploring Logo Without a Computer* (David Thornburg, Addison-Wesley Publishing)
4. demonstrate that different Logo procedures can produce the same drawing	*Interpretive Comprehension* Understand cause-effect relationships. *Critical Comprehension* Evaluate according to criteria (size, shape, and color).	Develop different procedures for creating same geometric shape.	
5. use Logo commands for individual exploration and experimentation	*Creative Comprehension* Elaborate upon changes and/or create ideas and programs.	Predict and record outcomes for set of commands. Keep journal of Logo discoveries.	

mation by touching the screen; this is particularly useful for students who have difficulty with the keyboard because of visual-motor difficulties. The modem (short for modulator-demodulator) is important for telecommunication. The modem allows the microcomputer to send and receive messages over the phone by converting electronic signals from the computer so that they can be transmitted over a telephone line. These signals are reconverted to an electronic computer code by a modem at the other end (Balajthy, 1986). Used not only to access computerized data bases (see Chapter 3) but also to transmit data such as electronic mail (see Chapters 3 and 8), modems have opened up the channels of communication among microcomputer users.

Two other input devices, card readers and sense sheets, detect patterns of holes and other markings so that multiple-choice exams, for instance, can be scored and stored. Publishing companies are developing computerized management systems to keep records of students' progress in basal reading series. For instance, the Macmillan series program has a computerized management program, RIMS, that attaches a card reader to an Apple computer. The card reader reads the information from each student's answer sheet, scores the task, and reports the student's reading strengths and weaknesses to the teacher. If you are using some form of Computer Managed Instruction (CMI), these systems should be investigated in terms of peripheral-hardware compatibility.

Output devices such as printers, plotters (devices for printing blueprints and charts), and synthesizers (devices that produce and control sound) (Flake, McClintock, & Turner, 1985), also should be considered. As with input devices, the output devices purchased need to be compatible with the hardware.

Other features such as color graphics, upper- and lower-case letters, and available languages also should be considered in relation to planned objectives. For example, color graphics are recommended if the computer will be used for CAI in reading/language arts; however, they may be unnecessary if the computer will be used mainly for CMI or word processing. The upper- and lowercase letter option on computers is important if the computer is to be used for report writing or student compositions.

The most essential hardware consideration in schools is the number of compatible software packages available. If the desired software is not compatible with the hardware purchased, all planning efforts will have been futile. Before settling on hardware, an investigation should be made of changing trends in software development and compatibility. The Apple hardware family has been the bellwether among K–12 educators, but it could become tomorrow's anachronism. While IBM is emerging quickly as the hardware of choice among college and business communities, it still seems to be in an embryonic stage for K–12 software developments. However, this could change.

Certain caveats are in order before making hardware decisions:

- Do not allow the national recognition of a well-publicized software package usable in only one type of machine to influence district-wide hardware decisions. Hardware companies operate on the clever premise that getting their foot in the door with one outstanding package for one segment of the population will result in district-wide adoption.
- Do not forfeit hardware quality for quantity. Many of those deals that could not be refused turn into public embarrassments because of their unidimensional curricular functions.
- Do not buy hardware whose vendors can offer you only well-intentioned promises of future developments. Those promised programs or equipment saviors may never appear during your career.
- Do not buy hardware without thinking about your present and future use of peripherals. Some hardware products may not be adaptable for enough of the peripherals desired.
- Do not wait for tomorrow's improvements. The technology is changing so rapidly that whatever is purchased may and probably will become obsolete within a few years.
- Comparison-shop with local computer stores, retail department stores, manufacturers, and mail-order outlets. If the school district must solicit bids for hardware, mail the bid specifications directly to those suppliers whose prices are lowest. If possible, coordinate purchasing efforts with other local school districts in order to purchase larger quantities of computers at reduced rates.

Indeed, a tremendous amount of time and effort is required to buy the right computer at the best possible price, but the rewards will be well worth the investment.

Software. The battle to keep up with software developments reflects the mercurial nature of the hardware industry and the publishers' efforts to keep abreast of current educational theories and practices. There is a burgeoning array of software available in almost every discipline, and reading is no exception. Certain suggestions are offered to help you plan for your reading/language arts software library.

- *Look for software that presents learning skills in a meaningful context and provides for students' active involvement.* Whether you are teaching reading from a subskill-list approach (isolating reading skills for instructional purposes) or a holistic approach (using realistic reading and writing situations to foster language subsystems on a need basis) (Miller & Burnett, 1985), software programs should use some type of contextual clues to help students acquire literacy. Older students should develop vocabulary, comprehension, and study skills as they apply their knowledge of semantic, syntactic, and graphophonic clues. Younger students should develop decoding strategies while associating the information presented with their life experiences. Even programs that teach or reinforce letter-recognition skills should contain representative words and pictures for each letter presented. Programs that do nothing more than drill skills in isolation do not prepare students to transfer these skills to realistic reading situations.

Because students also need to be significantly involved in the learning process, software programs should provide options for student control. Appropriate options for the number of items, level of difficulty, speed of presentation, sound effects, and other related factors should be offered. Teachers should be able to adjust these options according to the needs of various groups.

• *Think about how the software fits into your total curriculum.* According to Komoski (1984), when we view software through a broader lens, our focus will be on integrating the software into the curriculum rather than slotting our curriculum into software availability. While it is clearly more confusing to select from the vast array of software offerings than it is to choose from the more limited selection of textbooks, workbooks, and audiovisual equipment, we still need to match the software's objectives with our curriculum objectives. Therefore, the overriding question in evaluating software for its accurate, bias-free, graphically appropriate presentation of material should be "Where does the program fit into my curriculum?" (Senn, 1983).

• *Make sure that the software is appropriate for students' age and ability levels and takes students' interests into account.* When software does not meet the developmental needs of the learner, it is unlikely to be used successfully (Caissy, 1984). In addition to curricular concerns, wise software evaluation involves examining the degree to which the skills and materials covered approximate the specific learning needs and interests of your students, including directions, topic presentation, and accompanying activities.

We suggest using students of varying abilities to help with your assessment or following Flake, McClintock, and Turner's (1985) three-step process: (1) run the program briefly to become familiar with the flow, (2) execute the program as a serious, successful student, and (3) execute the program as an unsuccessful student to test how it handles student errors.

• *Keep a list of software that is available and on order, and coordinate efforts of all involved.*   Lists can be created in a number of ways: alphabetically, in content-area categories, by software type (for example, drill and practice, simulation), according to reading skill development, thematically or in any combination. For example, Modla (1985) created a list of software programs on drawing conclusions using a science fiction theme for fourth-graders. Included in her list were programs for drill and practice, simulation, creating signs and crossword puzzles, interacting with text, and word processing. Intended to encourage teachers to think in broad categories, this thematic approach to lists is useful for helping students to apply their skills in a number of ways.

As lists are created, think in terms of a primary location for the software collection, either classroom or computer lab, library media center, professional library, or display center. Lathrop and Goodson (1983) recommend practical ideas for circulation routines, backup policies, shelving arrangements, software catalogs, catalog cards, and direct on-line access to the software collection via the computer (see "Filing Systems for Information Management" in Chapter 3).

The library at Montclair-Kimberley Middle School has begun an interesting "lending library" policy with the software collection. Students can pay an annual five-dollar fee to borrow any software. The money is then used to maintain and enlarge the software collection.

We recommend that one person be responsible for ordering, organizing, storing, and circulating software. This avoids ordering redundancy and economizes on teachers' time. When Susan Ginsburg, computer coordinator for Irvington, New Jersey, created a software catalog by skill area and content area for the district, she found that teachers began to use software that they had previously ignored, probably because they did not know it was available.

• *When selecting software, use outside sources along with your district's evaluation procedures. This can give you a balanced, objective view and permit you to see how well your procedures fit in with those used by other professionals.*   Some excellent sources may be accessed through computer searches. *Microcomputer Index* contains digests of software reviews found in over forty microcomputer journals. Resources in Computer Education (RICE) includes *MicroSift Reviews* from participants in the Northwest Regional Lab. The *Texas Education Computer Cooperative* (TECC) offers both teacher and student evaluations of educational software. (See Chapter 3 for more information and sample printouts.)

Besides these on-line resources, you also can consult evaluation sources published in the form of printed guides and directories. *Software Reports: The Guide to Evaluated Education Software* is available from Allenbach Industries, 2101 Las Palmas Drive, Carlsbad, CA 92008, for $49.95 per year. An independent service board coordinates evaluations from parents, teachers, and students to rate educational programs in twenty subject areas, one of the largest being reading/language arts. Programs are given A-B-C-D ratings, with comments that are terse and easy to read. This is one of the few sources we know of that includes parents as evaluators. Evanston Educators, a group of parents, teachers, and children, publishes a selected catalog of widely tested software aimed at home and school use. You can receive their catalog and newsletter by sending $1.00 to *The Family Software Catalog*, 915 Elmwood Avenue, Evanston, IL 60202.

The Digest of Software Reviews: Education, School, and Home is published four times a year by School and Home Courseware Inc., 1341 Bulldog Lane, Fresno, CA 93710 ($52.92 per year). This resource prints digests of reviews found in educational journals, newsletters, and computer publications. Since it covers fifty programs each issue and organizes them by subject area, it can keep you abreast of new software packages that have been reviewed recently. The most comprehensive and in-depth source of information about educational software is *The Educational Software Selector* (TESS). Created from the Educational Products Information Exchange (EPIE) data base, the most recent edition contains over five thousand descriptive entries and cites over two thousand review sources. Best used to help you locate programs or to get information on hardware or costs, you can search for software by title or subject. Updated annually, this directory costs $49.95 and is published by Teachers College Press, Columbia University. It also is available on-line through CompuServe (see Chapter 3). EPIE is also the source for *Microcomputer Courseware Pro/Files*, the critical, in-depth reviews that are available to districts that belong to the EPIE system. We have referred to the EPIE reviews extensively throughout this book.

Two directories are available for Apple products. *The Blue Book of Apple Software* (Visual Materials, Gurnee, Illinois) provides information about hardware, peripherals, and software. *The Book of Apple Software* (The Book Company, Los Angeles, California) is a selective directory containing annotations and ratings based on evaluative testing and review. The education category includes many reading/language arts programs.

These sources, along with software reviews from computers-and-reading journals, computer organizations, and consortia, will help in locating and ordering the type of reading/language arts software needed.

Software evaluation forms have become a convenient framework for making decisions about software. Unfortunately, as Miller and Burnett (1985) have reported, most forms focus on the technical, practical, and record-keeping concerns rather than on the theoretical issues purportedly inherent in creating the software programs. These forms indicate that software developers, while mindful of educational practices, still focus on the technical characteristics. And, according to Komoski (1984), educational software still suffers from the cottage-industry mentality of designing technical exemplars without enough consideration for their educational implications. This becomes evident from the small number of packages that are highly recommended by EPIE.

Forms also can be quite extensive, demanding a great deal of time to use properly. Since time is precious for teachers, we need to have a limited number of theoretically sound factors to consider as we assess the value of a software package for our instructional situations. We offer the form in Figure 7.5 for software selection for those with a whole-language approach to reading/language instruction consonant with the philosophy of this book. Eventually, as in selecting textbooks and supplementary materials, you probably will modify the guide to suit your needs. But using such a guide will enable you to know quickly whether a selected software program can and should be used with your students.

Staff Development. We will discuss staff development on an individual and group basis. Individual staff development, usually an outgrowth of concerns or interests, provides teachers with the benefit of supervisory assistance on a one-to-one basis (Burg, Kaufman, Korngold, & Kovner, 1978) or the opportunity to pursue in-service, via workshops, conferences, and courses, in areas of interest. This helps the teacher to apply new techniques or suggestions to the classroom situation.

Information gleaned from individual staff development can serve as a springboard for developing a comprehensive staff development plan. Unlike individual staff development in which a specific need or interest has been identified, a comprehensive plan requires a concerted effort to reach a wider audience, some of whom regard staff development as unnecessary for professional responsibilities.

Recognized as a critical component for the successful utilization of computer technology (Cory, 1983), staff development cannot succeed unless a viable process is in operation. Consideration should be given to

Figure 7.5. Software evaluation form.

SOFTWARE EVALUATION CONSIDERATIONS

Name of Software Program:
Source:
Price:
Suggested Grade Level(s):
Description/Purpose:
Hardware/Peripherals Needed:
Evaluator:

1. Does the program fit into my curriculum?   Yes_____   To Some Degree_____
   No_____
   Comments:

2. Is the content presented in a meaningful context?   Yes_____
   To Some Degree_____   No_____
   Comments:

3. Is the content accurate?   Yes_____   To Some Degree_____   No_____
   Comments:

4. Does the program allow for the student's active involvement?   Yes_____
   To Some Degree_____   No_____
   Coments:

5. Is the program's content appropriate in difficulty and interest for the student?
   Yes_____   To Some Degree_____   No_____
   Comments:

6. Is the program free of technical errors?   Yes_____   To Some Degree_____
   No_____
   Comments:

7. Does the program present content as well as (or better than) material already being
   used?   Yes_____   To Some Degree_____   No_____
   Comments:

8. Is the program easy for students to use independently after they have been given
   the appropriate orientation?   Yes_____   To Some Degree_____   No_____
   Comments:

Weights (2, 1, 0) can be given to this scale so that a "Yes" answer equals 2, a "To Some
Degree" answer equals 1, and a "No" answer equals 0. A score of 13–16 may be considered "excellent," a score of 9–12 may be considered "fair," and a score of 0–8 may
be considered "poor." This rating should help you to answer the final question about
the software:

9. Does the software appear to be effective and appropriate for my students?
   Yes_____   No_____   Maybe_____

district in-service courses for credit, professional visitation days to conferences or other actively involved school districts, and workshops with local and outside talent.

Let's consider the staff development program in Irvington, New Jersey. As soon as computers were purchased for their Chapter I program, an intensive staff development program was planned. Since, at the time, the supervisor of reading was responsible for computer instruction in reading (he quickly developed his own computer expertise), he collaborated with the superintendent and the supervisor of math (responsible for computer instruction in math) to develop a weekly, hands-on, credit-bearing after-school in-service program to help the teachers learn how to use the machine and how to select appropriate software for Chapter I students. While teachers were crying out for help (they did not know the first thing about computers), the supervisor still was apprehensive about the level of participation and interest in the in-service course. Surprisingly, the in-service course was oversubscribed; the teachers wanted as much training as possible, even if it meant spending time after school. They liked being together as they learned by their mistakes, and they especially liked knowing that their supervisor was there to help them out with the bigger blunders.

Informal follow-up evaluations and visitations revealed that the teachers not only were more adept with the CAI concept but also were willing to explore new computer ideas with their students. Some even enrolled in other computer courses outside the district.

The following items need to be considered for effective staff development: identification of staff development needs, establishment of goals and objectives for the staff, assessment of resources, selection of in-service formats, scheduling of sessions, and evaluation of results. Each will be considered in turn.

Surveys, questionnaires, observations, or informal discussions will apprise the computer coordinator/supervisor or computer resource teacher of staff development needs and help to carve out the direction of present and future in-service pursuits. Midland Park, New Jersey, used a questionnaire to identify in-service needs for the district's computer program. How the district used the questionnaire was quite unique. The district identified a "dedicated dozen" of elementary school mothers who would receive free in-service training in exchange for working as volunteers in the district's innovative computer-aide program (Ashare, 1985). At a PTA-sponsored workshop for parents, the questionnaire was used to solicit interest in developing computer skills, which would later be applied in assisting teachers with one-on-one, hands-on lessons for students. The in-service course, based on the questionnaire responses, was used to give the parents enough information and knowledge to use the computer for reading and mathematics instruction.

In assessing resources, budget allocations should be matched with the types of activities, facilities, personnel, and equipment needed for various stages of staff development. In-service formats take into account previous in-service experiences as well as the experience impact desired. Specifically, if the teachers need an overview of a new idea (for example, the application of data-base-management systems to classroom learning), a lecture may be the format of choice. With a lecture format, teachers have little opportunity for content control, multisensory experiences, or two-way communication. If, however, the teachers have been exposed to data base management and need to see how it has been implemented for keeping records of reading assignments, classroom visitations may be a preferable format. This provides teachers with the opportunity to observe and communicate with other teachers, thereby providing them with more control of the content discussed and more opportunity for two-way communication.

The scheduling of sessions requires time to coalesce the bits and pieces of information collected previously. Finally, evaluation must be planned in order to know what works (Oliva, 1984). Designed to assess whether and how teacher and students have grown from their experiences, the evaluation process takes many forms. Initially, an evaluation form can be used to understand teachers' reactions to in-service sessions. Subsequently, an evaluation process, consisting of classroom observations and conferences, can be implemented to follow up on in-service. This follow-up helps the computer coordinator/supervisor or computer resource teacher to recognize the strengths and weaknesses of an in-service program in relation to classroom applications.

Facilities.   Computers usually are located in classrooms, computer labs, common building spaces (libraries or media centers), and offices on a permanent or rotating basis. According to Becker (1984), computer location decisions depend on the number of computer enthusiasts in a school or district, student characteristics (for example, age and socioeconomic status), and the degree of administrative and teacher influence in acquiring and implementing computers.

The impact and type of computer use must be considered before location decisions are made. For instance, placing computers in a regular classroom usually means that fewer teachers will use them and, possibly, that they will be used for a narrower range of instructional applications. Also, a broader range of students will have access but for a smaller amount of time. Placing computers in a computer lab usually suggests that a larger number of teachers will use them for a broader range of uses. However, while there is more computer use, it usually is heavy on programming for a narrower range of the student population. Rotating computers usually means that students will have more access but with less instructional impact (Becker, 1984).

Ideally, computers housed in both classrooms and labs (or central locations) would ensure widespread instructional use. Yet we recognize that few districts could afford this hardware luxury. We do recommend, though, that serious consideration be given to short-term and long-term plans for locating computers in the context of the districtwide curriculum and staff development needs.

Let's look at how one district, Teaneck, New Jersey, is handling its hardware situation. Presently, most of its computers are housed in computer labs. This primary location was selected to: (1) address the goals and objectives outlined in its computer curriculum, (2) serve the largest number of students possible, (3) ensure successful computer instruction by the most proficient staff members, and (4) provide for teacher training through modeling. As reported by John Cowen, director of curriculum and instruction, the district's long-range plan is to move computers into the regular classroom so that they become an integral part of classroom learning. Built into this plan is a cyclical review process of their computer curriculum, an intensive staff development training program, and a budgetary commitment for software and hardware acquisitions.

In addition to considering a district's pedagogical goals, certain practical issues arise in locating computer equipment in any room (see Figure 7.3). The availability and location of electrical sockets, windows, and chalkboards need to be addressed before computers are placed. Traffic patterns also need to be considered, particularly in regular classroom situations.

Another practical issue, particularly for computer labs, is networking. Networking, the interconnection of microcomputers by wires, is a strategic management device for downloading (transmitting a program from computer to computer) one piece of software to a number of computers. According to Flake, McClintock, and Turner (1985) and Balajthy (1986), current networking complications require a long, hard look at lab needs before networks are established. For example, networking with floppy disks usually means that the software program in the "master" microcomputer will appear on all the "slave" microcomputers. What does that mean in terms of differentiated instruction? Networking with hard disks usually means more variety in terms of software selection from the "master" microcomputers to the "slave" microcomputers, but software usually cannot be moved from a floppy to a hard disk without paying a special licensing fee. This cost factor, coupled with limited software choices, presents a different type of networking challenge.

Once computers are located, scheduling students for computer instruction must be considered in relation to instructional goals, size of student population, and the quantity of equipment available. In providing for equitable student access (see Chapter 8) timetables should be planned, through either teacher assignments or student choice (Caster, 1983), for individual or small-group computer work.

Government Mandates.   Government mandates for computers have been issued for teacher certification, teacher preservice and in-service, computer curriculum requirements in schools, and student test performance. According to the most recent "Survey of the States" by *Electronic Learning* (Reinhold & Corkett, 1985), twenty-six states have some form of computer literacy requirements. Nine of these states require a computer literacy course for all students, usually grades 7–12; however, only one state (Louisiana) requires students to pass a competency test. The remaining seventeen states mandate that schools either integrate computers into the curriculum, offer an optional computer course for students, or design a district-based standard for acquiring computer competency. This represents a dramatic shift in statewide mandates since 1983, when computer literacy requirements were practically nonexistent (Education Commission of the States, 1983).

While teacher certification requirements are appearing more slowly, nine states require business education, computer science, or programming teachers to take computer courses to be certified, and two states (plus the District of Columbia) require all teachers to take computer courses before they can be certified (Reinhold & Corkett, 1985).

Statewide computer mandates may become even more widespread when the National Assessment of Educational Progress (NAEP) begins to assess students for their computer prowess. According to the recent computer assessment draft (Tucker, 1985), three major categories (computer applications, computer science/programming, and computer knowledge/attitudes) will be assessed across three age and grade levels of students (age 9/grade 3, age 13/grade 7, and age 17/grade 11).

Even though national projects have been funded to address salient considerations for state policymakers (Fox, 1984), Slesnick (1984) has pointed out that these mandates, which affect our schools, are proliferating from legislators with little or no experience in education and from administrators with little or no experience in computers.

While it is difficult to exercise control over policy decisions, we need to be aware of and responsive to these mandates, particularly when mandates affect teacher eligibility for certain teaching positions or state approval of the district's computer instruction.

Budget. No doubt about it, computer equipment and adjunct materials require large budgetary expenditures, ultimately coming from taxpayers' dollars. Schools with model computer programs usually have substantial financial commitments from one or more sources. For example, the Fresno Academy of Technology (Computech for short) in Fresno, California, a school on the cutting edge of computer technology, already has spent roughly $700,000 on their computer equipment (Lyles, 1985). Their backing came from the federal government, state curriculum development budgets, bank loans, and savings from other district budget cuts.

To get the money needed, consider the following:

- Plan in terms of five-year cycles. Use all of the aforementioned factors (see Figure 7.3) to identify how money should be spent annually within a five-year period.
- Go for any government or foundation grant available, even if it means shifting your focus slightly. Use professional networks, conferences, and computer users' groups to find out about grant offerings. In 1983 alone, the U.S. Department of Education spent approximately $38 million on computer education projects (Klein, 1984).
- Tap businesses in need of public relations gestures through parents and the community.
- Document and publicize whatever works to convince others that your program is worth the investment.
- Think about leasing (rather than purchasing) computers if all else fails—at least your program can get started.

Support Systems. In addition to budgetary commitments, successful computer programs usually reflect a baseline level of support from district administrators and community representatives. Efforts to develop communication channels between these support systems (see Figure 7.3) will create the cooperative spirit needed to effect change.

The board of education, on behalf of the community at large, must be convinced of the necessity to channel the district's revenues into computer education. Allendale, New Jersey's exemplary computer program would not have developed as quickly as it did if the board of education, in response to a growing interest by the community, had not provided increased funds for microcomputer purchases or actively sought interested staff members for teaching computer education.

Similarly, building and district level administrators, as educational leaders for the school environment, determine the extent of cooperation and participation for any program change. How positive support can be translated into program accomplishments is demonstrated by the strides made in Demarest, New Jersey. Demarest has only two schools, one elementary (grades K–4) and one middle (grades 5–8), and the students are fed into a regional high school. According to the regional district curriculum guide, fourth-grade students should have some introduction to Logo and word processing. Although the fourth-grade teachers expressed interest in providing this instruction, there was no hardware and no plan in sight for responding to the guide.

Two instances of administrative support changed the situation considerably: (1) the superintendent, in acknowledging the need to find computer funds, used the money from an insurance settlement (the elementary school, County Road, had a leaky roof) to purchase six microcomputers; and (2) the principal, in response to the teachers' question, "What do we do when the computers arrive?," formed a "quality circle" to deal with such issues as where to house the computers, how to move them, what software to purchase, how to schedule use, and other implementation concerns. (Borrowed from American and Japanese business-management techniques, "quality circle" is a problem-solving approach in which five or six group members volunteer to meet to have brainstorming sessions which help to deal with questions involving day-to-day operations.) When the machines arrived, the school was ready to use them for word processing and Logo.

Besides planning, administrators need to take responsibility for monitoring computer instruction through observation reports. Whether part of the job description for the computer coordinator/supervisor (as in Ridgewood, New Jersey) or included in the principal's observation responsibilities, this supervisory support will help to solidify computer plans and also to address the next question, "How do we know how well we are doing?"

4. How Do We Know How Well We Are Doing?

This last question involves decision making about the relative value, effectiveness, and validity of your computer program. It requires an evaluation process, with provisions made to receive continuous feedback (Morphet, Johns, & Reller, 1974). Not unlike a baby's first steps, any curricular alterations with computers will be accompanied with hesitancy and minor bruises. Cautious, ongoing evaluation procedures help the district to avoid falling flat on its face in terms of financial waste and staff discontent.

As shown in Figure 7.6, evaluation should proceed after decisions are made about evaluation techniques, inside and outside evaluation sources, the people responsible for using the selected techniques, and the contents of the evaluation.

Many evaluations are done to gauge the effect of CAI on student reading achievement (Braun, 1985; Caster, 1983) by using standardized and informal test data. Even the program in Grand Rapids, Michigan, where parochial school remedial children are receiving computer-assisted reading and math instruction in the homes, will use a national exam of student achievement to evaluate the program's effectiveness ("Computers," 1985). Caution is advised in conducting only studies of this ilk for a few reasons: (1) conditions for doing this type of research in schools usually are less than optimal; (2) negative results may bias the staff, students, and community against computers, even if tested only for one use; and (3) positive results may lead people to believe that computers should be and are being used only for this type of instruction.

Some evaluations use results from their Computer Managed Instruction (CMI) program. With such results, students usually work for mastery of a certain number of reading skills. While districts, which use CMI to document how well remedial students are using the computer to acquire certain basic skills, may not be able to attribute students' learning improvement to computer-based instruction, they still are able to show reading growth.

Informal student assessments, particularly pupil attendance, self-reporting, and assignments, also serve an important purpose. Although not considered "hard data," these assessments reveal the cognitive and affective effects of computers on students. Just as teachers are being revitalized with computers, students are being attracted to the machine as to a magnet (Elmer-DeWitt, 1985). If nothing else, their attendance, commentaries, and assignments reflect a high level of interest in learning. With any evaluation, consider what it is that is most important to assess, and then communicate the results with the board of education and community.

One public school district in Connecticut already has embraced the idea of employing a computer coordinator for helping to integrate computers into all areas of study and, ultimately, evaluating its effectiveness. The district went the route of placing one computer in each elementary classroom while creating computer labs for the junior and senior high schools. Interestingly, this district also has a strong commitment to using Madeline Hunter's Mastery Teaching model (Brandt, 1985; Hunter, 1985), as reflected in all teacher observations.

The computer coordinator, Joe Tyler, in trying to design an evaluation procedure, realized that the teachers should begin to think in terms

(*Continued on page 164*)

Figure 7.6. *Considerations for answering question 4, "How do we know how well we are doing?"*

	COMPUTER SUPERVISOR/ COORDINATOR	COMPUTER RESOURCE TEACHER	CLASSROOM TEACHER
EVALUATION TECHNIQUES	Teacher observations and conferences On-site evaluations Survey questionnaires Review and analysis of standardized and informal test data Informal student assessments (report cards, pupil attendance, self-reporting, and assignments) Interviews Face-to-face communication with community, board of education, students, teachers, and districtwide administrators	Classroom observations Survey questionnaires Review and analysis of test data (including CMI) Informal student assessments (report cards, pupil attendance, self-reporting, and assignments) Teacher and student interviews Face-to-face communication with community, students, teachers, building administrator, and district coordinator	Student observations Student survey questionnaire Review and analysis of test data (including CMI) Informal student assessments (report cards, self-reporting, and assignments) Student interviews Face-to-face communication with community, other grade level and/or content-area teachers, building administrator, computer resource teacher and/or district coordinator
EVALUATION SOURCES	Administrators Teachers Students Community Outside consultants	Teachers Students Community Building administrator and district coordinator	Students Teachers (including computer resource teachers) Community Building administrator and district coordinator

EVALUATION RESPONSIBILITIES	Administrators Computer resource teacher Teachers	Same as computer supervisor/coordinator	Same as other two roles
CONTENTS OF EVALUATION	Hardware Software Curriculum Staff development Facilities Government mandates Support from teachers, administration, board of education, and community Student achievement attitudes and interests	Same as computer supervisor/coordinator	Same as other two roles
FOLLOW-UP	Program maintenance Transition plan Recommendations of evaluation	Same as computer supervisor/coordinator	Same as other two roles

of using Madeline Hunter's strategies for teaching with the computer. He wanted to try this at the elementary level. While it would take a few in-service sessions of demonstration, brainstorming, and problem solving with other teachers and administrators, he believed that this would be the ideal way of convincing teachers to focus on teaching and learning, as opposed to the technology.

Since the administrators already had to observe teachers using Madeline Hunter's model, they simply had to consider what to look for in terms of appropriate computer instruction for each grade level. (When one of the principals heard this, he commented in his inimitable fashion, "That's all, Joe!")

Six months later, Mr. Tyler was quite pleased with what was occurring. While it took a while for some of the teachers and administrators to accept this challenge, he still believed that it was worth the time and effort. The board of education obviously was impressed with this evaluation procedure. The teachers' observation reports contained evidence for the use of many things: computers, computer-curricular integration, and the integration of computers into the Madeline Hunter model.

As described above, only one evaluation technique was used by the building and district level administrators to evaluate the effectiveness of their computer program. While Mr. Tyler wants to conduct some informal student assessments and analyses, he feels that, for now, he is doing the right thing for his district.

Since evaluation is most useful when keyed to the original goals, the computer coordinator/supervisor, computer resource teacher, and classroom teacher should decide early in the program what they want to evaluate in terms of established goals and how they will proceed. This could entail, for instance, documenting the scheduling and student-access pitfalls of having only one computer in the classroom or creating a case for upgrading the original micros in the lab so that more memory and better reading/language arts software programs are available to students.

Any information gathered during evaluation should be used to maintain or modify the computer program's direction, keeping in mind that evaluation merely is another link to the continuous, cyclical process of program improvement. In answering this fourth question, "How do we know how well we are doing?," you are inviting opportunities to reflect on whether your answers to the first three questions continue to be suitable for your situation.

Vida Welsh, fourth-grade teacher and computer resource person at Montclair-Kimberley Academy, Montclair, New Jersey, includes her teachers' use of hardware and software as one means of evaluating the school's computer program. Most of the school's Apple microcomputers are located in the library (on rolling carts) or in the computer lab (eight are stationary; three are on rolling carts). Teachers can either sign up to bring the mobile micros to their classrooms or schedule time in the lab.

The software, arranged by content area in the library's card catalog system, also is available for teachers to borrow. Mrs. Welsh, in conjunction with the librarian, keeps careful records of the software borrowed and hardware used in the classrooms or the lab. Mrs. Welsh has used these records as part of her progress report at the monthly schoolwide computer committee meetings. This helps the committee to evaluate what her school needs in terms of hardware, software, budget, and teacher training. This evaluation procedure has helped her to build the school's computer program. As more teachers have begun to use the computer equipment as an integral part of their curriculum, she has encouraged her administrators to expand the school's hardware and software collection.

The people in the three roles, responsible for addressing the four questions, must be mindful that any change involves a slow evolutionary process so that enough time is budgeted for the system to endure the instructional mutations while striving for educational success.

<table>
<tr><td>□</td><td>SUMMARY</td><td>□</td></tr>
</table>

In describing three key roles in school districts — the computer coordinator/supervisor, the computer resource teacher, and the classroom teacher — this chapter has presented four questions to ask while going through the process of organizing the computer program for reading/language arts. Included in the questions are considerations for integrating the three instructional modes (tool, tutor, and tutee) with curriculum development, while using hardware and software resources. Also discussed is the need to use support systems while developing staff proficiencies, capitalizing on existing facilities, responding to government mandates, and developing realistic yet satisfactory budgets.

The next chapter will discuss some of the controversies surrounding computer use in schools. Computer trends also will be discussed in terms of what we can look forward to as we prepare our students for the holistic demands of society.

□8□

Issues and Trends

In this chapter we would like to share with you our ideas on some of the critical issues facing teachers of reading as they enter the computer age. The copying of commercial software is a problem once a school district begins to use computers in any significant way. What is the real issue and how can it be handled? This is one question we will address.

What about teaching children keyboarding? Some teachers find the kids pick up these skills easily and naturally and don't need direct instruction; others think that teaching children touch typing early will facilitate their use of the computer. And then there is the issue of whether or not computers belong in early childhood education. Can young children profit from using computers? If so, what kinds of software seem most appropriate?

Equal access to computers is another issue that faces educators. Do more boys than girls seek out computer opportunities? What about the children of the urban centers or poor rural areas? Often lack of funds or qualified staff precludes these children's exposure to computer-related activities. Will computers be another educational difference between students from affluent and those from poor districts? Between male and female students within districts?

Besides these key issues, we would like to highlight some trends that we believe will have an impact on the immediate future of computers in the reading/language arts classroom. These are trends in telecommunications, voice synthesis/recognition technology, interactive video systems, and artificial intelligence.

□   SOFTWARE AND THE COPYRIGHT LAWS   □

"Can I borrow your new word processing program tonight? I want to make a copy for myself," asked the tenth-grade English teacher. The middle-school reading.teacher can be overheard as she plans with the computer resource teacher, " We have twelve computers and only two disks for this reading comprehension program. I think it will be okay to make some copies if you can unlock the master. Then we could put a whole group into the program without waiting to purchase some additional disks with the next budget."

Conversations like these are not uncommon in schools today as teachers grapple with the difficult moral issue of duplicating software. There is no problem with public-domain software or software that is purchased with copy privileges; but commercial, copyrighted disks are another story. According to the Association of Data Processing Service Organizations (ADAPSO), two kinds of crime may be involved. "Softlifting" is being committed by the English teacher and those who copy programs not in the public domain either for themselves or their friends. "Software piracy" is being committed when the reading teacher and computer resource teacher deliberately decide to make multiple copies of a published program rather than purchase the number of copies needed. The situation is analogous to copying pages in a workbook rather than buying a class set, but the consequences can be worse over the long run in that companies may find it uneconomical to develop software for the school market.

The Law: Interpretation and Reactions

The Materials Council of the National Audio-Visual Association (NAVA) asked a law firm to clarify the terms of the United States copyright laws as they pertain to microcomputer software (Gould, 1981). The lawyers clearly advised that cassettes and disks cannot be reproduced without prior authorization of the copyright owner. Under Section 107 of the 1976 Copyright Reform Act, a school system may *not* purchase a cassette or disk and make multiple copies to be used at various locations; under "fair use," it *may* make *one copy* for archival or backup purposes. The law firm warned NAVA that successful prosecution of illegal copying could result in criminal fines and possibly imprisonment.

Apparently, some producers of software have been taking a hard line on allowing copying of any kind, even archival copies. This has led the Computer Using Educators (CUE) to issue a position paper on software purchasing/pricing policies (1981). CUE suggests that schools *not* purchase from commercial sources that fail to provide backups or prohibit the buyer from making a single archival copy.

They also anticipate the producers' "locking" of disks, citing the case of Personal Software Inc., which produced *Apple VisiCalc* with locks that made it impossible to copy. For $150, a school gets only one disk that is guaranteed against defects but not student abuse, machine malfunction, or other mutilation possibilities. CUE maintains that while this policy may be appropriate for business and industrial uses, it is not sensitive to school uses. It states, "The hazards that our computers and disks are exposed to daily far exceed the hazards that an industry installation might receive in a year" (CUE 1981, p. 53).

Another problem has been introduced with the appearance of Local Area Networks (LANs), which permit several computers to be serviced by one disk. Some producers have "locked" disks so that they cannot be used by networkers. The International Council for Computers in Education (ICCE) has responded to this trend among producers to prohibit the making of backups or use of disks in LANs by publishing a clearly written document called the "ICCE Policy Statement on Network and Multiple Machine Software" (1983). Developed by a team of educators, software publishers, and vendors, the statement asks that schools and software sellers cooperate and share the responsibility for reducing piracy.

Specifically, the ICCE calls for school districts to establish their own policies, offering a model document that may be adapted to local needs (see Figure 8.1). In their published policy statement, districts should agree to observe the copyright laws and explain how they will enforce them in their schools, designating specific educators to carry out the policies and to enter into licensing agreements with sellers. (Under a licensing agreement, schools may be permitted to make a specific number of copies for a special price.)

On the other hand, the ICCE statement says that producers and vendors should provide backup copies, allow and encourage previewing of software before purchase, offer special prices to schools that need multiple copies of disks but not multiple copies of documentation, and provide network-compatible versions of software at fair prices. The policy also encourages software and hardware vendors to work together to provide an encryption process (a way of locking disks so that they cannot be copied), which "avoids inflexibility but discourages theft."

Besides the school district policy statement sample, this ICCE source offers a community college sample and a suggested format for a licensing agreement. Also included is technical information on software encryption needed by districts that want to use LANs and/or develop licensing arrangements with producers and vendors.

What Can the Schools Do?

Schools have the obligation to respect and uphold the copyright laws. Educators must set the model for students and the community at large. If we flaunt the law, we do not deserve the respect of our students. Finkel

Figure 8.1. ICCE *model document for districts.*

Suggested District Policy on Software Copyright

It is the intent of _____ to adhere to the provisions of copyright laws in the area of microcomputer programs. Though there continues to be controversy regarding interpretation of those copyright laws, the following procedures represent a sincere effort to operate legally. We recognize that computer software piracy is a major problem for the industry and that violations of computer copyright laws contribute to higher costs and greater efforts to prevent copies and/or lessen incentives for the development of effective educational uses of micro-computers. Therefore, in an effort to discourage violation of copyright laws and to prevent such illegal activities:

1. The ethical and practical problems caused by software piracy will be taught in all schools in the District.

2. District employees will be expected to adhere to the provisions of Public Law 96-517, Section 7(b) which amends Section 117 of Title 17 of the United States Code to allow for the making of a back-up copy of computer programs. This states that "...it is not an infringement for the owner of a copy of a computer program to make or authorize the making of another copy or adaptation of that computer program provided:

    a. that such a new copy or adaptation is created as an essential step in the utilization of the computer program in conjunction with a machine and that it is used in no other manner, or

    b. that such a new copy and adaptation is for archival purposes only and that all archival copies are destroyed in the event that continued possession of the computer program should cease to be rightful."

3. When software is to be used on a disk sharing system, efforts will be made to secure this software from copying.

4. Illegal copies of copyrighted programs may not be made or used on school equipment.

5. The legal or insurance protection of the District will not be extended to employees who violate copyright laws.

6. _____ of this school district is designated as the only individual who may sign license agreements for software for schools in the district. (Each school using the software also should have a signature on a copy of the software agreement for local control.)

7. The principal of each school site is responsible for establishing practices which will enforce this policy at the school level.

(1983) likens duplicating copy-protected software to petty tax evasion: both seem innocuous but are illegal and punishable by fines or imprisonment. He cites the suit recently brought against New York University by the American Association of Publishers (AAP) in which the association charged university instructors with duplicating copyrighted print materials. This case was settled out of court in favor of the AAP.

Educators can also be hurting themselves by pirating commercial software rather than buying the required number of disks. If the software producers do not get a fair return on their research and development budgets, they may abandon the educational market. In fact, Finkel (1983) has noted a change in priorities given software development during the last few years. Instead of designing software for schools with derivatives for the home market, producers have been developing products for home use with spinoffs for school use. According to Finkel, "These new products are much more 'gamey' and entertaining and relate less and less to the subjects we teach" (p. 28).

The answer seems to be for educators, producers, and vendors to work together in an honest, open manner. For instance, at William Paterson College we were planning a controlled experiment with our college basic-skills classes. To see if students would gain more in comprehension/rate when they practiced reading continuous text on the computer screen rather than in traditional printed form, we decided to have one group work with the Davidson Associates' *Speed Reader II* in the computer lab (experimental) and one group use the same selections in paper form in their classrooms (control).

Having only a few *Speed Reader II* disks from the college tutoring lab, we were faced with the problem of getting enough disks for fifteen to twenty students to use in the Apple lab at one time. (Keeping the students together was necessary for scheduling purposes and for meeting the conditions of a controlled experiment.) A call to Davidson Associates resulted in a quick solution. In response to pressure from such groups as CUE and ICCE, they were planning to market "lab" or "school" packs that would be available in time for our project. These consisted of five disks plus one set of documentation for a discounted price of about $100, a far cry from the original $69.95 per program. We placed an order for three lab packs and were ready to go without resorting to elaborate scheduling schemes or illegal copying of software.

We recommend that schools follow the ICCE guidelines and set up a district policy on software and computer use. They should make it clear to their staff and students that illegal copying will not be condoned and should designate a person (usually the district computer coordinator or computer resource teacher) to enforce the policy and act as the representative in licensing agreements. They should deal only with producers and vendors who respect the ICCE's guidelines by such practices as providing backup copies, allowing previewing, and offering multiple copies (lab packs) and/or master disks for LANs at special prices.

Apparently, school districts and the commercial market are coming to mutual ground on this issue. A recent survey by Dick Ricketts (1984) found that softlifting and piracy have become "a diminishing problem." Most K–12 schools reported little or no copying; most secondary schools reported minimal copying by staff members but much student copying of games, though not necessarily at school.

Piracy was associated more with small districts with little money (usually hardware purchases had eaten up the budget) and districts just getting into computers, led by enthusiastic but naive initiators who didn't have much experience. Piracy was controlled in districts in which teachers were more experienced and more aware of the issue and its consequences; usually these districts had established and enforced a no-piracy policy and had provided for their software needs adequately in budget planning (see Chapter 7). Also, they had developed evaluation tools and were selecting software more critically (see Figure 7.5, Chapter 7). Ricketts also thinks that many vendors now are working with districts in offering discounts on multiple purchases and in entering into licensing agreements.

While the problem may be diminishing, it will not disappear until school administrators and district computer coordinators, along with school-level computer resource people and classroom teachers, take a strong stand against illegal copying of software within their own districts.

☐   **KEYBOARDING**   ☐

Keyboarding is a term used to describe the act of entering information into the computer through the use of a typewriterlike keyboard. Skill in keyboarding enables an individual to use a computer efficiently. With the increasing popularity of computers at home and in the classroom, the issues surrounding keyboarding and its role in the educational process have surfaced as a major concern. Some of the questions being asked by educators are: Who needs keyboarding? Should it be taught in an organized way? If so, when and how should instruction be introduced? Who should teach keyboarding? What level of competency is required?

We are convinced that everyone can benefit from some instruction in using the keyboard. As soon as students begin to use the computer with regularity, they should receive help with keyboarding techniques. This not only will assist them in completing their current tasks more effectively but can prevent the development of inefficient lifelong habits.

Although the two finger hunt-and-peck method may work for short response, such a method is not adequate when more lengthy keying is necessary. The two-finger habit requires looking back and forth from copy or instruction to the keys, searching for the right keys, then looking at the screen and back to copy. This habit is time consuming and, once formed, is difficult if not impossible to correct. (Kisner, 1984, p. 21)

Schools have approached keyboarding instruction in a variety of ways. Many now offer keyboarding in the upper elementary grades. Our experience, however, suggests that it is still more likely to be taught at the middle and high school levels. At these levels, instruction often occurs in a computer lab as one phase of a computer literacy program. Bortnick (1986) reports that all fifth-graders in Arlington Heights, Illinois, learn keyboarding so that major reports can be word processed thereafter. Keyboarding may also be offered as part of an elective course, in evening or late afternoon classes, or during summer programs. In many school districts, business education teachers are called upon to assist in teaching keyboarding. They may provide direct instruction to students or in-service to teachers in methods of teaching typewriting. Some teachers have developed a set of instructional procedures of their own. Others have made use of software designed expressly for that purpose.

MasterType: The Typing Instruction Game is an example of a computer-assisted learning package designed to teach keyboarding. The program includes seventeen lessons, five of which introduce new keystrokes. The remaining lessons provide sequenced drill on words or number/symbol combinations of increasing length. The lessons are sequenced from "easy" to "difficult." The program includes high-resolution graphics, sound effects, and an option for the creation of new lessons. The sound effects may be turned off if desired. Although *MasterType* has generally received good reviews, there have been criticisms as well. The program makes use of the arcade video games for its format, causing Lambrecht and Pullis (1983) to complain, "The random presentation of 'words' in the corners of the screen for rapid, accurate typing under the threat of enemy attack presents a stimulus so unlike actual keyboarding requirements that it may deter successful 'touch' typing" (p. 67). The unlikeliness of the presentation of single keystroke characters in the beginner's mode to encourage correct finger placement and the requirement that learners type single keys rather than key combinations while under "attack" have also been criticized as working against the intended results.

SuperKey is another, more recently developed program designed to teach keyboarding skills. One of its main advantages is that it allows the learner to type in any materials he or she chooses. The program has four main parts: "Posture," which introduces correct body and hand positions; "Finger Names," which teaches the terms used in the lessons and introduces the home row position; "Lessons," consisting of ten units for developing keyboarding technique; and "Skill Check," which provides practice, assesses progress, and suggests ways to improve. Designed for students eight years old to adult, the program is easy to follow. Numerous ideas for word games and other extended activities beyond *SuperKey* are given.

A number of other keyboarding programs are available, but most have received mixed reviews because of their advantages and disadvantages. The primary concern among educators has been that too often programming knowledge has taken precedence over care for the methodology applied to teaching typewriting. Lambrecht and Pullis (1983, pp. 67–68) list features that should be sought in a computer-assisted instructional package designed to be a typewriting tutor. We offer a slightly modified version of their suggestions to you as guidelines for the selection of software of this type:

- Keys should be introduced together with visual guidance on correct finger usage and technique for striking the keys.
- Meaningful letter combinations should be used as soon as possible after introducing a key. Words, phrases, and sentences should be composed of those letter/key combinations occurring most frequently in ordinary keyboarding use.
- While early key-location instruction may not accept error correction in preference to requiring that the correct key be struck, natural error correction should be possible during typing drills.
- Sound and sight should both be available to provide feedback about stroking accuracy. If preferred by the user, the sound should be capable of being turned off.
- Gross typing rates reported should include all strokes, correct and incorrect. Error-correction backspaces may also reasonably be part of these rates.
- Reports concerning typing success and judgments about quality of the speed or accuracy rate should be based on both individual learner progress and research-based error expectations at different typing rates.
- Provision should be made within the program for upper-and-lowercase letter display on the screen and the use of natural shift key operation for capital letters.
- Provision should be made within the program for allowing computer-controlled interval timing while learners type from copy of their own choice.

Even primary-grade teachers are beginning to introduce some keyboarding skills to their students. While they recognize that young children have neither the fine motor skills nor hands large enough to master touch typing, they have discovered that they can learn proper placement of the home keys—A, S, D, and F for the left hand and J, K, L, and ; for the right—as well as some basic rules of keyboarding. Paper keyboards are sometimes used for keyboarding practice. Teachers have found these useful for helping students remember and locate the home keys quickly and to acquaint them with the space bar and other frequently used keys. Most teachers at this level, however, simply prefer to use programs that are designed to help pupils become acquainted with the keyboard while they build other skills such as letter and number recognition, directional skills, and problem solving.

There are a number of software programs available that give young children practice on the computer keyboard as they learn about numbers and letters. In Chapter 4, we described *Muppet Learning Keys* as being a program of this type. It uses a separate keyboard with large, alphabetically arranged letters and includes three programs that allow children to explore colors, numbers, and letters. When children press certain designated keys, they can change the color and number of objects on the screen and add motion and sound. According to teachers, children have no difficulty transferring from this keyboard to the regular keyboard.

As long as computers use the standard typewriter keyboard as a device for input, there will be a need to help students master the skill of keyboarding as they are taught to make use of what the computer has to offer. Schools need to consider a developmental approach to the development of keyboarding skills as a part of the whole range of computer competencies that need attention.

☐   YOUNG CHILDREN AND COMPUTERS   ☐

The introduction of computers into early childhood classrooms represents one of the most significant changes in the education of young children in recent years. Extensive coverage of computer news in the popular press coupled with impressive advertising claims by software developers have stirred strong public interest in the educational potential of the computer for the young child. At a time when schools are constantly seeking ways to respond to parents' seemingly ever-growing eagerness to ensure their children the best possible start, the addition of computers into the early childhood curriculum was inevitable. Nevertheless, even those educators who have been at the forefront in providing computer-related experiences for their young students have expressed concern about entering a situation where so little is known about the long-term positive or negative effects. "Researchers have yet to answer the major question: What are appropriate experiences on microcomputers for young children? Many seem to look uncritically at the microcomputer as the latest solution to current needs and dilemmas" (Brady & Hill, 1984, p. 49).

Fortunately, more and more teachers and researchers are in the process of investigating the use of computers in early childhood settings. As their findings are shared, our ability to make informed decisions will grow. What are needed are both formal and informal observations of children's behavior and attitudes toward computers, their responses to various types of software, and the relative benefits, if any, of this type of instruction for the very young.

Current investigations of this type already are providing some direction. Observations made by Piazza and Riggs (1984) of kindergarten children's use of the computer to explore written language reveal that their explorations are in many ways like those involving pencil and paper. However, because the computer offers a unique stimulus for writing, children were observed to experiment with speech and writing in ways that were specific to the machine. The account below of a kindergartener named Selen shows her use of the machine to play with oral and written speech. Selen combines chanting and letter experimentation as she uses the SHIFT key, the cursor controls (I, J, K, M keys), and the RESET button. The researchers point out that Selen speaks to the computer in ways reminiscent of the language adults use in games in which they wish to control the outcome of the action of inanimate objects, such as a baseball or dice:

> I want a big D. Come on (to the computer). D, big D, then a little tiny a, little tiny a. I played on the computer today or not? (to the researcher). Where's the t? There. A (types "A"). Big B. I need a big . . . I know what happened. What did I want, a big B? Oh, big B, B, B, B, come on B, B, B, oops! Let me erase that so I can write after it, no B, B, ok. It's going to work or not? (to the researcher). (Types "B"). Ah, I need a big B again, push this and the N then push the big B, big B, what, wha, wha, wha (types "Y") . . . I want that to go up again (points to the cursor. She giggles as she uses the I, J, K, M keys to move the cursor around the screen). Oops, go back up again, M! Oops, get down, down, down, down! Oops, get back up, up, up! Wait there . . . I, I, up! . . . (There is a halt in her typing because the buzzer sounds as she hits the RESET BUTTON. She hits it again.) I tricked you, I tricked you bomble, bingle, dingle. (pp. 72–73)

According to Piazza and Riggs, opportunities to become engaged in word processing and keyboard functions allow young children to explore language in computer-specific ways. "This language play facilitates children's systematic organization of print, their formulating and testing of language hypotheses, and the stimulation and development of symbolic thought" (p. 64).

The use of Logo with young children has become increasingly popular, since many educators believe that it enhances their ability to think. However, the evidence is far from conclusive. We, like Bowman (1983), question whether students are old enough to have mastered certain skills such as an understanding of size (for example, twenty is bigger than ten) before they can experience power as a learner with Logo. Studies with six-year-olds (Clements & Gullo, 1984) and eight-year-olds (Gorman & Bourne, 1983), however, indicate that Logo may have some effect on children's abilities to monitor their own thinking and to perform on rule-learning tasks. As indicated in Chapter 6, we prefer to see other types of tuteelike programs used at this age, with Logo being introduced in the third or fourth grade.

The work of Smith-Willis, Riley, and Smith (as cited in Brady & Hill, 1984), among others, suggests that children can successfully acquire "reading readiness skills" through the use of microcomputers. Prinz and Nelson (1985) used the computer to improve the word-recognition and reading-comprehension abilities of hearing-impaired children two to five years old. Unfortunately, most skill-oriented software is very similar to workbooks. We agree with Cuffaro (1984), who states, "The question here is not 'Why use a microcomputer?' but rather 'Why use workbooks, animated or not, with young children?'" (p. 562).

Other areas of interest regarding microcomputers and young children include the computer's efffect on children's social interactions and their choice of free-play activities. Two studies by Muller and Perlmutter (1985) indicated that preschool children can engage in cooperative problem solving and instruction and that the technology might even stimulate social interaction in problem solving. Two recent studies by Lipinski (1984), in which a microcomputer and age-appropriate software were placed in classrooms for four-year-olds, revealed that although the presence of the microcomputer initially disrupted children's free-play choices, their free-play patterns returned to baseline levels after several weeks. Karen Burg (1984), a kindergarten teacher who had initially approached microcomputers with a high degree of skepticism, agrees:

> It is doubtful that microcomputers will ever replace blocks or dolls or trucks or crayons. But the microcomputer can provide children with

developmentally appropriate experiences. Most five-year-olds can play games on the microcomputer that provide opportunities to compare numbers, letters, words, shapes, colors, sounds, amounts, and other concepts. (p. 84)

Two good resources for obtaining information about new developments in the use of computers and young children are The Educational Research Information Center's Clearinghouse for Elementary and Early Childhood Education at the University of Illinois, 805 West Pennsylvania Avenue, Urbana, Illinois 61801 and The High/Scope Educational Research Foundation, High/Scope Press, 600 North River Street, Ypsilanti, Michigan 48197. Each publishes a newsletter, which can be obtained for a fee. The ERIC Clearinghouse also publishes a short report summarizing current practice and research, called *Microcomputers and Young Children*. It is available at no cost.

Despite the apparent positive outcomes of many of the recent studies concerning young children and microcomputers, most researchers are quick to suggest that teachers approach the new technology with caution. There are many questions and concerns to be addressed. Clearly no matter how one currently feels about the use of microcomputers with young children, there is no denying that the new technology will play a significant role in their lives — if not at school, in the home and through games and television programs and advertisements. Sheingold (1985) summarizes the issue well: "The concerns that the technology will take over and that teachers' behavior or beliefs will not matter are contradicted by existing research. Answering questions about microcomputer use by young children calls for a complex and cooperative enterprise among teachers, researchers, and developers" (p. 38).

□   EQUITY   □

Providing equitable distribution of computer resources is one of the biggest challenges facing those who plan computer education programs. The major problems center on equitable treatment for both low-income and affluent students, for girls as well as boys, and for low-achieving as well as academically able students. Concerned that the new technologies are widening the gap between the haves and the have-nots, educational policymakers find themselves with a brand new set of difficult and perplexing decisions to make. Ironically, like so many educational technologies and innovations preceding it, the microcomputer raised expectations for greater equity and quality in education. Unfortunately, for most school districts, the issues of quality and equity remain largely unresolved.

The imbalance in computer resources for rich and poor students is perhaps the most obvious and pressing aspect of the equity issue. It has certainly been the most well documented. In a review of the research on equity and quality in education for urban disadvantaged students, Ascher (1984) reports:

> According to the Johns Hopkins survey (CSOS 1983), the least likely owners of microcomputers are public schools in poorer districts and small parochial schools. Whereas 66 percent of the public schools in more affluent districts have them, only 41 percent of the schools in the least wealthy districts have any.
>
> . . . Schools already owning microcomputers were more likely to purchase additional ones than schools without any were to make an additional purchase. (p. 1)

Many feel that this latter finding may actually be of greater consequence than the ownership gap between rich and poor, since it implies that the poorer schools are not catching up. On the contrary, the wealthier schools are increasing their advantage. Special funding programs and monetary gifts for computer equipment can compound the problem:

> The real pressure for the use of computers comes mainly from predominantly white, middle class parents who want the district to help their children master the computer. This typically has two results. First, there is a budget and equipment imbalance, because these parents are paying for computers to be used in the schools their children attend, and schools attended mostly by low-income, minority students get far fewer machines. Second, many districts, when they do make computers available to low-income, minority students, use them mostly for drill and practice applications, while the white, middle class students get computer literacy programs. Thus, the children of the poor do not get the experience that will give them a competitive advantage in a high technology economy, while the rich kids do. (Tucker, 1983, p. 320)

School officials may do little or nothing to correct this type of imbalance. They fear that if the schools of the poor were compensated with tax funds to bring them up to the level of the schools that derive their computer funds from the gifts of middle-class parents, the incentive to provide those gifts would disappear (Tucker, 1983, p. 320).

Differences in the computer instruction offered to students of varying abilities often parallel those described for low- and middle-income students. In many districts, programming courses will be provided for students "good in math" and computer-assisted instruction will be offered to "disabled learners." In some cases the vast middle range of students may have no contact at all with computers. The educational assumptions behind ability-stratified usage patterns and the likely educational outcomes need careful examination (Sheingold et al., 1981, p. 102).

Komoski (1983) suggests the use of aggregated computer purchasing power to foster donations of computers by manufacturers for use in poorer schools and poverty-level homes. He advocates school and library cooperation in establishing wide software exchanges and programs to train parents of school-age and preschool children in the use of the computer. Komoski warns, however, that a strong federal commitment will be necessary to combat inequities due to fiscal restraints:

> To deal with computer equity, local and state officials must press for federal legislation that provides greatly increased funds for disadvantaged school systems aimed at providing computers and teacher and parent training to achieve effective school and home use of educational technology. The responsibility for active rather than reactive or retroactive policymaking belongs to all who are about excellence and equity through free public education — electronically or otherwise. (p. 4)

Another source of inequity related to computer education evolves from the differences in treatment afforded girls and boys. Studies suggest that girls and young women are often not given appropriate support and contexts for learning about this technology. Hawkins (1984) suggests three possible categories of concern: (1) the common identification of computers with mathematics and science; (2) concern about sex-related differences in science and mathematics, which also emerge in the area of computers; and (3) investigations of children's learning processes and computer use in education, particularly as it relates to sex differences. Several suggestions have been made to combat the problems associated with sex differences in computer instruction. Linn (1983) makes the point that females often come to the computer environment with less relevant experience than males and may therefore require more effective instruction to benefit equally. Hawkins (1984) stresses the need for using computers in classrooms as tools for a variety of goals. She stresses the need to match the goals and interests of individual children, along with appropriate support for learning about the technology. Our experience suggests that the sexual stereotypes surrounding the use of computers are gradually eroding. In schools where computers are used extensively for word processing as well as other types of activities, students readily see the usefulness of the computer in their lives. Young children learning Logo come with no preconceived ideas relating their sex and achievement. We agree that as the computer is given wider and more personal use in the curriculum it is less likely that these sexual distinctions will persist.

□   SOME TRENDS TO WATCH   □

Before we close, we would like to discuss some technological trends that could have significant implications for teaching reading/language arts.

Telecommunications

The area of telecommunications is exploding. Recently, one of our colleagues, Beva Eastman of the William Paterson College Mathematics Department, participated in an extraordinary event. By logging on to the World Logo Conference through CompuServe, she was able to read the papers of leaders such as Seymour Papert and David Thornburg and the reactions of hundreds of Logo enthusiasts from around the world. She also had the opportunity to interact when the moderator, situated in Vancouver, Canada, with ninety persons there present at the hub of the conference, announced that the conference was "open to the global floor." Conference etiquette had been spelled out so participants knew how to key in their requests and wait for a signal to go ahead.

Participants from the UK, Israel, Kuwait, Spain, and Australia joined peers in diverse parts of the United States in responding to the major presenters on such topics as the place of Logo in the classroom today and its future at all levels of education. Dr. Eastman, who downloaded most of the conference on disk to read at another time, found that she had reaffirmed her belief in Logo as a learning environment. All this without even leaving her home!

Through membership in the Educational Information Exchange System (EIES) developed by the New Jersey Institute of Technology (NJIT), we have been able to communicate with computer educators in higher education throughout the state. At a conference at NJIT on using computers in college-level basic-skills courses, we learned how to log on to read messages from people at other colleges in the network and to leave messages about such concerns as software we found to be worthwhile and peripherals we were trying out. This telecommunications network keeps us current on college computer use, especially for basic skills computer use in reading and writing courses, our special areas of interest.

Daiute (1985) extols the advantages of electronic mail, a component of telecommunications that may prove to be particularly useful for the schools. She sees it as providing "additional communication channels" and promoting writing and reading as people send messages to one another from across great distances.

Electronic mail is just beginning to appear in schools. Daiute cites a project based at the University of California at San Diego in which classes in suburban southern California have been exchanging messages with counterparts in rural Alaska. The researchers found that, because the lifestyles of the two pupil populations were so different, the students had to write clearly and with great detail to be understood. The project acted as a stimulus for interesting and realistic reading and writing episodes at both ends.

Deaf and hearing-impaired students in upstate New York are participating in an electronic mail project initiated by New York University to improve their reading and writing skills. Approximately thirty students in five school districts are communicating with each other and with students in other states and countries as far away as Great Britain and Israel. Each of the students has an individual "mailbox," a code within the network that belongs only to that student, and can display messages through another code, known as a "billboard," that is accessible to all. Summative evaluation is being conducted to assess the effect of the program on students' reading comprehension and writing skills such as sense of audience and logical flow of sentences within a piece of writing.

Quill, described in Chapter 2, has an electronic mail component called "Mailbag." This enables students to send messages through computers linked into a districtwide network. The teachers in Bridgewater-Raritan, New Jersey, are experimenting with *Quill* capabilities right now. As more schools begin to use *Quill* and tie into telephone lines with modems and memberships in services like CompuServe (see Chapter 3), reading and writing electronic messages will become a telecommunications activity promoting and requiring a high level of literacy.

Speech Synthesis/Recognition

Speech synthesizers, which give computers the ability to "speak" in a natural-sounding voice, and speech recognition systems, which give the computer the ability to recognize and respond to voice, are being developed rapidly for just about all computers. From the popular Borg-Warner *Ufonic Sound System* with its 2,000-word natural-language vocabulary to Street Electronics' *Echo II* 750-word natural-voice vocabulary with text-to-speech robotic voice, the peripherals necessary to support talking software for the Apple II family are available. Two synthesizers have recently been introduced for the Macintosh. While *Smoothtalker* allows you to specify whether you want your typed text to be read by a male or a female voice, *Kidtalk*, designed to be used by the very young, permits the selection of voice by sex, pitch, and volume. Children can have whatever they type in read back to them in human-sounding speech.

Innovative software to be used with these systems also is beginning to emerge. *Alphabet ReadAlong* speaks the words the child is reading but allows the child to turn off the speech so that the system speaks only those words the child selects. The *Story Mix Series* from the same producer (Bertamax) is a story generator capable of creating over four thousand different stories by asking the student to make selections at various points in the story. *Micro-Read*, which uses a human voice to model pronunciation, purports to drill reading comprehension, vocabulary, and study skills.

On the recognition side, Votan's *Voice Key Synthesizer* for the IBM PC and Borg-Warner's *Ufonic Speech Composer* for the Apple II family may be used to create voice-actuated software. *Voice-Based Learning System* (Scott Instruments) allows you to develop software in which students answer orally rather than by typing in responses.

A reading/language application that incorporates both recognition and synthesis is being developed jointly by the Educational Development Center, Koala Technologies, and Dragon Systems. The program reads a story to the child, stopping when a long word is encountered. The computer asks the child to say the word, and if the child errs, it pronounces the word three times, asking the child to repeat after it. A picture of the word appears to support the pronunciation task.

The potential for speech synthesis/recognition programs seems limitless. What better way to begin to teach children (or adults) to read than to add speech to what they can type or to have a system capable of recognizing their speech and turning it into print for them to read back? Here we have all the advantages of the Language Experience Approach (LEA) and word processing with voice-over added!

Interactive Video

The video cassette recorder (VCR) is fast becoming a mainstay in American homes. It is projected that VCRs will be found in 30 percent of our households by the end of 1986 (Goncharoff, 1985). (In fact, 50 to 60 percent may be a more realistic projection.) With the advent of the VCR has come the new market of educational video. Producers like Spinnaker, familiar to computer users, have been developing learning cassettes with accompanying print materials. Children's Television Workshop has been packaging segments of "Sesame Street" into videos to bring reading readiness activities into the home in a more direct way than they are encountered by children during regular TV viewing. Since the cassette can be played and replayed, placed on pause for discussion, and reviewed as many times as needed, the VCR can be a valuable teaching tool, and, for our television-oriented children, they are fun to learn from and watch.

Add a computer to a video playback system with remote control and you have interactive video. You need a special interface board to permit the computer to send signals through the remote-control connector on the playback system. The computer then can control the video output, selecting segments to be played, reversed, and replayed at varying speeds; it can present text alone on the monitor or text combined with video.

Donna Alvermann (1985) showed an innovative application for interactive videocassette use in training reading teachers. She and colleagues at the University of Georgia used an authoring language presently available to prepare an interactive videocassette to help teach preservice teachers how to administer and interpret an Informal Reading Inventory (IRI). Students were guided through the protocols as they went from videos of teachers administering IRIs to questions that appeared on the monitor. These teachers in training could choose to go through a video again if they could not respond adequately after one viewing episode. Based on preliminary evaluations, Alvermann said that the materials had worked successfully for her. She cited two menu-driven authoring languages, _Ghost Writer_ and _Insight,_ that are available now for teachers who want to experiment with writing interactive videos for educational purposes.

While interactive videocassettes were favored early in the development of this medium, interactive videodisk, which resembles a phonograph record, is rapidly gaining attention because of its technological advantages (faster, sharper, and more storage, to mention a few). Manning et al. (1983) point out that videodisk is especially suited for educational purposes because it allows the use of both still and motion pictures and does not degrade the image in the still-frame mode. Also, since the radial surface of the disk permits random access, any frame can be recalled from anywhere on the disk without going through intermediate frames. Among the other features that make videodisks appealing are parallel soundtracks, synchronization of sound and picture, frame-by-frame movement, and easy editing.

Mosenthal (1985) described an authoring language called _Handy_ that has been developed by Don Nix for IBM. By means of a demonstration disk of a comprehension lesson based on a folktale, Mosenthal showed how you can create a "display unit," enter text and graphics, and add speech to your video text. If a user wasn't able to answer a question posed by the computer, the video portion clarifying that episode would be rerun.

With this menu-driven, natural-language program, reading teachers will be able to write their own interactive videodisk lessons, combining the exciting, moving visuals of TV with the interactive teaching capabilities of the computer. This technology, which permits text to be surrounded and interspersed with animated, technicolor graphics plus sound to provide full context, offers great potential for teaching beginners at any age and second-language learners to read.

Artificial Intelligence

Artificial intelligence (AI), a branch of computer science attempting to simulate the human cognitive processes of problem solving, reasoning, and understanding natural language, has become a buzzword in the personal computer industry (Juliussen, 1984). As numerous companies are developing AI-based software for personal computers, there also are several firms dedicated to creating computers that have the processing power and memory required to run AI-based products. In fact, as we write this book, Thinking Machines Corporation is getting ready to unveil the Connection Machine, an AI prototype (Rothenberg, 1985). The creator of this architectural innovation, Daniel Hillis, has systematically combined the processing and memory functions of the computer in a structure known as parallel processing. This will enable machines to process vast stores of information all at once rather than one element at a time, resulting in the fastest computers ever developed.

While Hillis already is being applauded by AI enthusiasts for his ability to bridge the gap between the thinking man and the thinking machine, he still will be challenged by many AI skeptics. The controversy has to do with the nature of thought—in other words, as Waldrop (1985) asks, "What is it that we do up there in our skulls? And how, exactly, do we do it?"

The AI enthusiasts believe that the mind, like the computer, is a system for manipulating symbols—for processing information. Their task is to discover how this processing occurs through formal rules (Rose, 1985). Even MIT linguist Noam Chomsky agrees that grammar, or the structure of language, also can be described according to formal principles. The AI skeptics, on the other hand, argue that perception, understanding, and learning are not a matter of following rules; they are dynamic, holistic processes that make possible our status as human beings. The skeptics claim that even if the computer had efficient means of building new knowledge bases, it still would not be capable of simulating the insightful, intuitive, and inspirational part of our minds.

AI and Reading

Given the sobering acknowledgment that so-called intelligent machines are probably hundreds of years away, where are we today in terms of reading/language arts software packages and what can we expect with future developments?

Current reading/language arts software packages interact with students in two ways, either by exact-match responses or by open-ended responses (Balajthy 1985). Exact-match programs, usually the foundation of drill-and-practice programs, examine the student's input for a certain response. If the student's response matches any of the responses put into the program, the computer will acknowledge this response accordingly. For example, if the student types in Sacramento when asked for the capital of California and the computer recognizes this input, the computer might respond, Correct, Sacramento is the capital of California. If not recognized, the computer might be programmed to say, No, try again or whatever else has been programmed for "no-match" input.

Even a conversational-type program such as *Eliza* (see Chapter 6) is programmed to respond to certain keywords. For example, if the student kept typing yes after every question or comment, *Eliza* would respond with certain phrases such as, You are sure?, You seem quite positive, I see, and I understand. *Eliza* does not know how to continue with the conversation; it simply matches the input with certain key phrases.

Open-ended programs respond nonjudgmentally to a student's input. For example, if a student typed in today's date as January 41, 2001, the computer would write, Today's date is January 41, 2001. The computer has not been programmed to respond to the input in a meaningful way, so it merely regurgitates students' input. Software such as *The Puzzler* and some prompt programs (see Chapter 5) are open-ended because students can type in any response without being judged right or wrong.

Criticisms abound for both program types because of their restrictive (exact-match) and mindless (open-ended) response to natural language. The essence of AI research is to produce computers that will eventually eliminate these natural-language barriers.

Until (if ever) this is realized, we still can anticipate certain software program improvements in reading because of current advances in AI research. Vast improvements in memory storage and processing, coupled with the research in "expert systems," will help to create these changes. (The "expert systems" approach to AI programs the computer to become an expert about a specific topic of interest and then the computer uses elementary reasoning power—"if-then" rules—to make decisions.)

The combination of these two factors in reading software programs would help with both diagnosis and instruction. Similar to the *Mycin* program for diagnosing infectious diseases by Feigenbaum (Waldrop, 1985), a diagnostic reading software package could be developed which combines data from various standardized and informal tests as well as survey information on physical, environmental, emotional, and cognitive factors. The program could score the tests and reason through various pieces of data to suggest students' reading levels, strengths, weaknesses, and contributing factors for any reading difficulties noted. Containing data on a vast array of reading materials, it could match each student's reading abilities and interests to a list of suggested materials to use.

An important instructional application has to do with creating software that is more interactive so that realistic dialogues are created between the computer and the user. Even simple reading-comprehension packages could analyze students' responses and subsequently create a dialogue about students' responses, offering appropriate information about the topic presented.

Taking the "dynabook" concept (see Chapter 5) one step further, students not only could have choices in terms of what they want to learn but also could discuss what they know so that the computer could fill in schematic gaps. For example, if students read a passage about Pearl Buck and they chose to have more background information presented about the author, the computer might ask them to describe what they know. If they had only one association (such as the publication of her book *The Good Earth*), the computer would acknowledge this fact and continue to offer more information about her childhood, her missionary work, and her writing career.

Almost like a Directed Reading Lesson, the computer could elicit what students know, fill in the gaps to help students read the passage, and follow up with a discussion related to students' responses.

While these futuristic developments are not yet available, strides in AI research have allowed us to predict how it might be applied to the reading field.

☐   SUMMARY   ☐

We have discussed our positions on a few major issues that confront teachers who want to use computers in their reading/language arts programs. For instance, we strongly believe that schools should encourage respect for the copyright laws and seek to work with producers and vendors to arrive at fair pricing policies so that the need for illicit copying is eliminated. As for the equity issue, we are deeply concerned about the widening gap between rich and poor schools and between talented and underachieving students. We agree with those who suggest that this may be a broader issue than many local school districts can handle alone. State and federal initiatives may be needed to guard against the development of a technological underclass. Inequities related to sex role distinctions should be rectified at the local level. Sufficient research information is available for school districts to carefully consider this problem and to take appropriate steps, where necessary, to adjust policy and curriculum.

Turning from ethical issues to teaching decisions of a pragmatic nature, we support the direct teaching of keyboarding skills, specifically touch typing, to students even at the elementary level (as early as grades 3 and 4). Then, opportunities to use these skills must be built into the reading/writing/computers curriculum. If students are to use the computer to its fullest potential, they should have some degree of automaticity with its principal access device, the keyboard.

As for the computer's place in the early childhood curriculum, we are somewhat cautious. While we think that *teachers* can use this tool effectively when working on beginning literacy with the young child (see the sections on word processing and the language experience approach in Chapter 2), we think that the amount of time that young children spend at computer terminals, rather than engaging in the concept-building and socializing experiences included in a traditional early childhood program, is open to question. Certainly exploring and manipulating language in unstructured sessions with a word processor or gamelike activities such as early tutee applications like *Facemaker* (see Chapter 6) have their place, but drill and skill readiness software do not warrant large blocks of time in the already overcrowded early childhood curriculum.

In this closing chapter we also pointed out trends that could affect the way computers may be used by reading teachers. The exploding telecommunications field offers a dynamic context in which to teach reading and writing as students compose and read messages transmitted electronically from sources as close as the next classroom to those as far away as Asia, Africa, or Australia.

Voice synthesis/recognition technology and interactive video systems, which are rapidly becoming more sophisticated and less expensive, promise to add a total-language context to our efforts to develop reading and writing in meaningful milieux.

Artificial intelligence is paving the way for the development of software that focuses on reading as a dynamic, holistic process. Combined with advances in telecommunication and voice synthesis/recognition technology, AI-based software products will begin to simulate "ideal" instructional reading situations for students of all ages.

This is an exciting time to be involved in the teaching of reading and writing. To the tremendous research base on how we develop as thinkers and learn language by ear and by eye is being added a new technology to add in the delivery of our instructional practices. It is indeed a time to explore, experiment, reflect, and celebrate as we begin to use the best applications of the computer as tool, tutor, and tutee in our reading/ language arts programs.

GUIDE TO RESOURCES

REFERENCES

GLOSSARY

INDEX

Guide to Resources
Software, Peripherals, and Data Bases

Resources are listed in alphabetical order for each chapter. Keep the following information in mind as you use this list.

When a resource is discussed more than once in the text, it will be listed under each chapter in which it is mentioned. A full description will appear under the first chapter in which it is discussed.

Although one source is mentioned for each product, other sources may also be available. Catalog prices are listed but may vary according to the source used and the hardware configuration needed.

When exact grade levels have not been assigned by the developer, the terms primary, elementary, and secondary may be used. *Primary* indicates grades prekindergarten through 3, *elementary* indicates grades 4 through 6, and *secondary* indicates junior/senior high school and adult.

The "Apple II Family" hardware configuration consists of the following Apple computer models: Apple II +, Apple IIe, and Apple IIc.

☐   **CHAPTER 2**   ☐

TITLE: *AppleWorks*
SOURCE: Apple Computer, 20525 Mariani Avenue, Cupertino, CA 95014
PRICE: $200
SUGGESTED GRADE LEVEL: High School–Adult
DESCRIPTION: An integrated package that includes word processing, data base, and spreadsheet programs
HARDWARE: Apple II Family

TITLE: *Bank Street Storybook*
SOURCE: Mindscape, Inc., 3444 Dundee Road, Northbrook, IL 60062
PRICE: $39.95

Suggested grade level: 3–9
Description: Users can select from a file of predrawn graphics and add text
Hardware: Apple II Family, IBM, Commodore 64 (requires joystick)

Title: *Bank Street Writer*
Source: Scholastic Software, Scholastic Inc., P.O. Box 7502, 2531 E. McCarty Street, Jefferson City, MO 65102
Price: $95
Suggested grade level: 3 and up
Description: A menu-driven, easy-to-use word processor
Hardware: Apple II Family, Commodore 64, Atari, IBM

Title: *Crossword Magic*
Source: L & S Computerware, P.O. Box 70728, Sunnyvale, CA 94087
Price: $49.95
Suggested grade level: 4–Adult
Description: A utility program to create crossword puzzles
Hardware: Apple II Family, Atari, Commodore 64, IBM

Title: *Format II*
Source: Kensington Microwave, 251 Park Avenue South, New York, NY
Price: $150
Suggested grade level: Secondary
Description: An easy-to-learn word processing package that prints out the page exactly as it is seen on the computer screen
Hardware: Apple II Family

Title: *Ghost Writer*
Source: MECC, 3490 Lexington Avenue North, St. Paul, MN 55126-8097
Price: $89; 10-diskette lab kit, $314
Suggested grade level: 6–Adult
Description: A text editing program that can be used with the following popular word processors: MECC *Writer, Bank Street Writer, Apple Writer II, Writing Workshop, Magic Window II, Pie-Writer*
Hardware: Apple II Family

Title: *Language Experience Recorder*
Source: Teacher Support Software, P.O. Box 7125, Gainesville, FL 32605-7125
Price: $75
Suggested grade level: Used with beginning readers at all levels
Description: Teacher tool for recording text generated by students
Hardware: Apple II Family

TITLE: *MacWrite*
SOURCE: Apple Computer, 20525 Mariani Avenue, Cupertino, CA 95014
PRICE: Distributed free with the Macintosh
SUGGESTED GRADE LEVEL: All
DESCRIPTION: Word processing program with a "mouse" pointer and pull-down
    help windows
HARDWARE: Macintosh

TITLE: *Magic Slate*
SOURCE: Sunburst Communications, 39 Washington Avenue, Pleasantville, NY
    10570
PRICE: $65
SUGGESTED GRADE LEVEL: 2–Adult
DESCRIPTION: Word processing program that offers three type sizes to accom-
    modate various ages and stages: 20-, 40-, and 80-column levels
HARDWARE: Apple II Family (80-column card needed for 80-column level)

TITLE: *Moxley's Writing and Reading Programs for Children* (in development)
SOURCE: Roy Moxley, Division of Education, West Virginia University, Morgan-
    town, WV 26506
PRICE: Consult source
SUGGESTED GRADE LEVEL: Primary
DESCRIPTION: Developed with Logo, this series of programs develops beginning
    writing and reading skills
HARDWARE: Apple II Family

TITLE: *Newsroom*
SOURCE: Springboard, 7807 Creekridge Circle, Minneapolis, MN 55435
PRICE: $49.95
SUGGESTED GRADE LEVEL: 4–Adult
DESCRIPTION: Users create their own newspapers with graphics and banners
HARDWARE: Apple II Family, IBM PC, Commodore 64

TITLE: *Notewriter* (in development)
SOURCE: Richard Marius, Harvard University Composition Program, Harvard
    University, Cambridge, MA
PRICE: Consult source
SUGGESTED GRADE LEVEL: Developed for college composition courses
DESCRIPTION: A commenting program that permits instructors to write notes on
    a text written on a computer

TITLE: *Personal Filing System (PFS): Write*
SOURCE: Software Publishing Corporation, 1901 Landings Drive, Mountain View, CA 94043
PRICE: $125
SUGGESTED GRADE LEVEL: 4–Adult
DESCRIPTION: A screen-oriented word processing program
HARDWARE: Apple II Family, IBM

TITLE: *Quill*
SOURCE: D. C. Heath, 125 Spring Street, Lexington, MA 02173
PRICE: $150
SUGGESTED GRADE LEVEL: 3–12
DESCRIPTION: Integrated writing program that includes "Planner" for prewriting, "Library" for storing information, "Writer's Assistant" for editing text, and a message system called "Mailbag"
HARDWARE: Apple Family, TRS-80 Model III/IV

TITLE: *Sensible Speller*
SOURCE: Sensible Software, Inc., 6619 Perham Drive, West Bloomfield, MI 88033
PRICE: $125
SUGGESTED GRADE LEVEL: 4–Adult
DESCRIPTION: A spelling checker containing 80,000 words to be used with all Apple word processing programs
HARDWARE: Apple II Family

TITLE: *Story Maker: A Fact and Fiction Tool Kit*
SOURCE: Scholastic Software, Scholastic Inc., P.O. Box 7502, 2531 E. McCarty Street, Jefferson City, MO 65102
PRICE: $125
SUGGESTED GRADE LEVEL: Primary/Elementary
DESCRIPTION: Enables children to write creative stories and illustrate them either by drawing their own graphics or by choosing pictures from a gallery of 65 figures
HARDWARE: Apple II Family

TITLE: *Talking Screen Textwriting Program*
SOURCE: Computing Adventures Ltd., 9411 N. 53 Street, Glendale, AZ 85302
PRICE: $299 including speech synthesizer; $159 for software alone
SUGGESTED GRADE LEVEL: Used with beginning readers at all levels
DESCRIPTION: Teacher tool for recording text generated by students; voice synthesizer may be added so students can also hear stories
HARDWARE: Apple II Family, speech synthesizer

TITLE: *Writer's Workbench*
SOURCE: Bell Laboratories, 190 River Road, Summit NJ 07901
PRICE: $1,700
SUGGESTED GRADE LEVEL: High School–Adult
DESCRIPTION: An editing package that includes programs to check spelling and
    grammar (split infinitives, punctuation) and diction (wordy phrases, clichés)
HARDWARE: UNIX operating system, AT&T 3B2 computer

TITLE: *Word Perfect*
SOURCE: Satellite Software International, 288 West Center Street, Orem, UT
    84057
PRICE: $495
SUGGESTED GRADE LEVEL: High School–Adult
DESCRIPTION: A sophisticated word processing program with excellent formatting
    options
HARDWARE: IBM PC

☐   **CHAPTER 3**   ☐

Software

TITLE: *Appilot II*
SOURCE: MUSE Software, 347 N. Charles Street, Baltimore, MD 21201
PRICE: $99.95
SUGGESTED GRADE LEVEL: 1–12
DESCRIPTION: Authoring language that includes high- and low-resolution graphics,
    built-in timer, light pen input, and voice output
HARDWARE: Apple II Family

TITLE: *Apple SuperPILOT*
SOURCE: Apple Computer, 20525 Mariani Avenue, Cupertino, CA 95014
PRICE: $150
SUGGESTED GRADE LEVEL: All
DESCRIPTION: Sophisticated authoring language program with the ability to pro-
    duce graphics and sound effects
HARDWARE: Apple II Family

TITLE: *Cloze Generator* (in development)
SOURCE: University of Quebec in Montreal, Department des Sciences de l'Edu-
    cation, P.O. Box 8888, Succursale A, Montreal (Quebec), Canada H3C 3P8

PRICE: Consult source
SUGGESTED GRADE LEVEL: Intermediate
DESCRIPTION: Informal cloze generator with a variety of cloze options available

TITLE: *Computer-based Reading Assessment Instrument (CRAI)*
SOURCE: Kendall Hunt Publishing Company, 2460 Kerper Boulevard, P.O. Box
    539, Dubuque, IA 52001
SUGGESTED GRADE LEVEL: 1–8
DESCRIPTION: A computerized informal reading inventory
PRICE: $39.95
HARDWARE: Apple II Family, IBM PC

TITLE: *Create–Lessons*
SOURCE: Hartley Courseware Inc., 123 Bridge Street, Box 419, Dimondale, MI
    48821
PRICE: $29.95
SUGGESTED GRADE LEVEL: 1–6
DESCRIPTION: Mini-authoring language for writing lessons, drill sequences, tests,
    or tutorials. Hint or explanation frame may be used after each question
HARDWARE: Apple II Family

TITLE: *Create—Vocabulary*
SOURCE: Hartley Courseware Inc., Box 431, Dimondale, MI 48821
PRICE: $40
SUGGESTED GRADE LEVEL: 1–3
DESCRIPTION: Editor program for including desired word list. Format allows stu-
    dent to read word displayed on video screen and, a moment later, the cas-
    sette recorder pronounces the word. Student decides whether the word was
    pronounced correctly
HARDWARE: Apple II Family, also requires cassette control device and cassette
    recorder

TITLE: *Crossword Magic* (see Chapter 2)

TITLE: *Exam Builder*
SOURCE: A. U. Software, P.O. Box 597, Colleyville, TX 76034
PRICE: $99.95
SUGGESTED GRADE LEVEL: 1–12
DESCRIPTION: Teacher utility package for creating a data base of exam questions
    in 5 user-defined subjects
HARDWARE: Apple II Family, Radio Shack TRS-80 Mod I/III/IV, IBM PC

TITLE: *E-Z Pilot*
SOURCE: Teck Associates, Inc., P.O. Box 8732, White Bear, MN 55110
PRICE: $34.95
SUGGESTED GRADE LEVEL: 4–16
DESCRIPTION: A simple computer language created for teachers to write lessons. Contains only 12 commands
HARDWARE: Apple II Family

TITLE: *Fiction Finder*
SOURCE: Michael McKenna, Director of the Reading Center, The Wichita State University, Wichita, KS 67208
PRICE: Consult source
SUGGESTED GRADE LEVEL: All
DESCRIPTION: Easy-to-use data base system for identifying fiction titles commonly found in school libraries
HARDWARE: Apple II Family

TITLE: *Informal Reading Placement Test*
SOURCE: Educational Activities Inc., P.O. Box 392, Freeport, NY 11520
PRICE: $49.95
SUGGESTED GRADE LEVEL: 1–6 (Developmental), 1–12 (Remedial), or Special Education
DESCRIPTION: Informal assessment of word and passage comprehension for reading placement purposes
HARDWARE: Apple II Family, TRS-80, Commodore 64, Atari, IBM

TITLE: *Jabbertalky*
SOURCE: Automated Simulations, 1988 Leghorn Street, Mountain View, CA 94043
PRICE: $29.95
SUGGESTED GRADE LEVEL: All
DESCRIPTION: Mini-authoring system with 4 game options for sentence scrambling and word scrambling
HARDWARE: Apple II, TRS-80, IBM PC

TITLE: *Kid Bits™ Words Fair*
SOURCE: Potomac Micro Resources Inc., P.O. Box 277, Riverdale, MD 20737
PRICE: $100
SUGGESTED GRADE LEVEL: Pre-K–4
DESCRIPTION: A mini-authoring system for primary children that allows teachers to tailor lessons to classroom needs
HARDWARE: Apple II Family

TITLE: *Micro Power and Light Readability*
SOURCE: Micro Power and Light, 12820 Hillcrest Road, Suite 224, Dallas, TX 75230
PRICE: $45
SUGGESTED GRADE LEVEL: All
DESCRIPTION: Yields readability levels from 9 popular formulas
HARDWARE: Apple II Family, IBM

TITLE: *Mystery Sentences*
SOURCE: Scholastic Software, Scholastic Inc., P.O. Box 7502, 2531 E. McCarty Street, Jefferson City, MO 65102
PRICE: $49.95
SUGGESTED GRADE LEVEL: 3 and up
DESCRIPTION: Sentences are provided (with and without clues) with missing parts for students to complete. Contains editor program for inserting clues
HARDWARE: Apple II Family

TITLE: *The O'Brien Vocabulary Placement Test*
SOURCE: Educational Activities Inc., P.O. Box 392, Freeport, NY 11520
PRICE: $29.95
SUGGESTED GRADE LEVEL: K–7
DESCRIPTION: Informal assessment of word opposites for reading placement purposes
HARDWARE: Apple II Family, TRS-80, Commodore 64, Atari, IBM

TITLE: *Personal Filing System (PFS):FILE*
SOURCE: Software Publishing Corporation, 1901 Landings Drive, Mountain View, CA 94043
PRICE: $79.95–$140 (depending on hardware)
SUGGESTED GRADE LEVEL: Elementary and up
DESCRIPTION: Information management software package that allows user to create data bases
HARDWARE: Apple II Family, Commodore 64, IBM PC, Macintosh

TITLE: *The Print Shop*
SOURCE: Beagle Bros. Micro Software, 4315 Sierra Vista, San Diego, CA 92103
PRICE: $44.95
SUGGESTED GRADE LEVEL: 6 and up
DESCRIPTION: Allows user to create invitations, greeting cards, signs, personal stationery, banners, and advertising material
HARDWARE: Apple II Family, Commodore 64, Atari

TITLE: *The Professional Sign Maker*
SOURCE: Sunburst Communications, 39 Washington Avenue, Pleasantville, NY
10570
PRICE: $59
SUGGESTED GRADE LEVEL: All
DESCRIPTION: Teacher utility package for creating signs and posters
HARDWARE: Apple II Family

TITLE: *The Puzzler* (word search puzzles)
SOURCE: TARA Ltd., P.O. Box 118, Selden, NY 11784
PRICE: $52
SUGGESTED GRADE LEVEL: All
DESCRIPTION: Teacher utility package for creating word search puzzle of 3 dif-
ferent sizes
HARDWARE: Apple II Family, Commodore PET

TITLE: *Quizley Test Worm*
SOURCE: Classified Software, 8986 S. Overhill, DeSoto, KS 66018
PRICE: $29
SUGGESTED GRADE LEVEL: 1–12
DESCRIPTION: Teacher utility package for creating up to 1,000 objective questions
(multiple-choice, true-false, fill-in-the-blank) which can be coded by objec-
tive number, topic, and level
HARDWARE: Apple II Family

TITLE: *School Utilities*, Vol. 2
SOURCE: Minnesota Educational Computing Consortium (MECC), 3490 Lexing-
ton Avenue North, St. Paul, MN 55126-8097
PRICE: $45
SUGGESTED GRADE LEVEL: All
DESCRIPTION: Easy-to-use program that yields readability estimates by the Spache,
Dale-Chall, Fry, Raygor, Flesch, and Gunning-Fog formulas
HARDWARE: Apple II Family

TITLE: *Teacher Utilities*, Vols. 1, 2, 3, and 4
SOURCE: Minnesota Educational Computing Consortium (MECC), 3490 Lexing-
ton Avenue North, St. Paul, MN 55126-8097
PRICE: $40 (Vol. 1), $100 (Vols. 2, 3, and 4 total)
SUGGESTED GRADE LEVEL: All
DESCRIPTION: Mini-authoring system to create crossword puzzles, hidden word
puzzles, posters, and tests
HARDWARE: Apple II Family

TITLE: *Vanilla Pilot*
SOURCE: Tamarack Software, Inc., P.O. Box 247, Darby, MT 59829
PRICE: $29.95
SUGGESTED GRADE LEVEL: 3–16
DESCRIPTION: Full-featured PILOT language interpreter, including Turtle Graphics
HARDWARE: Commodore PET, Commodore 64, Commodore VIC-20

TITLE: *Wiz Works, Idea Invasion, Master Match* (Arcademic Drill Builders)
SOURCE: Developmental Learning Materials (DLM), 1 DLM Park, Allen, TX 75002
PRICE: $44
SUGGESTED GRADE LEVEL: K–12
DESCRIPTION: Drill-and-practice exercises in game format. Contains an editor pro-
     gram to modify content
HARDWARE: Apple II Family

TITLE: *Wordsearch*
SOURCE: Hartley Courseware, Box 431, Dimondale, MI 48821
PRICE: $27
SUGGESTED GRADE LEVEL: All
DESCRIPTION: Teacher utility package for creating word search puzzles. The teach-
     er can control difficulty by specifying whether or not words can overlap or
     appear backwards or along diagonals
HARDWARE: Apple II Family

TITLE: *Words for the Wise*
SOURCE: TYC Software, 40 Stuyvesant Manor, Geneseo, NY 14454
PRICE: $35
SUGGESTED GRADE LEVEL: 1–6
DESCRIPTION: Features 5 separate spelling activities—filling in missing letters, word
     scrambles, letter matching, alphabetizing, and hangman. Contains 1,000-word
     vocabulary with editor program for teachers to create their own lists
HARDWARE: TRS-80

TITLE: *Word Wise*
SOURCE: Total Information for Educational Systems (TIES), 1925 West County
     Road 32, St. Paul, MN 55113
PRICE: $74.95
SUGGESTED GRADE LEVEL: 1–3
DESCRIPTION: Authoring system for creating sight vocabulary exercises for pri-
     mary-level students
HARDWARE: Apple II Family

TITLE: ZES *Authoring System*
SOURCE: Avante-Garde Creations, P.O. Box 30160, Eugene, OR 97403
PRICE: $250
SUGGESTED GRADE LEVEL: All
DESCRIPTION: Authoring system with branching capabilities. Times student responses and records the responses
HARDWARE: Apple II Family

Information Data Bases

TITLE: BRS
SOURCE: Bibliographic Retrieval Services, 1200 Route 7, Latham, NY 12110
DESCRIPTION: Offers over 80 data bases including ERIC, RICE, TECC, and *Academic American Encyclopedia*

TITLE: CompuServe
SOURCE: H&R Block, 5000 Arlington Center Boulevard, P.O. Box 20212, Columbus, OH 43220
DESCRIPTION: Time-sharing service offering features such as electronic mail, a national bulletin board, a general-purpose encyclopedia, and *The Educational Software Selector* (TESS) from EPIE

TITLE: DIALOG
SOURCE: DIALOG Information Services, Inc., 3460 Hillview Avenue, Palo Alto, CA 94304
DESCRIPTION: A comprehensive system offering over 200 data bases including ERIC and *Microcomputer Index*

TITLE: *Dow Jones News/Retrieval Service*
SOURCE: Dow Jones News/Retrieval Service, P.O. Box 300, Princeton, NJ 08540
DESCRIPTION: This on-line data base carries stock/bond quotes, information on leading companies, medical reports, weather, sports, movie reviews, an encylopedia, and current news updates

TITLE: ERIC (Educational Resources Information Center)
SOURCE: Available on DIALOG and BRS
DESCRIPTION: Over a half million educational citations (articles, speeches, research reports, books) with over 6,000 on computers in education

TITLE: *Barron's Computer SAT Study Program*
SOURCE: Barron's Educational Series, 113 Crossways Park Drive, Woodbury, NY 11797
PRICE: $89.95
SUGGESTED GRADE LEVEL: High School
DESCRIPTION: Exercises to prepare for the SAT
HARDWARE: Apple II Family, IBM PC, Commodore 64

TITLE: *Children's Carrousel*
SOURCE: Dynacomp, Inc., 1427 Monroe Street, Rochester, NY 14618
PRICE: $19.95
SUGGESTED GRADE LEVEL: Prekindergarten/Kindergarten
DESCRIPTION: Collection of 9 readiness activities, including programs for exploring keyboard
HARDWARE: Apple II Family

TITLE: *Cloze-Plus (A Context Analysis Program)*
SOURCE: Milliken Publishing Company, 1100 Research Boulevard, St. Louis, MO 63132
PRICE: $425 (12 diskettes—Levels C-H), $635 (12 diskettes with backups), $150 (4 diskettes—any single level)
SUGGESTED GRADE LEVEL: 3–8
DESCRIPTION: Comprehension and vocabulary development with structured cloze activities and vocabulary-in-context activities
HARDWARE: Apple II Family

TITLE: *Comprehension Power*
SOURCE: Milliken Publishing Company, 1100 Research Boulevard, St. Louis, MO 63132
PRICE: $1700 (48 disks—HiABC-JKL), $425 (12 disks in one set), $150 (4 disks—single level)
SUGGESTED GRADE LEVEL: 4–Adult
DESCRIPTION: Inductive comprehension-building program with focus on 25 major comprehension skills
HARDWARE: Apple II Family

TITLE: *Computer Preparation for the SAT*
SOURCE: Harcourt Brace Jovanovich, 1250 Sixth Avenue, San Diego, CA 92101
PRICE: $79.95
SUGGESTED GRADE LEVEL: High School
DESCRIPTION: Exercises to prepare for the SAT

HARDWARE: Apple II Family, Atari, IBM PC, Commodore 64, TRS-80 III, IV

TITLE: *88 Passages*
SOURCE: College Skills Center, 320 West 29 Street, Baltimore, MD 21211
PRICE: $149.95 per pkg.; $279.95 for the two
SUGGESTED GRADE LEVEL: Adult (Pkg. 1—6.0–9.3 readability levels; Pkg. 2—8.0–15.0 readability levels)
DESCRIPTION: Comprehension improvement exercises for college/adult student; mature content
HARDWARE: Apple II Family, TRS-80 III, IV

TITLE: *English SAT I*
SOURCE: Micro Lab Learning Center, 2310 Skokie Valley, Highland Park, IL 60035
PRICE: $30
SUGGESTED GRADE LEVEL: High School
DESCRIPTION: Exercises to prepare for the verbal portion of the PSAT and SAT
HARDWARE: Apple II Family

TITLE: *Fundamental Word Focus*
SOURCE: Random House, 2970 Brandywine Road, Atlanta, GA 30341
PRICE: $165
SUGGESTED GRADE LEVEL: 4–9
DESCRIPTION: Drill and practice on structural analysis
HARDWARE: Apple II Family, TRS-80

TITLE: *The Hinky Pinky Game*
SOURCE: Evanston Educators, Inc., 915 Elmwood Avenue, Evanston, IL 60202
PRICE: $39.95
SUGGESTED GRADE LEVEL: Elementary
DESCRIPTION: Word game for teaching vocabulary and rhyming skills
HARDWARE: Apple II Family

TITLE: *Homonyms I* and *Homonyms II*
SOURCE: Milliken Publishing Company, 1100 Research Boulevard, St. Louis, MO 63132
PRICE: $80
SUGGESTED GRADE LEVEL: 3–9
DESCRIPTION: Drill-and-practice program for teaching the use of homonyms in context
HARDWARE: Apple II Family

TITLE: *Juggles' Rainbow*
SOURCE: The Learning Company, 4370 Alpine Road, Portola Alley, CA 94025

PRICE: $29.95
SUGGESTED GRADE LEVEL: Prekindergarten–Primary
DESCRIPTION: Reading and math readiness
HARDWARE: Apple II Family, Atari, TRS-80

TITLE: *Kindercomp*
SOURCE: Spinnaker Software Corporation, 215 First Street, Cambridge, MA 02142
PRICE: $24.95
SUGGESTED GRADE LEVEL: Pre-K–3
DESCRIPTION: Collection of 6 educational games: Scribble, Names, Sequence, Letter, Draw, and Match
HARDWARE: Apple II Family, Atari, Commodore 64, IBM PC and PCjr

TITLE: *Mastering the SAT*
SOURCE: CBS Software, 521 Fifth Avenue, New York, NY 10175
PRICE: $109
SUGGESTED GRADE LEVEL: High School
DESCRIPTION: Exercises to prepare for the SAT
HARDWARE: Apple II Family, IBM PC, Commodore 64

TITLE: *M-SS-NG L-NKS*
SOURCE: Sunburst Communications, 39 Washington Avenue, Pleasantville, NY 10570
PRICE: $49
SUGGESTED GRADE LEVEL: 4 and up
DESCRIPTION: Word puzzle format in which students fill in letters from passages of nonfiction or children's classics
HARDWARE: Apple II Family, Atari 800, IBM PC

TITLE: *Muppet Learning Keys*
SOURCE: Sunburst Communications, 39 Washington Avenue, Pleasantville, NY 10570
PRICE: $69.95
SUGGESTED GRADE LEVEL: Ages 3 and up
DESCRIPTION: Specially designed keyboard and accompanying software package to help young children learn colors, letters, and numbers
HARDWARE: Apple IIe and Apple IIc, Commodore 64

TITLE: *Owlcat SAT Preparation Course*
SOURCE: Digital Research, Inc., 60 Garden Court, Pacific Grove, CA 93950
PRICE: $89.95, 15 hour course; $249.95, 30 hour course
SUGGESTED GRADE LEVEL: High School

DESCRIPTION: Exercises to prepare for the SAT
HARDWARE: Apple II Family, IBM PC

TITLE: *The Perfect Score*
SOURCE: Mindscape, 3444 Dundee Road, Northbrook, IL 60062
PRICE: $69.95
SUGGESTED GRADE LEVEL: High School
DESCRIPTION: Exercises to prepare for the SAT
HARDWARE: Apple II Family, IBM PC, Commodore 64

TITLE: *Pick-A-Dilly*
SOURCE: Actioncraft, P.O. Box 6087-C, Anaheim Hills, CA 92806
PRICE: $34.95
SUGGESTED GRADE LEVEL: Primary
DESCRIPTION: High-resolution color graphics and musical sounds are used in this "Concentration" game format to promote visual and sound memory association
HARDWARE: Apple II Family

TITLE: *Power of Words*, Vols. 1 and 2
SOURCE: Funk Vocab-Ware, 4825 Province Line Road, Princeton, NJ 08540
PRICE: $29.95
SUGGESTED GRADE LEVEL: Secondary
DESCRIPTION: Vocabulary improvement program
HARDWARE: Apple II Family

TITLE: *Reinking's Passages* (in development)
SOURCE: Milliken Publishing Company, 1100 Research Boulevard, St. Louis, MO 63132
PRICE: Consult source
SUGGESTED GRADE LEVEL: Elementary and up
DESCRIPTION: Passages presented with options to get definitions, background information, main ideas, or passage presented at lower readability level
HARDWARE: Apple II Family

TITLE: *Return to Reading Series*
SOURCE: Media Basics, Charles Clark Co., Inc. (Distributor), 168 Express Drive South, Brentwood, NY 11717
PRICE: $70 per title (approximately 100 titles available)
SUGGESTED GRADE LEVEL: Secondary
DESCRIPTION: After reading a literary book, students use computer for comprehension development
HARDWARE: Apple II Family

TITLE: *Sentence Combining*
SOURCE: Milliken Publishing Company, 1100 Research Boulevard, St. Louis, MO
    63132
PRICE: $95
SUGGESTED GRADE LEVEL: 4–8
DESCRIPTION: Tutorial and practice exercises for building complex sentences
HARDWARE: Apple II Family

TITLE: *66 Passages*
SOURCE: College Skills Center, 320 West 29 Street, Baltimore, MD 21211
PRICE: $149.95 per pkg.; $279.95 for the two
SUGGESTED GRADE LEVEL: Adult (Pkg. 1 – 3.0–5.7 readability levels; Pkg. 2 – 3.3–8.0
    readability levels)
DESCRIPTION: Practice comprehension exercises for college students/adults read-
    ing at elementary school levels; mature content
HARDWARE: Apple II Family, TRS-80 III, IV

TITLE: *Speed Reader II*
SOURCE: Davidson & Associates, 6069 Groveoak Place No. 12, Rancho Palos
    Verdes, CA 90274
PRICE: $69.95
SUGGESTED GRADE LEVEL: High School–College
DESCRIPTION: Offers instruction and practice in increasing rate of reading
HARDWARE: Apple II Family, IBM PC, Commodore 64

TITLE: *Speed Reading (Sack-Yourman)*
SOURCE: College Skills Center, 320 West 29 Street, Baltimore, MD 21211
PRICE: $99.95; unprotected copy (means you can make multiple copies), $200
SUGGESTED GRADE LEVEL: College–Adult
DESCRIPTION: Interesting selections with comprehension questions to improve
    reading rate
HARDWARE: Apple II Family, TRS-80

TITLE: *Speed Reading . . . The Computer Course*
SOURCE: Bureau of Business Practice, 24 Rope Ferry Road, Waterford, CT 06385-
    9985
PRICE: $150
SUGGESTED GRADE LEVEL: College–Adult
DESCRIPTION: Tutorial and practice exercises for rate improvement
HARDWARE: Apple IIe, IBM PC

TITLE: *Sticky Bear ABC*
SOURCE: Xerox Education Publications, 245 Longhill Road, Middletown, CT 06457
PRICE: $39.95
SUGGESTED GRADE LEVEL: Prekindergarten–Early Primary
DESCRIPTION: Alphabet recognition and matching games
HARDWARE: Apple II Family, Atari

TITLE: *Success with Reading*
SOURCE: Scholastic Software, Scholastic Inc., P.O. Box 7502, 2531 E. McCarty Street, Jefferson City, MO 65102
PRICE: $99.95 for one grade level; $219 for all levels
SUGGESTED GRADE LEVEL: 3–6
DESCRIPTION: Cloze passages from accompanying books; has an option to create your own cloze passages
HARDWARE: Apple II Family, Commodore

TITLE: *Tutorial Comprehension*
SOURCE: Random House, 201 E. 50 Street, New York, NY 10022
PRICE: $247.50 for each series (main idea, critical reading, sequence, inference)
SUGGESTED GRADE LEVEL: 1–3
DESCRIPTION: Drills students in main idea, sequencing, details, inference, and recognizing fact or opinion
HARDWARE: Apple II Family, TRS-80

TITLE: *Word Attack*
SOURCE: Davidson & Associates, 6069 Groveoak Place No. 12, Rancho Palos Verdes, CA 90274
PRICE: $49.95
SUGGESTED GRADE LEVEL: Secondary
DESCRIPTION: A vocabulary-building program
HARDWARE: Apple II Family, IBM PC

TITLE: *Word Blaster*
SOURCE: Random House, 201 E. 50 Street, New York, NY 10022
PRICE: $150
SUGGESTED GRADE LEVEL: 3–6
DESCRIPTION: Arcade-type game for using cloze-type activity to teach/reinforce reading comprehension and vocabulary development
HARDWARE: Apple II Family, TRS-80, Atari 400 or 800, IBM

TITLE: *The Writing to Read System*
SOURCE: IBM, P.O. Box 1329, Boca Raton, FL 33422
PRICE: Through sales representatives
SUGGESTED GRADE LEVEL: Kindergarten–Primary
DESCRIPTION: Multimedia beginning reading/writing program, using computers, typewriters, and workbooks
HARDWARE: IBM PCjr

☐   **CHAPTER 5**   ☐

TITLE: *Alice in Wonderland, The Swiss Family Robinson, Below the Root, Treasure Island, Robin Hood, The Wizard of Oz*
SOURCE: Windham Classics, One Kendall Square, Cambridge, MA 02139
PRICE: $26.95
SUGGESTED GRADE LEVEL: 10 and up
DESCRIPTION: Interactive adventure game using literary classics
HARDWARE: Commodore 64, Apple II Family, IBM

TITLE: *Apple*—Elementary, Vol. 3—Social Studies (History, Economics, and Geography)
SOURCE: Minnesota Educational Computing Consortium (MECC), 3490 Lexington Avenue North, St. Paul, MN 55126-8097
PRICE: $48
SUGGESTED GRADE LEVEL: Elementary/Junior High
DESCRIPTION: Simulates the operation of an apple stand; a lesson on pricing
HARDWARE: Apple II Family

TITLE: *Bicycle*—Elementary, Vol. 3—Social Studies (History, Economics, and Geography)
SOURCE: Minnesota Educational Computing Consortium (MECC), 3490 Lexington Avenue North, St. Paul, MN 55126-8097
PRICE: $48
SUGGESTED GRADE LEVEL: Elementary/Junior High
DESCRIPTION: Simulates the management of different bicycle shops
HARDWARE: Apple II Family

TITLE: CARIS (Computer Animated Reading Instruction System)
SOURCE: Britannica Computer-Based Learning, 425 North Michigan Avenue, Chicago, IL 60611
PRICE: $74
SUGGESTED GRADE LEVEL: K–1

DESCRIPTION: Introduces the reading and spelling of an initial vocabulary by using animated cartoons to illustrate simple sentences
HARDWARE: Apple II Family

TITLE: *Catch*
SOURCE: Colette Daiute, School of Education, Harvard University, Cambridge, MA
PRICE: In development
SUGGESTED GRADE LEVEL: Junior/Senior High and Adult
DESCRIPTION: Prompt program to guide revision and editing
HARDWARE: Apple II Family

TITLE: *Civil*—Elementary, Vol. 3—Social Studies (History, Economics, and Geography)
SOURCE: Minnesota Educational Computing Consortium (MECC), 3490 Lexington Avenue North, St. Paul, MN 55126-8097
PRICE: $48
SUGGESTED GRADE LEVEL: Elementary/Junior High
DESCRIPTION: Simulates 14 battles of the Civil War. One student may assume the role of the Confederate commander while another student assumes the role of a Union commander as they learn to weigh the problems faced by a commander in the Civil War
HARDWARE: Apple II Family

TITLE: *Composition Strategy: Your Creative Blockbuster*
SOURCE: Behavioral Engineering, 230 Mt. Herman Road, Suite 207, Scotts Valley, CA 95066
PRICE: $39.95
SUGGESTED GRADE LEVEL: Suggested for all ages (authors suggest High School–Adult)
DESCRIPTION: Prompt program to help writers to write connected narrative with a sense of voice/audience and sensory orientation
HARDWARE: Apple II Family

TITLE: *Cranston Manor*
SOURCE: Sierra On-Line, Inc., 36575 Mudge Ranch Road, Coarsegold, CA 93614
PRICE: $40
SUGGESTED GRADE LEVEL: 9–12
DESCRIPTION: An adventure in which players must collect 16 treasures as they explore a manor house full of mazes, secret rooms, mysterious passages, and other dangerous pitfalls
HARDWARE: Apple II Family

TITLE: *Creatures of the Night*
SOURCE: Troll Associates, 320 Route 17, Mahwah, NJ 07430
PRICE: $39.95
SUGGESTED GRADE LEVEL: 2–4
DESCRIPTION: *I Can Read* books and word-for-word cassettes are teamed up with
     microcomputer software. Software uses word attack, vocabulary develop-
     ment, and reading comprehension to reinforce content from books
HARDWARE: Apple II Family

TITLE: *Death in the Caribbean*
SOURCE: Micro Lab, Inc., 2699 Skokie Valley Road, Highland Park, IL 60035
PRICE: $40 approximately
SUGGESTED GRADE LEVEL: 9–12
DESCRIPTION: In this adventure game, players must use courage and cunning to
     find the buried treasure and survive a journey through a lush tropical island
HARDWARE: Apple II Family

TITLE: *Kidwriter*
SOURCE: Spinnaker Software Corporation, 215 First Street, Cambridge, MA 02142
PRICE: $34.95
SUGGESTED GRADE LEVEL: Primary–Elementary
DESCRIPTION: Children create an illustrated story
HARDWARE: Apple II Family, IBM, Commodore, Atari

TITLE: *Language Experience Recorder* (See Chapter 2)

TITLE: *Lemonade* — Elementary, Vol. 3 — Social Studies (History, Economics and
     Geography)
SOURCE: Minnesota Educational Computing Consortium (MECC), 3490 Lexing-
     ton Avenue North, St. Paul, MN 55126-8097
PRICE: $48
SUGGESTED GRADE LEVEL: Elementary/Junior High
DESCRIPTION: A simulation in which students make decisions similar to those they
     would make running a real lemonade stand
HARDWARE: Apple II Family

TITLE: *Microzine*
SOURCE: Scholastic Software, Scholastic Inc., P.O. Box 7502, 2531 E. McCarty
     Street, Jefferson City, MO 65102
PRICE: $49.95 — School version (includes teacher's manual, student handbook,
     and backup disk)
SUGGESTED GRADE LEVEL: 3 and up

DESCRIPTION: Each issue contains a variety of programs, including Twistaplots, designed to improve reading skills, decision making, and vocabulary skills
HARDWARE: Apple II Family

TITLE: *Nucleus*
SOURCE: Nucleus, 20 Buckingham Road, Swindon, Wiltshire, England
PRICE: Consult source
SUGGESTED GRADE LEVEL: Primary
DESCRIPTION: Software for use with a concept keyboard (an extra keyboard with an array of touch sensitive key areas)
HARDWARE: Acorn

TITLE: *Odell Lake* — Elementary, Vol. 4 — Math/Science (Ecology, Astronomy, and Arithmetic)
SOURCE: Minnesota Educational Computing Consortium (MECC), 3490 Lexington Avenue North, St. Paul, MN 55126-8097
PRICE: $49
SUGGESTED GRADE LEVEL: 2–6
DESCRIPTION: Simulates a typical food web found in lakes in North America
HARDWARE: Apple II Family

TITLE: *Odell Woods* — Elementary, Vol. 4 — Math/Science (Ecology, Astronomy, and Arithmetic
SOURCE: Minnesota Educational Computing Consortium (MEEC), 3490 Lexington Avenue North, St. Paul, MN 55126-8097
PRICE: $49
SUGGESTED GRADE LEVEL: 2–6
DESCRIPTION: Simulates animal survival in woods
HARDWARE: Apple II Family

TITLE: *Oregon* — Elementary, Vol. 6 — Social Studies (Simulations)
SOURCE: Minnesota Educational Computing Consortium (MECC), 3490 Lexington Avenue North, St. Paul MN 55126-8097
PRICE: $49
SUGGESTED GRADE LEVEL: 3–6/Junior High
DESCRIPTION: Simulates trip by covered wagon from Independence, Missouri, to Oregon City in 1847
HARDWARE: Apple II Family

TITLE: *Play Writer: Tales of Me*
SOURCE: Woodbury Software, 127 White Oak Lane, Old Bridge, NJ 08857
PRICE: $39.95

SUGGESTED GRADE LEVEL: Elementary
DESCRIPTION: Students answer a series of questions that are used to compose a
    personalized story
HARDWARE: Apple II Family

TITLE: *The Puzzler (Prediction Strategies)*
SOURCE: Sunburst Communications, 39 Washington Avenue, Pleasantville, NY
    10570
PRICE: $55
SUGGESTED GRADE LEVEL: 3–6
DESCRIPTION: Presents 5 intriguing stories that actively engage students in prob-
    lem-solving process of reading for meaning
HARDWARE: Apple II Family

TITLE: *Questions and Story*
SOURCE: American Micro-Media, P.O. Box 306, Red Hook, NY 12571
PRICE: $9.95
SUGGESTED GRADE LEVEL: Primary
DESCRIPTION: Personalized story created according to student's responses to com-
    puter-generated questions
HARDWARE: Apple II Family

TITLE: *Robot Odyssey I*
SOURCE: The Learning Company, 545 Middlefield Road, Menlo Park, CA 94025
PRICE: $49
SUGGESTED GRADE LEVEL: Secondary
DESCRIPTION: A problem-solving game in which players escape from an under-
    ground city by designing circuit chips and building robots to help them
HARDWARE: Apple II Family

TITLE: *Story Machine*
SOURCE: Spinnaker Software Corporation, 215 First Street, Cambridge, MA 02142
PRICE: $34.95–$39.95
SUGGESTED GRADE LEVEL: Kindergarten–Primary
DESCRIPTION: Child composes text using supplied vocabulary
HARDWARE: Apple II Family, Atari, IBM, Commodore

TITLE: *Story Maker*
SOURCE: Bolt, Beranek and Newman, Inc., 10 Moulton Street, Cambridge, MA
    02238
PRICE: $30
SUGGESTED GRADE LEVEL: 4–8

DESCRIPTION: Stories branch according to student-selected responses with goals used to guide students. Student-generated responses are encouraged with certain stories
HARDWARE: Apple II Family

TITLE: *Story Tree*
SOURCE: Scholastic Software, Scholastic Inc., P.O. Box 7502, 2531 E. McCarty Street, Jefferson City, MO 65102
PRICE: $75
SUGGESTED GRADE LEVEL: 4 and up
DESCRIPTION: Considered a "story processor," this program is used to enhance writing and reading skills by encouraging children to read, write, and extend their own stories with unlimited endings
HARDWARE: Apple II Family, Commodore 64, IBM

TITLE: *That's My Story*
SOURCE: Learning Well, 200 South Service Road, Roslyn Heights, NY 11577
PRICE: $59.95
SUGGESTED GRADE LEVEL: 2–8
DESCRIPTION: Students use story starters to write their own stories
HARDWARE: Apple II Family, IBM

TITLE: *Topoi or Aristotle's Topics*
SOURCE: Captain Hugh Burns, Dr. George Culp, RASSL Learning Services, University of Texas, Austin, TX
PRICE: Consult source
SUGGESTED GRADE LEVEL: High School–Adult
DESCRIPTION: A prompt program designed to help students write persuasive essays
HARDWARE: Apple II Family

TITLE: *Writing a Character Sketch*
SOURCE: Minnesota Educational Computing Consortium (MECC), 3490 Lexington Avenue North, St. Paul, MN 55126-8097
PRICE: $43
SUGGESTED GRADE LEVEL: 9–12
DESCRIPTION: A prompt program for creating a character sketch; includes examples and understanding checks students may try before writing their own ideas
HARDWARE: Apple II Family

TITLE: *Writing a Narrative*
SOURCE: Minnesota Educational Computing Consortium (MECC), 3490 Lexington Avenue North, St. Paul, MN 55126-8097
PRICE: $43
SUGGESTED GRADE LEVEL: 7–9
DESCRIPTION: A prompt program to encourage idea-storming and prewriting to prepare students to write a draft of a narrative
HARDWARE: Apple II Family

☐   **CHAPTER 6**   ☐

TITLE: *Apple Logo*
SOURCE: Apple Computer, 20525 Mariani Avenue, Cupertino, CA 95014
PRICE: $100
SUGGESTED GRADE LEVEL: Elementary and up
DESCRIPTION: Logo program designed to run on Apple computer, using Turtle Graphics to introduce programming
HARDWARE: Apple II Family

TITLE: *Children's Carrousel* (See Chapter 4)

TITLE: *Delta Drawing*
SOURCE: Spinnaker Software Corporation, 215 First Street, Cambridge, MA 02142
PRICE: $39.95
SUGGESTED GRADE LEVEL: Pre-K–7
DESCRIPTION: User creates colorful drawings on the computer screen using single-key commands to control the Delta Cursor
HARDWARE: Apple II Family, Atari, Commodore 64, IBM

TITLE: *Eliza*
SOURCE: Artificial Intelligence Group, 921 North LaJolla, Los Angeles, CA 90046
PRICE: $25 (protected); $45 (unprotected)
SUGGESTED GRADE LEVEL: Elementary and up
DESCRIPTION: Simulates Carl Roger's approach to psychotherapy by encouraging computer user ("patient") to converse with computer ("doctor")
HARDWARE: Apple II Family, IBM

TITLE: *E-Z Logo*
SOURCE: Minnesota Educational Computing Consortium (MECC), 3490 Lexington Avenue North, St. Paul, MN 55126-8097
PRICE: $48

SUGGESTED GRADE LEVEL: Preschool–3
DESCRIPTION: Simple commands used to help children explore Logo's Turtle Graphics
HARDWARE: Apple II Family

TITLE: *Facemaker*
SOURCE: Spinnaker Software Corporation, 215 First Street, Cambridge, MA 02142
PRICE: $24.95
SUGGESTED GRADE LEVEL: Pre-K–3
DESCRIPTION: Student selects features to create face and, subsequently, programs the face to do various facial movements. Game similar to "Simon" is part of program
HARDWARE: Apple II Family, Atari, Commodore 64, IBM PC and PCjr

TITLE: *The Friendly Computer*
SOURCE: Minnesota Educational Computing Consortium (MECC), 3490 Lexington Avenue North, St. Paul, MN 55126-8097
PRICE: $46
SUGGESTED GRADE LEVEL: K–3
DESCRIPTION: Contains 5 programs that introduce students to the computer. The "Picture" program allows students to create drawings, using single keystroke commands
HARDWARE: Apple II Family, Commodore 64

TITLE: *Getting Started with Logo*
SOURCE: Developmental Learning Materials (DLM), 1 DLM Park, Allen, TX 75002
PRICE: $45
SUGGESTED GRADE LEVEL: Elementary/Secondary
DESCRIPTION: Introduces Apple Logo with simple activities and reference charts
HARDWARE: Apple II Family

TITLE: *Introducing Logo to Primary Children*
SOURCE: Houghton Mifflin, One Beacon Street, Boston, MA 20108
PRICE: $99, entire kit (includes teacher's manual, program disk, activity cards, and charts); $46.50, disk only
SUGGESTED GRADE LEVEL: K–3
DESCRIPTION: Collection of activities and ideas for introducing fundamental Logo concepts
HARDWARE: Apple II Family

TITLE: *Kindercomp* (See Chapter 4)

TITLE: *Learning Through Logo*
SOURCE: Sunburst Communications, 39 Washington Avenue, Pleasantville, NY 10570
PRICE: $49.95
SUGGESTED GRADE LEVEL: 3–6
DESCRIPTION: Uses activity cards to work with Logo so that students are introduced to turtle graphics
HARDWARE: Apple II Family, Commodore 64, IBM

TITLE: *Moxley's Writing and Reading Programs for Children* (See Chapter 2)

TITLE: *Mr. Pixel's Programming Paint Set*
SOURCE: Mindscape, Inc., 3444 Dundee Road, Northbrook, IL 60062
PRICE: $39.95
SUGGESTED GRADE LEVEL: 3–8
DESCRIPTION: Allows students to create pictures by using commands on bottom of the screen
HARDWARE: Apple II Family, Commodore 64, IBM

☐ CHAPTER 8 ☐

TITLE: *Alphabet ReadAlong*
SOURCE: Bertamax, Inc., 101 Nickerson Street, Suite #550, Seattle, WA 98109
PRICE: $24.95
SUGGESTED GRADE LEVEL: Primary
DESCRIPTION: Speaks words as child reads
HARDWARE: Apple II Family, speech synthesizer

TITLE: *Eliza* (See Chapter 6)

TITLE: *Master Type*
SOURCE: Scarborough Systems, Inc., 25 North Broadway, Tarrytown, NY 10591
PRICE: $29.95–$49.95
SUGGESTED GRADE LEVEL: Elementary–Secondary
DESCRIPTION: Typing instruction in game format
HARDWARE: Apple II Family, Atari, Commodore, IBM

TITLE: *Micro-Read*
SOURCE: American Educational Computer, 2450 Embarcadero Way, Palo Alto, CA 94303
PRICE: $595

Suggested grade level: 1–8
Description: Drills reading comprehension, vocabulary, and study skills
Hardware: Apple II Family

Title: *Muppet Learning Keys* (See Chapter 4)

Title: *Story Mix Series*
Source: Bertamax, Inc., 101 Nickerson Street, Suit #550, Seattle, WA 98109
Price: $24.95
Suggested grade level: Primary or beginning readers of all ages
Description: A story generator
Hardware: Apple II Family, speech synthesizer

Title: *Superkey*
Source: Bytes of Learning, Inc., 150 Consumer's Road, Suite 202, Toronto, Ontario, Canada M2J 1P9
Price: $69.95
Suggested grade level: Elementary and up
Description: Basic keyboarding package
Hardware: Apple II Family

Speech Synthesizer/Recognition Devices

Title: *Echo II*
Source: Street Electronics, 1140 Mark Avenue, Carpinteria, CA 93013
Price: $129.95
Suggested grade level: All
Description: Speech synthesizer with 750-word natural-voice vocabulary and text-to-speech robotic voice
Hardware: Apple II Family

Title: *Kidtalk*
Source: First Byte, 2845 Temple Avenue, Long Beach, CA 90806
Price: $149.95
Suggested grade level: All
Description: Speech synthesizer on which sex, pitch, and volume of voice can be specified
Hardware: Apple Macintosh

Title: *Smoothtalker*
Source: First Byte, 2845 Temple Avenue, Long Beach, CA 90806
Price: $149.95

SUGGESTED GRADE LEVEL: All
DESCRIPTION: Speech synthesizer that reads orally what has been typed in
HARDWARE: Apple Macintosh

TITLE: *Ufonic Sound System*
SOURCE: Borg-Warner, 600 West University Drive, Arlington Heights, IL 60004
PRICE: $495
SUGGESTED GRADE LEVEL: All
DESCRIPTION: Speech synthesizer with 2,000-word natural-voice vocabulary
HARDWARE: Apple II Family

TITLE: *Ufonic Speech Composer*
SOURCE: Borg-Warner, 600 West University Drive, Arlington Heights, IL 60004
PRICE: $225
SUGGESTED GRADE LEVEL: All
DESCRIPTION: Speech authoring system (speech recognition)
HARDWARE: Apple II Family

TITLE: *Voice-Based Learning System*
SOURCE: Scott Instruments, 1111 Willow Springs Drive, Denton, TX 76205
PRICE: $99.95
SUGGESTED GRADE LEVEL: All
DESCRIPTION: Speech authoring system (speech recognition)
HARDWARE: Apple II Family

TITLE: *Voice Key Synthesizer*
SOURCE: Votan, 4487 Technology Drive, Fremont, CA 94538
PRICE: $500
SUGGESTED GRADE LEVEL: All
DESCRIPTION: Speech authoring system (speech recognition)
HARDWARE: IBM

References

Alvermann, D. (1985). *Interfacing microcomputers with videocassettes: A program for teaching the IRI.* Paper presented at the College Reading Association Conference, Pittsburgh, PA.

Armbruster, B. B. (1984). The problem of inconsiderate text. In G. G. Duffy, L. R. Roehler, & J. Mason (Eds.), *Comprehension instruction: Perspectives and suggestions* (pp. 202–217). New York: Longman.

Ascher, C. (1984). *Microcomputers: Equity and quality in education for urban disadvantaged students.* New York: ERIC Clearinghouse on Urban Education. (ERIC Document Reproduction Service No. ED 242 801)

Ashare, E. (1985, May 8). Parents byte into pupils' Apple. *The Record,* Hackensack, NJ, sec. C, p. 5.

Balajthy, E. (1984). Computer simulations and reading. *The Reading Teacher, 37,* 590–593.

Balajthy, E. (1985). Artificial intelligence and the teaching of reading and writing by computers — Can computers respond "intelligently" to our students? *Journal of Reading, 29,* 23–32.

Balajthy, E. (1986). *Microcomputers in reading and language arts.* Englewood Cliffs, NJ: Prentice-Hall.

Becker, H. J. (1984). *School uses of microcomputers.* Baltimore, MD: Johns Hopkins University Center for Social Organization of Schools. (ERIC Document Reproduction Service No. ED 249 886)

Bitter, G. G., & Watson, N. R. (1983). *Apple Logo primer.* Reston, VA: Reston.

Blanchard, J. (1985, May). *Design issues in computer-based reading.* Paper presented at the meeting of the International Reading Association, New Orleans, LA.

Bortnick, R. (1986, April). *Beyond word processing to writing processing and reading.* Paper presented at the meeting of the International Reading Association, Philadelphia, PA.

Botel, M. (1968). *Botel reading inventory: Word opposites test.* Chicago: Follett.

Bowman, B. (1983, November). *Research in early childhood education: The most urgent research question.* Paper presented at the National Association for the Education of Young Children Annual Conference, Atlanta, GA.

Bradley, V. (1982). Improving students' writing with microcomputers. *Language Arts, 59,* 732–743.

Brady, E., & Hill, S. (1984). Young children and microcomputers. *Young Children, 39*(3), 49–61.

219

Brandt, R. (1985). On teaching and supervising: A conversation with Madeline Hunter. *Educational Leadership, 42*(5), 61–66.

Braun, R. J. (1985, July). Computer questioned as teaching panacea. *The Star-Ledger,* Newark, NJ, pp. 1, 8.

Bridge, C., Winograd, P., & Haley, D. (1983). Using predictable materials vs. pre-primers to teach beginning sight words. *The Reading Teacher, 36,* 884–891.

Broida, A. (1985). *Computer software review.* (Research Rep.). William Paterson College of New Jersey.

Brown, A. (1982). Learning how to learn from reading. In J. Langer & M. Smith-Burke (Eds.), *Reader meets author/bridging the gap* (pp. 26–54). Newark, DE: International Reading Association.

Bruce, B., Michaels, S., & Watson-Gegeo, K. (1985). How computers can change the writing process. *Language Arts, 673,* 143–149.

Burg, K. (1984). The microcomputer in the kindergarten. *Young Children, 39*(3), 28–33.

Burg, L. A., Kaufman, M., Korngold, B., & Kovner, A. (1978). *The complete reading supervisor: Tasks and roles.* Columbus, OH: Charles E. Merrill.

Caissy, G. A. (1984). Evaluating educational software: A practitioner's guide. *Phi Delta Kappan, 66,* 249–250.

Calkins, L. (1983). *Lessons from a child.* Portsmouth, NH: Heinemann.

Carlson, E. H. (1982). *Kids and the Apple.* Chatsworth, CA: Datamost.

Casey, J. (1983). Talking screen textwriting program. *Computers, Reading and Language Arts, 1,* 51–53.

Casteel, C. P. (1984). Computer skill-banks for classroom and clinic. *The Reading Teacher, 38,* 294–297.

Caster, T. (1983). *The use and effectiveness of computers in the elementary classroom.* Athens, GA: Georgia Association for Childhood Education. (ERIC Document Reproduction Service No. ED 248 886)

Clements, D. H., & Gullo, D. F. (1984). Effects of computer programming on young children's cognition. *Journal of Educational Psychology, 76,* 1051–1058.

Computers as classroom management aids. (1984, March). *Computers in Education* (Special Supplement No. 5 — Teacher's Edition), 3–6.

Computers bridging gaps for schools in Michigan. (1985, October 7). *The New York Times,* sec. B, p. 2.

Computer Using Educators (CUE) position paper on commercial software pricing policies. (1981). *The Computing Teacher, 8*(6), 53–56.

Cory, S. (1983, November). A 4-stage model of development for full implementation of computers for instruction in a school system. *The Computing Teacher, 11*(4), 11–16.

Cuffaro, H. (1984). Microcomputers in education: Why is earlier better? In D. Sloan (Ed.), *The computer in education: A critical perspective* (pp. 21–30). New York: Teachers College Press, 1984, 1985.

Daiute, C. (1985a). *Writing and computers.* Reading, MA: Addison-Wesley.

Daiute, C. (1985b, March). *Using computers in the language arts.* Paper presented at Writing, Reading, and Computers conference, William Paterson College, Wayne, NJ.

Dale, E., & Chall, J. S. (1948). A formula for predicting readability: Instructions. *Educational Research Bulletin, 27,* 11-20, 27-54.

Davison, A. (1984). Readability formulas and comprehension. In G. G. Duffy, L. R. Roehler, & J. Mason (Eds.), *Comprehension instruction: Perspectives and suggestions* (pp. 128-143). New York: Longman.

Doyle, P. (1985). *Software evaluation: Preschool through first grade.* (Research Rep.). William Paterson College of New Jersey.

Dreyer, L. (1984). Readability and responsibility. *The Reading Teacher, 27,* 334-338.

Duffelmeyer, F. A. (1985). Estimating readability with a computer: Beware of the aura of precision. *The Reading Teacher, 38,* 392-395.

Durkin, D. (1981). What is the value of the new interest in reading comprehension? *Language Arts, 58,* 23-43.

Dwyer, T. A., & Kaufman, M. S. (1973). *A guided tour of computer programming in BASIC.* Boston: Houghton Mifflin.

Education Commission of the States. (1983). *A 50-state survey of initiatives in science, mathematics and computer education* (No. SM-83-1). Denver, CO: Author.

Eiser, L. (1985, February). Can kids outgrow word processing programs? *Classroom Computer Learning, 5*(6), 52-55.

Elmer-DeWitt, P. (1985, September 16). Tools in the hands of kids. *Time, 126*(11), 77-78.

Farstrup, A. (1985, May). *Introduction to a student authoring system.* Paper presented at the meeting of the International Reading Association, New Orleans, LA.

Feeley, J. T. (1985, July). *The computer as a resource in teaching reading: Now and tomorrow.* Paper presented at the meeting of the United Kingdom Reading Associated Conference, University of Reading, Reading, UK.

Feeley, J. T. (1986). The computer as a resource for teaching reading: Now and tomorrow. In B. Root (Ed.), *Resources for reading: Does quality count?* (pp. 206-219). London: Macmillan.

Finkel, L. (1983). When is a pirate a thief? *Electronic Learning, 3*(2), 26-28.

Flake, J. L., McClintock, C. E., & Turner, S. V. (1985). *Fundamentals in computer education.* Belmont, CA: Wadsworth.

Flesch, R. (1962). *The art of readable writing.* New York: Collier.

Foley, K. M. (1984, May). *Hooked on books—by a computer!* Paper presented at the meeting of the International Reading Association, Atlanta, GA.

Foley, K. M. (1985). *A closet is no place for a computer.* Menlo Park, CA: Addison-Wesley.

Fortier, G., & Berthelot, S. (1984, October). *The microcomputer cloze generator: A new tool raising new questions.* Paper presented at the meeting of the College Reading Association, Washington, DC.

Fox, J. (1984). Effective computers in school: State issues and options. In S. S. Klein (Ed.), *Computer Education: A catalog of projects sponsored by the U.S. Department of Education, 1983* (p. 221). Washington, DC: National Institute of Education.

Fry, W. (1977). Fry's readability graph: Clarifications, validity, and extension to level 17. *Journal of Reading, 21*(3), 242–251.

Geoffrion, L. D., & Geoffrion, O. P. (1983). *Computers and reading instruction.* Reading, MA: Addison-Wesley.

Geoffrion, L. D., & Geoffrion, O. P. (1985, May). *Beyond the electronic workbook.* Paper presented at the meeting of the International Reading Association, New Orleans, LA.

Giblin, L., & Giblin, J. (1985, May). *E-Z Logo.* Workshop presented at William Paterson College, Wayne, NJ.

Glossbrenner, A. (1983). *The complete handbook of personal computer communications: Everything you need to go on line with the world.* New York: St. Martin's Press.

Goldenberg, E. P., Russell, S. J., Carter, C. J., Stokes, S., Sylvester, M. J., & Kelman, P. (1984). *Computers, education and special needs.* Reading, MA: Addison-Wesley.

Goodman, K. (1984). Unity in reading. In A. Purves & O. Niles (Eds.), *Becoming readers in a complex society* (pp. 79–114). Chicago: National Society for the Study of Education.

Goodman, K., & Burke, C. (1980). *Reading Strategies: Focus on Comprehension.* New York: Holt, Rinehart and Winston.

Goncharoff, K. (1985, November 19). Educational "kid-vid": *Fall Educational Survey of the New York Times,* pp. 10–11.

Gorman, H., & Bourne, L. (1983). Learning to think by learning Logo: Rule learning in third grade computer programmers. *Bulletin of the Psychonomic Society, 21,* 165–167.

Gould, T. M. (1981). Copyright laws. *The Computing Teacher, 8*(5), 22.

Graves, D. (1983). *Writing: Children and teachers at work.* Portsmouth, NH: Heinemann.

Gunning, R. (1952). *The technique of clear writing.* New York: McGraw-Hill.

Hall, J. (1983). Sentence combining. *Educational Technology, 23*(9), 58.

Hall, M. (1981). *Teaching reading as a language experience.* Columbus, OH: Charles E. Merrill.

Hawkins, J. (1984). *Computers and girls: Rethinking the issues.* New York: Bank Street College of Education Center for Children and Technology. (ERIC Document Reproduction Service No. ED 249 922)

High/Scope Educational Research Foundation. (1985). Software reviews. *Key Notes: The High/Scope Early Childhood Computer Learning Report, 1*(1), 5–6.

Holbrook, H. T. (1985). ERIC/RCS report: A content for vocabulary. *Journal of Reading, 28,* 642–644.

Hoover, T., & Gould, S. (1983). The many roles of the school district microcomputer coordinator. *Educational Technology, 23*(5), 29–30.

Howitt, D. (1984, October 29). Experimental software boosted: IBM's "Writing to Read" gets nod from Educational Testing Service. *InfoWorld,* pp. 29–30.

Hunt, K. W. (1970). *Syntactic maturity in school children and adults.* Chicago: Society for Research in Child Development, University of Chicago Press.

Hunter, B. (1983). *My students use computers: Learning activities for computer literacy.* Reston, VA: Reston.

Hunter, M. (1985). What's wrong with Madeline Hunter? *Educational Leadership,* 42(5), 57–60.

ICCE policy statement on network and multiple machine software. (1983). *The Computing Teacher,* 11(2), 18–22.

Instructional resources. (1985). *TechTrends,* 30, 68.

Jarchow, E., & Montgomery, J. (1985). Dare to use adventure games in the language arts classroom. *English Journal,* 74, 104–106.

Jenes, T. (1984a). Writing a narrative. *Computers, Reading and Language Arts,* 2(1), 50–51.

Jenes, T. (1984b). Writing a character sketch. *Computers, Reading and Language Arts,* 2(1), 51–52.

Juliussen, E. (1984). Personal computers in 1990. *Creative Computing* 10(11), 258–267.

Kibby, M. W. (1981). Test review: Degrees of reading power. *Journal of Reading,* 24, 416–429.

Kisner, E. (1984). Keyboarding—A must in tomorrow's world. *The Computer Teacher,* 11(6), 21–22.

Klein, S. S. (Ed.). (1984, April). *Computer education: A catalog of projects sponsored by the U.S. Department of Education, 1983.* Washington, DC: National Institute of Education.

Komoski, P. K. (1983). 4XE—Equitable electronic educational excellence. Washington, DC: National School Boards Association, Educational Policies Service. (ERIC Document Reproduction Service No. ED 239 377)

Komoski, P. K. (1984). Educational computing: The burden of insuring quality. *Phi Delta Kappan,* 66, 245–248.

Lambrecht, J., & Pullis, J. (1983). Computer assisted instruction in typing. *Educational Computer Magazine,* 3(3), 42–45, 66–68.

Lathrop, A., & Goodson, B. (1983). *Courseware in the classroom: Selecting, organizing and using educational software.* Menlo Park, CA: Addison-Wesley.

Linn, M. C. (1983). Fostering equitable consequences from computer learning environments. Berkeley: University of California, Lawrence Hall of Science. (ERIC Document Reproduction Service No. ED 242 626)

Lipinski, J. M. (1984). *Competence, gender and preschoolers' free play choices when a microcomputer is present in the classroom.* (ERIC Document Reproduction Service No. ED 243 609)

Littlefield, P. (1984). Littlefield on software: Creative writing. *Computers, Reading and Language Arts,* 1(4), 41–42.

Lombardi, J. (1983). Sentence combining courseware from Milliken. *Infoworld,* 5(23), 42–48.

Lyles, R. M. (1985). A school on the cutting edge. *Classroom Computer Learning,* 6(1), 57–60.

Mandler, M., & Johnson, N. (1977). Remembrance of things parsed. Story structure and recall. *Cognitive Psychology,* 9(1), 111–151.

Mangiapane, S. (1983). Software review: *Crossword Magic. Computers, Reading and Language Arts,* 1(3), 48–50.

Manning, D. T., Ebner, D. G., Brooks, F. R., & Balson, P. (1983). Interactive videodiscs: A review of the field. *Viewpoints in Teaching and Learning, 59*(2), 28–40.

Mason, G. (1984). Using teacher utility programs — Moving toward the idea. *The Reading Teacher, 37,* 809–810.

Mason, G. E. (1985). Why not make your own? *The Reading Teacher, 38,* 598–599.

Mathis, J. (1985, May). *Reading and Logo.* Paper presented at the meeting of the International Reading Association, New Orleans, LA.

May, F. B. (1982). *Reading as communication.* Columbus, OH: Charles E. Merrill.

McConkie, G. (1984). The reader's perceptual processes. In G. G. Duffy, L. R. Roehler, & J. Mason (Eds.), *Comprehension instruction: Perspectives and suggestions* (pp. 10–25). New York: Longman.

McKenna, M. C. (1985, May). *Developing your own library retrieval system.* Paper presented at the meeting of the International Reading Association, New Orleans, LA.

McWilliams, P. (1983). A guide to word processing. *Family Computing, 1*(4), 58–65.

Miller, J. W. (1985, May). *Conducting research with your own diagnostic data base.* Paper presented at the meeting of the International Reading Association, New Orleans, LA.

Miller, L. (1984, June). *Computers and the language arts.* Paper presented at the Colloquium on Canadian Research in Reading and Language Arts, University of Lethbridge, Lethbridge, Alberta.

Miller, L., & Burnett, D. (1985, April). *Theoretical considerations in selecting language arts software.* Paper presented at the Symposium on Computer Assisted Learning, Nottingham, UK.

Modla, V. (1984). Writing a program to reinforce reading skills. *Computers, Reading and Language Arts, 1*(4), 27–29.

Modla, V. (1985, October). *Software programs related to a science fiction unit for fourth graders.* Paper presented at the meeting of the College Reading Association, Pittsburgh, PA.

Moore, M. L. (1985a). *Computer problems of the week: Exploring logo graphics.* Palo Alto, CA: Creative Publications.

Moore, M. L. (1985b). *Logo discoveries: Investigating numbers, words and lists.* Palo Alto, CA: Creative Publications.

Morphet, E. L., Johns, R. L., & Reller, T. L. (1974). *Educational organization and administration: Concepts, practices and issues* (3rd ed.). Englewood Cliffs, NJ: Prentice-Hall.

Mosenthal, P. (1985). *Handy: A new utility program for instruction and research.* Paper presented at the Center for the Study of Reading Sixth Annual Conference on Reading Research, New Orleans, LA.

Moxley, R. (1984, May). *Writing and reading programs for Logo.* Paper presented at the International Reading Association Convention, Atlanta, GA.

Muller, A. A., & Perlmutter, M. (1985). Preschool children's problem-solving interactions at computers and jigsaw puzzles. (ERIC Document Reproduction Service No. ED 248 013)

Nessel, D., & Jones, M. B. (1981). *The language experience approach to reading.* New York: Teachers College Press.

Newman, J. (1985). Online: Vision and wisdom. *Language Arts, 62,* 295–300.

Nobil, C. (1983). Fundamental word focus. *Interface Age, 2*(6), 93.

Nucleus Newsletter. (1984). Nucleus Software, Swindon, Wiltshire, UK.

Ohanian, S. (1984). Hot new item or same old stew? *Classroom Computer Learning, 5,* 30–31.

O'Hare, F. (1973). *Sentence combining* (Research Report No. 15). Urbana, IL: National Council of Teachers of English.

Okun, G. (1984). *The writing–word processing connection.* Unpublished manuscript, William Paterson College, Wayne, NJ.

Oliva, P. F. (1984). *Supervision for today's schools* (2nd ed.). New York: Longman.

Papert, S. (1980). *Mindstorms: Children, computers and powerful ideas.* New York: Basic Books.

Patterson, J. L., & Patterson, J. H. (1983). *Putting computer power in schools: A step-by-step approach.* Englewood Cliffs, NJ: Prentice-Hall.

Pearson, P. D., & Spiro, R. (1982). The new buzz word in reading: Schema. *Instructor, 91,* 46–48.

Petty, W., Herold, C., & Stoll, E. (1968). *The state of knowledge about the teaching of vocabulary.* Urbana, IL: National Council of Teachers of English.

Phenix, J., & Hannan, E. (1984). Word processing in the grade one classroom. *Language Arts, 61,* 804–812.

Piazza, C., & Riggs, S. (1984). Writing with a computer: An invitation to play. *Early Child Development & Care, 17*(1), 63–76.

Poirot, J. L. (1983). *Forty easy steps to programming in BASIC and Logo.* Austin, TX: Sterling Swift.

Prinz, P. M., & Nelson, K. E. (1985). A child-computer-teacher interactive method for teaching reading to young deaf children. (ERIC Document Reproduction Service No. ED 247 720)

Raygor, A. L. (1977). The Raygor readability estimate: A quick and easy way to determine difficulty. In P. D. Pearson (Ed.), *The 26th Yearbook of the National Reading Conference.* Clemson, SC: National Research Council.

Reinhold, F., & Corkett, K. (1985, October). Mandates: Yes, no, maybe. *Electronic Learning, 5*(2), 25–31.

Reinking, D. (1985). *Reading, computers and a new technology of print.* Manuscript submitted for publication.

Reinking, D., & Schreiner, R. (1985). The effects of computer-mediated text on measures of reading comprehension and reading behavior. *Reading Research Quarterly, 20,* 536–552.

Ricketts, D. (1984). Software piracy—A diminishing problem? *The Computing Teacher, 11*(9), 5.

Rose, F. (1985, March). The black knight of AI. *Science 85, 7*(3), 46–51.

Rosenblatt, L. (1978). *The reader, the text, the poem.* Carbondale: Southern Illinois University Press.

Rothenberg, R. (1985, December). Daniel Hillis on artificial intelligence. *Esquire,* pp. 214–216.

Rubin, A., & Bruce, B. (1984, February). *Quill: Reading and writing with a micro-*

computer (Report No. 5410). Cambridge, MA: Bolt, Beranek and Newman.

Rumelhart, D. (1977). *Introduction to human information processing.* New York: John Wiley and Sons.

Sangston, B. (1983, March). Foreword. In B. Hunter, *My students use computers: Learning activities for literacy* (pp. 13–14). Reston, VA: Reston.

Schubert, N. A. (1985). Reading teacher as programmer: Writing computer assisted instruction. *The Reading Teacher, 38,* 930–932.

Schweitzer, P. (1985, August). *Computer curriculum course guides, grades 3–5.* Unpublished report, Teaneck Public Schools, Teaneck, NJ.

Seise, J. J. (1985). *Inside three districts.* Unpublished manuscript, William Paterson College, Wayne, NJ.

Senn, P. R. (1983). Six checklists to prepare your classroom for technology. *Social Education, 47*(5), 317–320.

Sheingold, K. (1985). *The microcomputer is a medium for young children* (Technical Report No. 26). New York: Bank Street College.

Sheingold, K., et al. (1981). Study of issues related to implementation of computer technology in schools. New York: Bank Street College of Education, Children's Electronic Laboratory. (ERIC Document Reproduction Service No. ED 210 634)

Shelly, M. (1983). Review of *Word Blaster. Educational Technology, 23*(1), 48–49.

Sickert, J. (1983). Software review: *Microzine. Computers, Reading and Language Arts, 1*(3), 43–45.

Slesnick, T. (1984). Mandates aren't good enough: Here's an alternative. *Classroom Computer Learning, 4*(1), 26–27.

Smith, C. B. (1985). How teachers use microcomputers for reading instruction. *The California Reader, 18,* 11–15.

Smith, F. (1982). *Understanding reading.* New York: Holt, Rinehart and Winston.

Smith, F. (1983). *Essays into literacy.* Portsmouth, NH: Heinemann Educational Books.

Smith, P. (1985). *A survey of the Willard School computer program with an emphasis on reading.* (Research Rep.). William Paterson College of New Jersey.

Spache, G. D. (1974). *Good reading for poor readers.* Champaign, IL: Garrard Publishing.

Squire, J. R. (1983). Composing and comprehending: Two sides of the same basic process. *Language Arts, 60,* 581–589.

Staples, B. (1985). SAT packages: An update. *Creative Computing, 2*(4), 86–89.

Stauffer, R. (1980). *The language experience approach to the teaching of reading.* New York: Harper & Row.

Stotsky, S. (1982). The role of writing in developmental reading. *Journal of Reading, 25,* 330–340.

Taylor, R. (Ed.). (1980). *The computer in the school: Tutor, tool, tutee.* New York: Teachers College Press.

Thomas, D. M. (1985). A teacher makes his own. *The Reading Teacher, 38,* 600–602.

Thornburg, D. (1985). *Discovering Apple Logo.* Reading, MA: Addison-Wesley.

Thornburg. D. (1985). *Exploring Logo without a computer.* Reading, MA: Addison-Wesley.

Tucker, M. (1983). Computers in schools: A plan in time saves nine. *Theory into Practice, 22,* 313–320.

Tucker, M. S. (Ed.). (1985, October). *Objectives for computer competence.* Princeton, NJ: National Assessment of Educational Progress.

Vacca, R. T. (1981). *Content area reading.* Boston: Little, Brown.

Waldrop, M. M. (1985, March). Machinations of thought. *Science 85, 7*(3), 38–45.

Warasch, B. G. (1984, May). *Computer language experience approach.* Paper presented at the International Reading Association Convention, Atlanta, GA.

Watt, D. (1983). *Learning with Logo.* New York: McGraw-Hill.

Watt, D. (1984). *Learning with Apple Logo.* New York: McGraw-Hill.

Wepner, S. B. (1983). Computer flowcharts: Road maps to reading skills. *Computers, Reading and Language Arts, 1*(2) 14–17.

Wepner, S. B. (1986). Logo and comprehension: A dynamic combination for thinking skills. Manuscript submitted for publication.

Wepner, S. B. (in press). Logo and comprehension: A dynamic combination for thinking skills. *Computers, Reading, and Language Arts.*

Wepner, S., & Kramer, S. (1984). *Designing your computer curriculum: A process approach.* (ERIC Document Reproduction Service No. ED 247 900)

Wepner, S. B., & Kramer, S. (1986). The computer supervisor. *The Reading Instruction Journal, 29*(2), 13–16, 21.

Whaley, J. (1981). Story grammar and reading instruction. *The Reading Teacher, 34,* 762–771.

Wheeler, F. (1983). *The Puzzler:* An answer to the reading riddle? *Classroom Computer Learning, 4*(1), 46–50.

Willis, J., & Kuchinskas, G. (1983). Simulations = fun & language learning. *Computers, Reading and Language Arts, 1*(3), 24–26.

Wright, E. G., & Forcier, R. C. (1985). *The computer: A tool for the teacher.* Belmont, CA: Wadsworth.

Yin, R. (1985). Update: Where does research responsibility rightfully lie in discovering appropriate application for computer technology in education? *ASCD Update, 27*(6), 5.

Glossary

ANIMATION. The creation of "movement" of an object across the computer screen by lighting different parts of the screen very rapidly.

APPLICATION PROGRAM. Software designed to perform specific tasks in, for example, education, business, or entertainment.

ARTIFICIAL INTELLIGENCE. A study or "model" of how people learn so that machines can be built to perform like the human mind in terms of learning, adapting, reasoning, self-correction, and automatic improvement.

AUTHORING LANGUAGE. Software that enables the user to develop computer-assisted instruction without an understanding of programming logic. Once a set of commands is learned, the user can create lessons, characters, graphics, and sound.

AUTHORING SYSTEM. Software that enables the user to create drill-and-practice activities, games, and tests within a tightly structured framework.

BASIC. An acronym for *Beginner's All-Purpose Symbolic Instruction Code*, the most popular high-level programming language.

BIT. An abbreviation for *bi*nary digi*t*, representing a single entry of 0 or 1 in a binary number system or "on" or "off" in digital electronics.

BOOT. Process of loading part or all of the disk operating system into the computer so that the computer is ready to work.

BRANCHING. A modification of the usual line-by-line execution of a program. Unconditional branching does not depend on any conditions; conditional branching occurs only if certain conditions are met.

BYTE. A unit of information most commonly composed of eight bits "read" by the computer as a string of electric pulses ("ons" and "offs").

COMPATIBLE. Able to be used with another mechanism without special equipment, codes, or programs; for example, a computer program is "compatible" with a computer that can run it.

CARD READER. A computer input device that reads information from a punched card by sensing patterns of holes and other card markings and stores these patterns as data.

CENTRAL PROCESSING UNIT (CPU). The "heart" or "brain" of a computer system, which coordinates and controls all other units within the computer system. It performs the arithmetic and logical processes necessary.

CLOZE PROCEDURE. The deletion of every *n*th word in a passage for the purpose of measuring comprehension. Used as a teaching or testing tool, the student must provide closure by inserting the proper words according to context clues.

COMPUTER ASSISTED INSTRUCTION (CAI) or COMPUTER AIDED LEARNING (CAL). The process of using computers to help students learn, practice, and increase skills.

COMPUTER MANAGED INSTRUCTION (CMI). The process of using the computer to keep records of students' work.

COMPUTER LITERACY. Computer awareness — an understanding of how computers are used and their effects upon our lives.

COURSEWARE. Computer software used for instruction (*see* Software).

CURSOR. A position indicator, usually a blinking square, that shows where you are on the video screen.

DATA BASE or DATA BANK. A large collection of data that can be accessed in a computer system.

DIRECTED READING LESSON (DRL). Developmental reading lesson, usually involving readiness, directed silent reading, discussion, silent and/or rereading and follow-up activities. Directed Reading-Thinking Activity (DRTA) is similar but encourages predicting from title, pictures, subtitles, and continuous text rather than teacher-posed prereading questions.

DISK. A circular, Mylar-coated object used to store computer information.

DOT MATRIX PRINTER. A printer whose characters are patterns of dots.

DOCUMENTATION. Information about a particular computer or computer program, available on the screen or in a manual; user's guide.

DRILL AND PRACTICE. The repetition of a process or set of skills in order to develop skill proficiency.

ELECTRONIC MAIL. A method of sending and transmitting messages through electronic devices, generally sending messages from one computer connected to another via phone lines.

EXACT MATCH PROGRAMS. Computer programs that examine the user's input for specific responses.

EQUITY. An issue related to computer access (boys and girls; all socioeconomic status levels) and ways in which computers are used.

FLOWCHART. A diagram that represents the flow of information and decision points within a program.

FORMAT. 1. The arrangement of material on a typed page, including margins, indentations, etc. 2. The organization of data on a disk so that the data can be stored and retrieved easily.

GRAPHICS. Pictures, graphs, diagrams, and maps generated by the computer and appearing on the screen.

GRAPHICS TABLET. A flat peripheral device connected to the computer on which you draw pictures for the computer screen with a special pen.

GRAPHOPHONIC CLUES. A strategy for decoding printed words to oral words by using letter-sound correspondences.

HARD COPY. A copy of any information from a computer file that is printed on paper.

HIGH-RESOLUTION GRAPHICS. Graphics that use many thousands of pieces of screen space to create illustrations with great detail and smooth, curved lines.

HOLISTIC APPROACH. A teaching-learning approach emphasizing the whole of subject matter and the integration of parts with wholes.

INFORMAL READING INVENTORY. A series of graded passages used to identify independent, instructional, and frustration reading levels as well as listening level.

INFORMATION RETRIEVAL. The ability to find a specific fact from a large mass of data.

INFORMATION UTILITY. A service, such as The Source, which offers access to data bases of electronically stored and delivered information, computer programs, electronic mail, etc.

INPUT. The data that is put into the computer through the keyboard or other devices.

INTERACTIVE. Engaging in a conversation; asking and answering questions.

INTERFACE. An instrument or device that enables adjacent components, circuits, or equipment to acquire or transmit data between themselves.

JOYSTICK. A lever-type device connected to the computer that, when moved in various directions, controls the movement of the cursor on the screen by sending coded signals to the computer.

KEYBOARDING. Typing characters on the keyboard, an input device resembling a typewriter; touch typing.

KILOBYTE. A measure of how much information a computer can store; equals 1,024 bytes.

LIGHT PEN. A pen-shaped device attached to the computer that allows the user to draw or move images on the computer screen by transforming sensed light waves on the monitor into digital signals read by the computer.

LOGO. A high-level computer language that uses a "turtle" to draw colorful, detailed graphics on the screen.

LOW-RESOLUTION GRAPHICS. Graphics that use a few thousand pieces of screen space to produce illustrations that show curves as sets of straight lines.

MEMORY. The capacity of a computer to store information in the form of binary numbers or images for further use.

METACOGNITION. The study of thought processes.

MICROCOMPUTER. The smallest and cheapest type of computer that can take information outside itself (input), work on that information by following a set of instructions, and show or display results (output); also referred to as "home," "personal," or "desk-top" computer.

MICROPROCESSOR. A central processing unit contained on a single silicon chip.

MISCUE. An oral reading response that deviates from the written text.

MODEM. (*modulator-demodulator*) A device that enables computers to communicate over telephone lines.

MONITOR. A television or cathode ray tube used to display computer information. Monitors usually are monochrome (black-and-white, green, or amber) or color.

MOUSE. A desk-top input device that controls cursor movement, providing the user with an alternative to the keyboard.

NETWORK. A set of microcomputers connected together by various communication links so that messages can be sent from one station to another; sometimes called a Local Area Network (LAN).

OPEN-ENDED PROGRAMS. Computer programs designed to respond nonjudgmentally to computer users' input.

OPERATING SYSTEM. Instructions that are a permanent part of the computer. It controls and manages computer operations, including control of input-output procedures, file management operations, and data conversion routines.

OUTPUT. Anything that is displayed on the video screen or sent to a peripheral.

PERIPHERAL DEVICES. Devices attached to a computer for input, output, or storage.

PRAGMATICS. A component of linguistics in which language usage is studied in terms of the influence of social or cultural conditions.

PRIOR KNOWLEDGE. The degree of previous learning, development, and experience that precedes a learning situation.

PROGRAM. A set of instructions stored in the computer's memory that tells a computer how, when, and in what fashion a specific task should be performed.

PSYCHOLINGUISTICS. An interdisciplinary field of psychology and linguistics in which language behavior is studied by understanding cognitive development and the structure of language.

READABILITY. Level of reading difficulty of reading material, usually ascertained with readability formulas. Readability formulas use a prescribed method for analyzing vocabulary load, word structure, sentence composition, and sentence length.

SCHEMA. (pl., schemata). Conceptual system for understanding something.

SEMANTIC CLUES. Clues provided by the meaningful relations among words which help in identifying an unknown word.

SENSE SHEETS. Marked sheets that allow input or a hand-coded form to be sensed from the sheet. For example, with many multiple choice exams, the computer uses the sense sheets to read the answers, correct the exam, and store the information.

SIMULATION. A computer program that recreates a real event, an imaginary event, or a model of some event.

SOFT COPY. Anything displayed on a computer screen.

SOFTWARE. The programs and instructions that control the computer. Software includes programs written by the computer user and programs purchased on disks and tape.

SPEECH SYNTHESIS. The ability of the computer to produce electronic speech, either by using digitized speech (human voice sounds are prerecorded) or by recognizing typed voices.

SPELLING CHECKER. A program that matches words in a text with a dictionary data base, presenting any nonmatches as words to check for misspelling.

STORY GRAMMAR. A particular kind of scheme, conceptualized in terms of predictable settings, characters, plots, episodes, and resolutions, all of which provide a frame for the construction and understanding of stories.

SUBSKILLIST APPROACH. A teaching-learning approach that focuses on skills that are part of more complex skills or body of skills.

SYNTACTIC CLUES. Grammatical clues or signals provided by word endings, function words, and word order that help in identifying unknown words.

TEACHER UTILITIES. Computer programs designed to help teachers create instructional materials and deal with instructional management.

TELECOMMUNICATIONS. Data transmission between computers and remotely located devices.

TOOL MODE. The mode in which the computer assists the computer user in accomplishing specific tasks.

T-UNIT (minimal terminable unit). One main clause plus any subordinate clauses attached to or embedded in it.

TURTLE GRAPHICS. The ability to "draw" complicated computer graphics with a minimal number of commands to the "turtle," usually a triangle on the computer screen.

TUTEE MODE. The mode in which the computer user functions as a teacher to the computer.

TUTORIAL. A computer program designed to teach new ideas.

TUTOR MODE. The mode in which the computer functions as a teacher for the computer user.

VIDEO DISK. A round plastic object, resembling a stereo record, that is capable of storing vast amounts of textual and graphic information.

VIDEO TAPE. A magnetic tape for recording the electronic impulses of the video and audio portions of a television program.

VOICE RECOGNITION. The ability of the computer to recognize or respond to spoken words.

USER FRIENDLY. Software that is easy to use because of clear on-screen instructions and carefully programmed error traps.

WRITING AS PROCESS. Stages of writing that usually include prewriting, drafting, revising, and editing.

WORD PROCESSING. The use of a computer to compose and store any text created. Word processing programs accept and manipulate text on command from the user.

Index